THE CHURCH ARCHITECTURE OF RICHARD TWENTYMAN

CHRIS KENNEDY & AIDAN RIDYARD

Photographs by John East

Preface by Dr A David Owen OBE

Foreword by Professor Hilary J Grainger OBE

ALL SAINTS DARLASTON CHANCEL

To the Reverend Prebendary John and Norma Ridyard

EMMANUEL BENTLEY WEST FRONT

CONTENTS

	PREFACE	VII
	FOREWORD	IX
	INTRODUCTION	2
	FOUNDATIONS	10
2	THE CHURCHES & MODERNISM	24
3	RECONSTRUCTION & EXPANSION	44
4	INTERWAR CHURCHES 1937-9	52
5	A CHANGE IN STYLE THE 1950s	82
6	NEW DIRECTIONS THE 1960s	150
7	THE 'UNKNOWN' TWENTYMAN CHURCHES	180
8	THE CREMATORIUM CHAPELS	196
9	CONCLUSIONS & REFLECTIONS	234
	LIST OF TWENTYMAN CHURCHES & CREMATORIA	243
	LOCATIONS OF TWENTYMAN'S CHURCHES & CREMATORIA	244
	ILLUSTRATION CREDITS	245
	INDEX	246
	ACKNOWLEDGEMENTS	247
	ABOUT THE AUTHORS	248

EMMANUEL BENTLEY ORGAN & CHOIR

PREFACE

It is a real privilege to be asked to write the preface to this book on the architecture of Richard Twentyman. There are so many aspects of our Christian life that he celebrates through his architecture.

When our company, Rubery Owen, responded to Staffordshire County Council's request to provide funds for a new Best Kept Village competition in Staffordshire, I always remember that it was the village church which was the focal point of each village that I visited. Twentyman has brought this vision to every place where his churches have been built in our past twentieth century. This may be on a new housing estate such as Bentley or in an area which had no church where residents could worship and meet together.

Because of his understanding architecturally of what a new church should bring to a community, each church that he built quickly became a place where the community could gather. The three churches that I know, St Gabriel, Walsall, All Saints, Darlaston, and Emmanuel, Bentley, each have a tower and are surrounded by beautifully-mown green grass. When the church bells ring, it is as if the Good Shepherd is drawing His flock together for worship and spiritual nourishment.

Richard Twentyman's churches have tall windows bringing in natural light with the nave leading to the focal point at the east end where worshippers can look up to the Cross, a Crucifix, or a tapestry when taking Holy Communion. It was important too that he used new building materials in his architecture which would provide employment for local businesses and would enable maintenance work to be done in the future.

He also saw the need for community activities and provided architecturally attractive linked buildings such as a church hall with catering facilities, and smaller rooms for all sorts of events and activities for both young and old, like film shows, birthday parties and local society meetings.

My father, Sir Alfred Owen, had a strong association with both All Saints, Darlaston and Emmanuel, Bentley. He was Chairman of Darlaston Council when the rebuilt All Saints was dedicated in 1952 by the Bishop of Lichfield. My father admired that church as a building and I am sure that is why he asked Richard Twentyman to design and build Emmanuel Church at Bentley – 'The Church on a Hill' – in memory of his father, Alfred Ernest Owen.

This book is a landmark for church and community architecture in the twentieth century and a time for great celebration.

Dr A David Owen OBE

David Owen was Chairman of the Rubery Owen Company from 1969-2010, succeeding his father Sir Alfred Owen whose family funded the building of Emmanuel, Bentley as a memorial to Alfred Ernest Owen (1869-1929), the founder of Rubery Owen. David plays an active role in local community, arts, and religious charities.

ST NICHOLAS RADFORD NAVE & CHANCEL

FOREWORD

All too often provincial architects are eclipsed and escape the critical acclaim that their work deserves. Richard Twentyman's private houses, commercial buildings, public houses and schools, built between the 1930s and early 1970s, are woven indelibly into the dense urban fabric of the West Midlands, lending character and distinctiveness to suburbs. His eleven churches and two crematoria, which form the subject of this book, have an enduring physical, spiritual and psychological presence. They are the places where generations of worshippers and mourners have come together. The distinctive bell towers of Twentyman's postwar churches punctuate the skylines of the neighbourhoods they were designed to serve. They continue to resonate with the tangible optimism of the period. Bushbury and Redditch crematoria are unique places in which the lives of thousands have been narrated, mourned and remembered. There is a strong sense of place and social purpose in Twentyman's architecture brought about by the meaningful relationships he forged between urban, and in the case of his crematoria, natural landscapes.

With his entire career dedicated to his native Wolverhampton and environs, Twentyman might be provincial, but he was by no means parochial. From the outset, he was well-attuned and responsive to progressive ideas in Britain and Europe. A measured assimilation and thoughtful interpretation of contemporary architectural thinking, tempered by an intelligent approach to tradition, equipped Twentyman to fulfil admirably Sir Basil Spence's call for the 'great social need for good architecture'.

Twentyman's churches illustrate eloquently his ability to negotiate the competing architectural and liturgical imperatives of the time. His talents found early endorsement in both architectural and ecclesiastical circles. His two interwar churches, St Gabriel, Walsall and St Martin, Wolverhampton, were included in McNally's *Fifty Modern Churches* (1947). Both acknowledge the red brick massing of Willem Dudok and the Nordic Classicism of Alvar Aalto. At St Martin these elements combine with a sturdy Neo-Romanesque and at St Gabriel with echoes of Germanic stripped classicism, all reinterpreted and abstracted through contemporary structure and construction. Both accommodate large congregations of 300 and point to Twentyman's skill, not only in handling the often challenging and restrictive demands of urban sites.

The 1950s and 1960s constituted a particularly inventive period in church architecture. The Liturgical Movement called for a radical rethink on church planning and exhorted the church to draw nearer to the people by shifting the emphasis from mass and liturgy to create spaces designed to foster different relationships between the

ST ANDREW WHITMORE REANS

congregation, both individually and collectively, with one another and with God. Twentyman's 1950s churches skilfully negotiated a balance between the fundamental functionalist views of Peter Hammond and the more spiritual and mystic aspirations of Edward Maufe. His final two churches, both dating from 1965, St Andrew, Whitmore Reans, and St Andrew, Runcorn, responded more directly to the demands of the Liturgical Movement with a more functional approach privileging the interior spatial configurations in service of the congregation.

One of Twentyman's strengths was his ability to judge the relationship between the boundaries of the sacred and secular. Handisyde and Starks's Trinity Congregational Church (1950-1) designed as part of the Festival of Britain had provided a much-publicised model of combining religious and social services, with its integrated halls and school rooms. At All Saints, Darlaston (1952) and Emmanuel, Bentley (1955-7), Twentyman balanced the sacred and the social so as never to jeopardise the primacy of worship. The Good Shepherd, Castlecroft, Wolverhampton (1955) is a particularly fine example of a dual-purpose church/hall of the type reflected in the models included in McNally's 1956 conspectus, *Sixty Post-War Churches: Churches, Church Centres and Dual-Purpose Churches*. This church, although simpler and more functional than some others, nevertheless resonated accents appropriate for a church.

Twentyman brought the instinct of an artist to his architecture through an innate understanding of the power of volume, light and contemporary colour palettes. A high premium was placed on quality of materials and detailing and the incorporation of contemporary art where budgets and sensibilities allowed, and he often designed his own well-judged schemes of church and crematorium furniture.

The modulation of light was central to his work. With increasing mastery, he tied his church interiors to the outside world by capturing natural light while in no way denying a sense of the mystical. At All Saints, Darlaston, Emmanuel, Bentley, and St Chad, Rubery, prominent windows make the interior activities legible from the outside, thereby denying any sense of isolation and separateness from the surrounding community. By 1965, Twentyman's orchestration of light reached new heights. St Andrew, Whitmore Reans, is his only church to employ stained glass, by his friend John Piper and partner Patrick Reyntiens.

Bushbury and Redditch crematoria allowed Twentyman to step onto the national stage. He became one of the handful of architects that included Sir Basil Spence, Thomas Cordiner, Potter and Hare and (closer to home) Holland W. Hobbiss who were designing both churches and crematoria. Twentyman published one of the first postwar articles on crematorium design in which he showed remarkable sensitivity to the paradoxical and ambiguous nature of crematoria, being at once religious and secular, functional and symbolic, and required to meet the practical and emotional needs of all faiths and none. Bushbury, like its contemporary, Thornhill Crematorium, Cardiff, pioneered the move away from the stylistic pluralism of the 1930s towards a 'humane' contemporary idiom so appropriate for the expression of the modernity of cremation and for the assuaging of fear by means of familiarity. His adroit handling of the idiom, incorporation of sparing sculpture and beautiful landscaping, obviated any hint of the municipal. Twentyman also acknowledged Gunnar Asplund's iconic Woodland Crematorium, Stockholm (1935-40) which had been the first to exploit the power of nature in providing solace for mourners, allowing them to reflect beyond the immediacy of their grief. At Bushbury, Twentyman followed the lead of Sanger and Rothwell at Oldham in 'opening up' the chapel by removing the side wall to look onto a private garden. Two decades later at Redditch he followed J. D. Wilkinson's 1961 precedent at Bath Crematorium, of creating a glass wall behind the catafalque. This feature, allowing views across the Arrow Valley, remains much admired and emulated.

This insightful and beautifully illustrated book will surely prompt further consideration of Twentyman's work, allowing him to step out of the shadows and take his rightful place in the wider context of British architecture.

Professor Hilary J Grainger OBE

Professor Emerita of Architectural History at University of the Arts London and Honorary Professor in the Department of Theology and Religion at Durham University, Hilary Grainger specialises in late nineteenth- and twentieth-century architecture and design and has published widely in these areas.

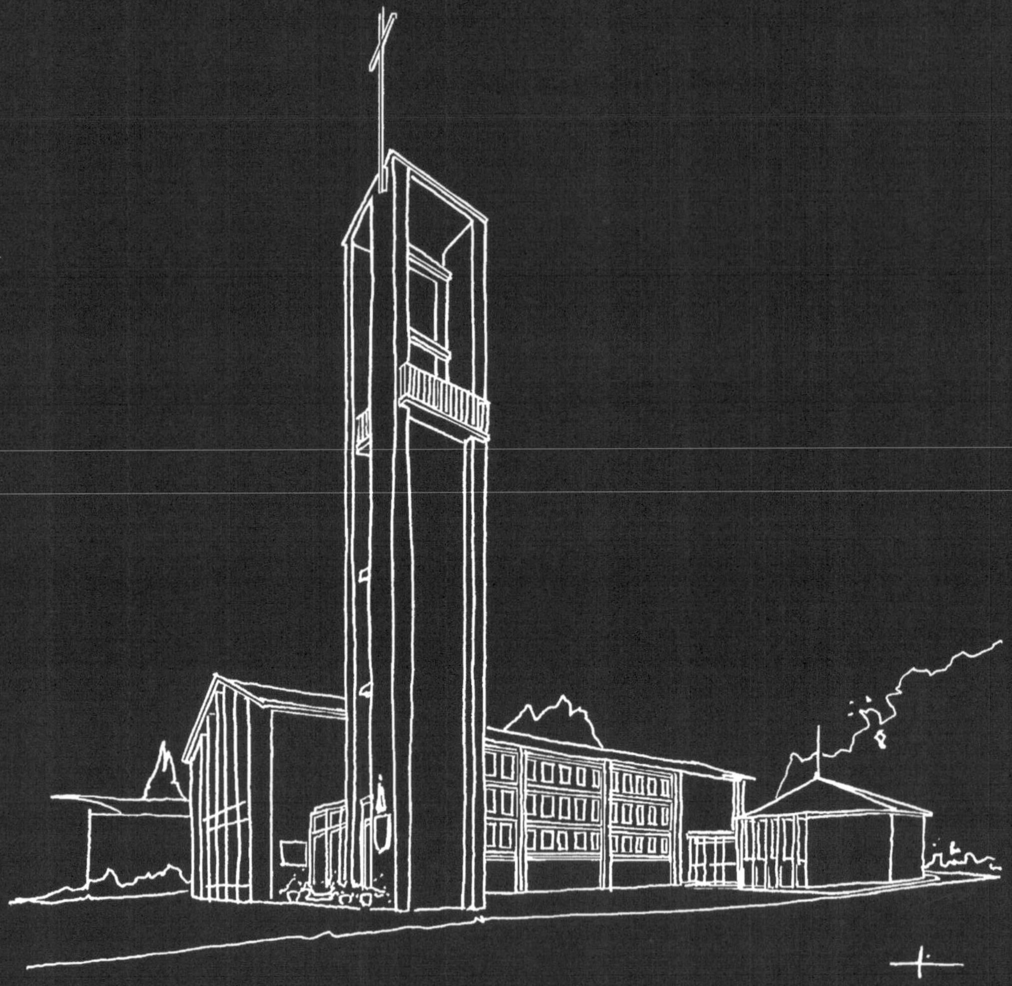

INTRODUCTION

INTRODUCTION

By unending attention to detail, he would develop a plan of great clarity into a finished building that was always elegant, well-mannered, and never dull.

J. Hares, 'Richard Twentyman' (Obituary), *RIBA Journal*, 87, 4, April, (1980), p.29.

Richard Twentyman (1903-79) was a principal partner in a Wolverhampton architects' practice, Lavender and Twentyman, from 1933, reconstituted as Lavender, Twentyman and Percy from 1942, and Twentyman, Percy and Partners from 1960. The practice was involved in several architecture projects including houses, schools, hospitals, public houses, and offices, but it is churches for which Twentyman is particularly known. From 1937 to 1973 he designed ten Anglican churches and one Methodist and two crematorium chapels in the West Midlands, mainly around the Wolverhampton area.

We focus on the social, political, and religious contexts of the eleven churches and the two crematorium chapels, and describe Twentyman's overall designs, use of materials, decorative effects, and integration of art works within the buildings. Although there is no surviving central Twentyman archive, and documentation is scarce and dispersed, texts, photos, drawings, plans, and maps were collected through site visits to the individual churches; local church archives; face-to-face and email conversations with clergy, churchwardens, and parishioners; and relatives and friends who knew Twentyman. We consulted primary and secondary literature from libraries, including that of the Royal Institute of British Architects (RIBA); the Birmingham, Chester, Shropshire, Stafford, Walsall, and Wolverhampton Record Offices; and Wolverhampton Art Gallery. Visits to sites and archive resources took place between 2019 and 2022. Original photographs were taken by John East, and line drawings of the churches, a particular innovative feature of the book, are the work of Aidan Ridyard. Since some Twentyman churches are aligned north-south, rather than east-west, a traditional liturgical orientation has been adopted for all church descriptions, i.e. the altar position is regarded as liturgical east.

Our aim is to investigate the architecture of Richard Twentyman, specifically trying to answer three questions: how did new church building in England, and in the specific case of Twentyman, in the interwar and postwar periods, reflect the main socio-political, economic, and religious influences of the time; what were the architectural parallels and possible influences on Twentyman both from within the UK and mainland Europe; and how did Twentyman's designs respond to their unique suburban locations, to the functions expected of a religious space, and to the liturgical demands of the time?

Churches are part of a system of interlinked components, including historical context and environment; religious requirements; form; ambience (elements such as light, sound, and heating); and building technology including materials.[1] Elements of this system underlie much of our description and discussion of Twentyman's work. The content includes sections on architectural

0.1
ST CHAD RUBERY CHOIR & CHANCEL

0.2
ST CHAD RUBERY TOWER & SOUTH AISLE

developments and materials from the 1930s onwards, ecclesiastic reactions to them, and the influence of liturgical reform on church architecture and church art. We describe West Midlands interwar and postwar housing expansion, the stimulus for new church building, and diocesan responses, and finally, consider aspects of Twentyman's churches, including two churches our research claims to have 'discovered'.

We identify three periods of evolutionary development of the churches, from an interwar monumental phase, to a postwar modernist period of lighter, more accessible churches, and a final phase in the 1960s of greater design experimentation. Common features of Twentyman's churches are simple but effective designs involving a subtle use of sculpture; wide naves and no aisles; the effective use of natural light; and an holistic view of church design, from the materials used to the details with which they were crafted.

We have chosen to write about Twentyman not only because his designs are worthy of study in themselves, revealing his own interpretations of the modernist movement in Britain, but also because he has been relatively neglected,[2] and is not a member of the accepted canon of national and international architects. Such neglect may be partly due to geography and attitude, Wolverhampton still suffering during Twentyman's time from its physical and cultural distance from the London metropolis,[3] or Twentyman's personal preference. Twentyman was not good at promoting his own work, and may have been content to maintain a relatively relaxed and financially secure lifestyle while running a successful regional practice in an expanding West Midlands market. An added factor is that European architects, both those who remained in Europe and those who, like Gropius, left primarily for the USA prior to and after World War II (WWII), were quicker to accept and promote modernism, and have received greater attention in architectural histories, though Darling has tried to redress the balance.[4]

The intention is not to isolate Twentyman from other English or European architects designing churches at the time, nor is there any suggestion that Twentyman should be regarded in a 'heroic' light. No doubt without his architectural skill and creativity, his churches would not have been built in the way they were, but there were other agents working together with him as a community who all played their roles, including practice colleagues, patrons, clergy, church committees, parishioners, financiers, surveyors, builders, engineers, artists, and city planners.[5] Inevitably, given such a constellation of interested parties, there was not always agreement on ways forward, and consensus, if reached at all, was achieved through negotiation, persuasion, or compromise, and sometimes simply through gradual familiarity with the building in use. Each church case study in Christ-Janer and Foley's book, for example, concludes with a personal view on the design and production process from a member of the clergy concerned with the church in question, a view which clearly demonstrates users' developing attitudes,[6] showing the complexity of interests involved in creating church architecture.

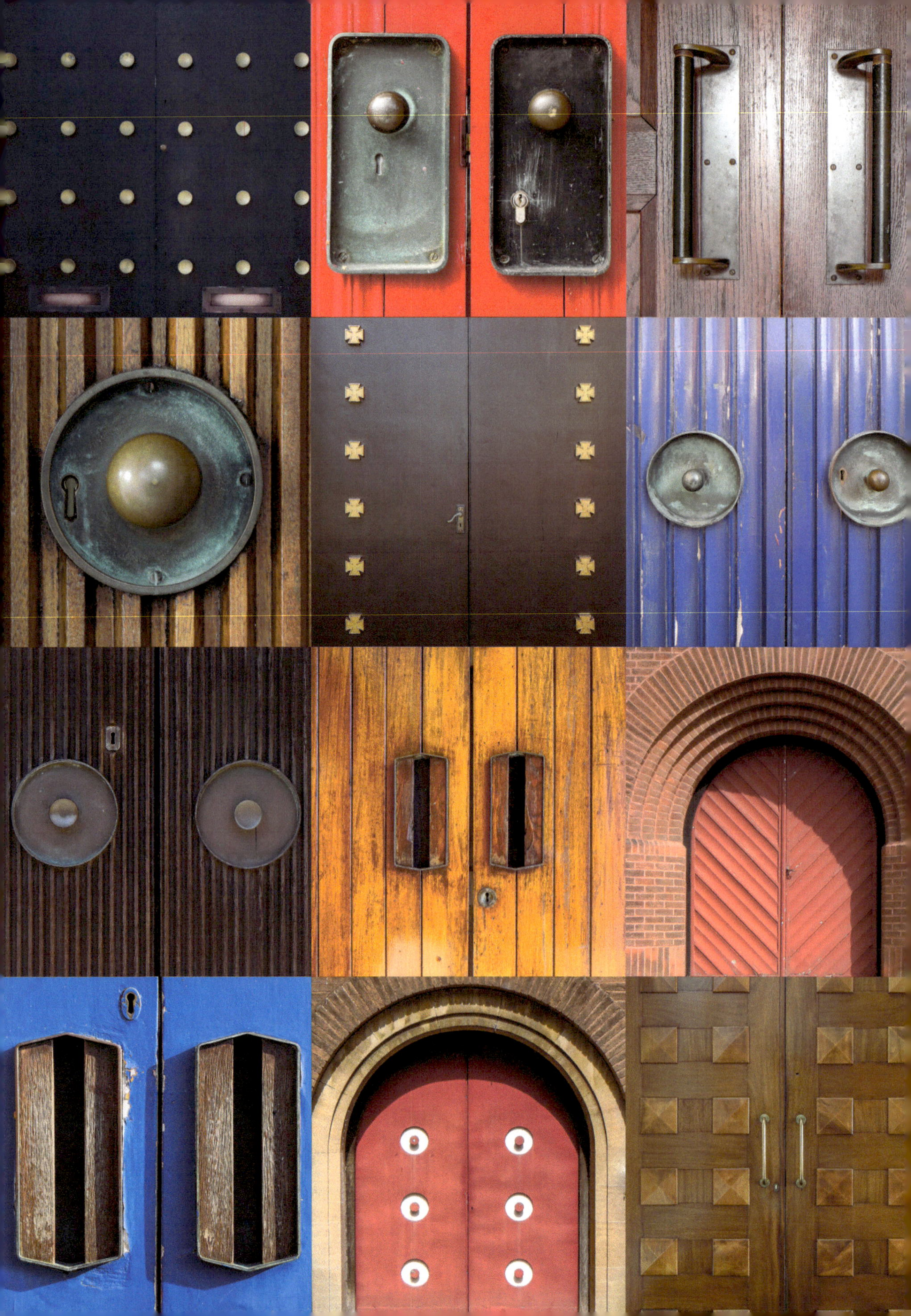

Notes

1. A. Geva, *Frank Lloyd Wright's Sacred Architecture* (London: Routledge, 2012), pp.13-15.

2. The only publications on Twentyman are: D. Billingsley, 'The churches and chapels of Richard Twentyman', *West Midlands RIBA Yearbook* (London: RIBA, 1994), pp.8-11, and J.Wallbridge, *The Churches of Richard Twentyman*. Online. http://www.historywebsite.co.uk/articles/Twentyman/Churches.htm. His work is referenced in A. Foster et al., *Birmingham and the Black Country* (London: Yale University Press, 2022).

3. Lethaby reports that Philip Webb (1831-1915) 'hated' Wolverhampton while working for Bidlake and Lovatt in 1854, and left after four weeks to return to Oxford. He was horrified by living and working conditions in industrial Wolverhampton: 'the herding of labouring men like herrings in a barrel'. In W. R. Lethaby, *Philip Webb and his Work* (London: Raven Oak Press, 1935, reprinted 1979), pp.10-11.

4. E. Darling, *Reforming Britain* (London: Routledge, 2007).

5. J. Walker, *Design History and the History of Design* (London: Pluto Press, 1990).

6. A. Christ-Janer and M. Foley, *Modern Church Architecture* (New York: McGraw-Hill, 1962).

CHAPTER ONE

1 FOUNDATIONS

RICHARD TWENTYMAN'S BACKGROUND

(Alfred) Richard Twentyman (1903-79), known to friends and colleagues as Dick, ran his successful West Midlands architects' practice in Wolverhampton until his retirement in 1977. He and his younger brother Anthony or Tony (John Anthony Twentyman 1906-88) were the only children of Colonel Harold Edward Twentyman (1869-1946) and Grace Evill (1867-1954). They were brought up in the Manor House, built in 1805, in the village of Bilbrook near Wolverhampton (1.1) from 1908 until 1958 when the unmarried brothers moved together to Woodfield House on the outskirts of Claverley village, Shropshire, a few years after the death of their mother. They remained there until Richard's death in December 1979, when Anthony moved into the village, living in Willowbrook House in Church Street, a substantial detached house in its own grounds with river views, until his death in November 1988. The local All Saints Church has memorials to the brothers in the churchyard, Richard's probably having been designed by his brother, Anthony (1.12).

The Manor House in Bilbrook was sold and demolished in the 1960s to make way for a small housing development around the present Manor House Park Road, house numbers 42 and 44 marking the former site of the Manor House.[1]

Richard and Anthony's father, H. E. Twentyman, worked with his two brothers at their grandfather's local family engineering firm of Henry Rogers, Sons and Company Ltd. in Wolverhampton. He was employed initially as an industrial draughtsman,

1.1 BILBROOK MANOR

1.2
PORTRAIT OF H.E. TWENTYMAN

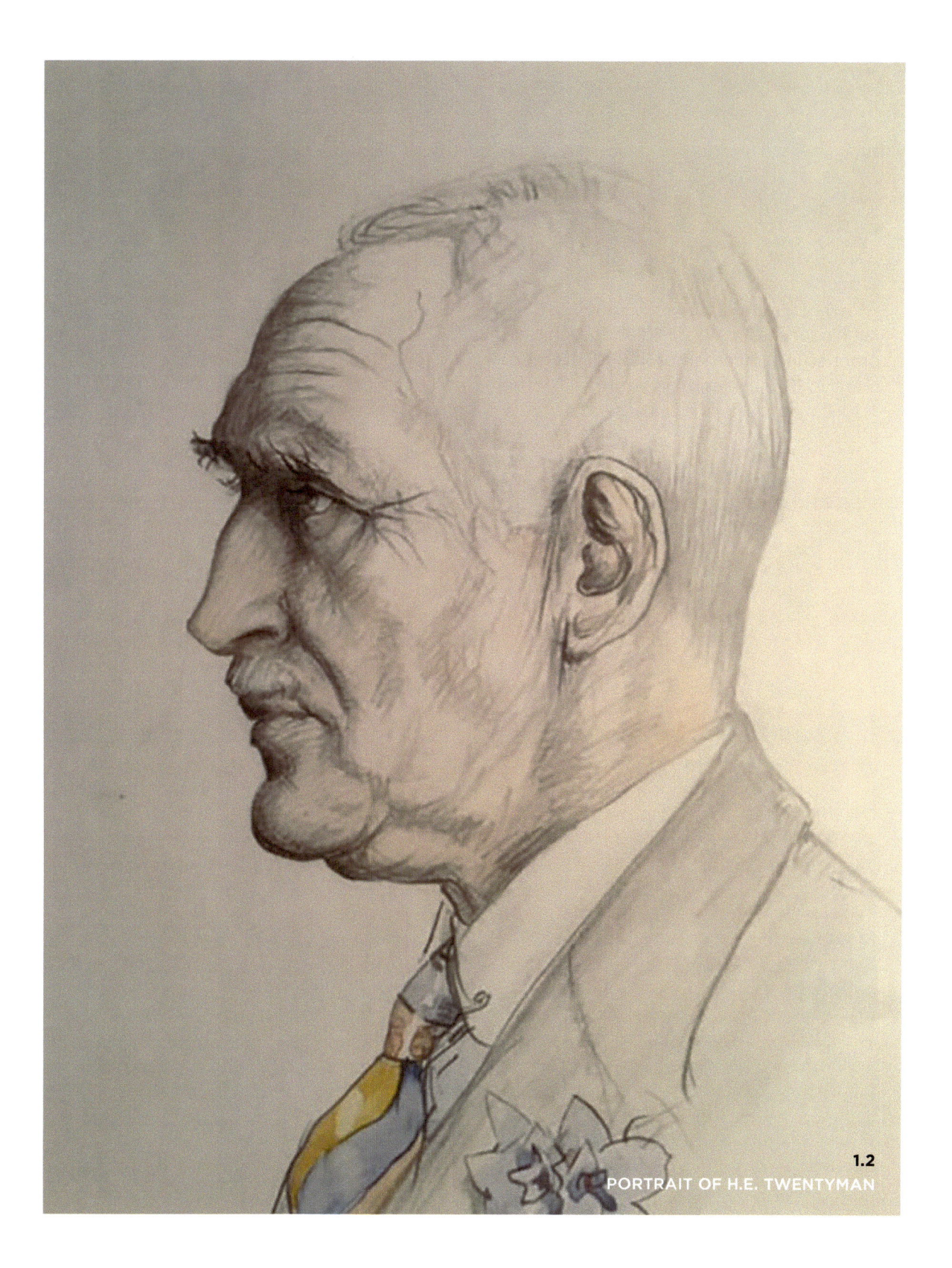

1.3 (BELOW)
Anthony & Richard Twentyman

designing cotton mills in Brazil and other industrial buildings in the UK and overseas, and later became the firm's Managing Director and Chairman. He was also a skilful woodturner, in 1955 becoming a Master of the Worshipful Company of Turners, with a competition still named after him. H. E. Twentyman took his position in the village seriously and was churchwarden of the local Holy Cross Church from 1908 till 1945 (1.2). After his death, the parishioners built a porch at the church to commemorate his work and a plaque at the entrance records his contribution. He also donated a field to the village, now a pleasant public recreation area known as the Twentyman Playing Fields where Bilbrook Village Hall is situated.

The brothers had a privileged upbringing in a household with a governess, family chauffeur, gamekeeper, gardener, and house servants (1.4 with mother). They were inseparable, and developed a code between themselves, referring to their parents, for example, as 'The Corkers' and the family firm as 'Annie's'.[2] Throughout their lives they shared a love of motorcycles and fast cars. Anthony's preference was for a Porsche, Richard's an Aston Martin, and they regularly competed in hill-climbs and races at Prescott near Cheltenham, Shelsley Walsh in Worcestershire, and Oulton Park in Cheshire. Nick Arber, a cousin, recalls the brothers' visit to the Nürburgring in 1937 and their willing acceptance of considerable alcoholic refreshment from the Bonn Oberbürgermeister. Whether Richard took advantage of the opportunity to visit any of the modern churches in the nearby German cities is not known.

Both brothers enjoyed a drink and were

1.4 (BELOW)
Anthony and Richard with their mother Grace

good company together. Anthony seems to have been the more outgoing of the two, and would compose amusing verses and notes. Neither was particularly institutionally religious, but, according to Anthony, making a rare comment on his brother Richard's work, they were brought up quite strictly:

> **...neither of us** (Anthony and Richard) **managed to shake off altogether the effect of our rather, and our parents' very, puritanical upbringing. Dick I think clings to** *constructional purity*...[3]

Richard's work patterns were somewhat different from those we might experience today. He went to the office about 10.30, and had lunch at the Conservative Club before returning about 3pm. He enjoyed playing bridge and tennis, read widely, and held political views to the right of centre.[4]

1.5 Bilbrook Manor in the 1940s

FOUNDATIONS

1.6 (RIGHT)
Richard Twentyman with two of his paintings

1.7 (OPPOSITE TOP)
Sketch of Bidart Church in south-west France 1930

1.8 (OPPOSITE BOTTOM)
'Spaceframe' by Anthony Twentyman 1985 at Dudmaston Hall

Richard and Anthony were originally destined to follow in their father's footsteps and join the family engineering firm on completion of their formal education. They were educated at Wellington College, Berkshire, and both read engineering at Pembroke Colleges, Richard at Cambridge and Anthony at Oxford. Anthony, who was a short, stocky man, acted as cox for the University Rowing Club, but did not finish his degree and initially joined the family firm, involving travel to the firm's tea plantations in Sri Lanka. The work did not suit his temperament, however, and after the war he spent more time developing his artistic career, eventually leaving the firm in the hands of his cousin Jack Twentyman, and becoming a professional artist and sculptor.

Anthony's influential artistic contacts proved useful to his brother Richard who, after finishing his engineering degree, decided, unexpectedly at least to his father, to become an architect. He studied at the Architectural Association (AA) in London between 1925 and 1931, where he found his engineering background helpful. At the time of Twentyman's attendance, the AA was a lively place to study, well-known for providing an excellent academic training for the architecture profession. One of its most successful alumni, Cachemaille-Day, had studied there from 1912-20, and later Board members included Atkinson, Goodhart-Rendel, and Maufe.

The formal curriculum that Twentyman followed would have included a traditional study of Greek, Roman, and Gothic architecture, followed in the subsequent years of his course by a greater emphasis on drawing and detailed design projects with varied subjects ranging from museums, to swimming pools, to warehouses. Examples of student work in Twentyman's time show some signs of moving towards more modern design, one commentator on students' work even warning against a reliance on American and European models: '...if England will but remember that she is

BIDART CHURCH 1930

English, and not either French, American, or Swedish, we need have no fear of the future'.[5] Life at the AA was eclectic during this period: schemes for a car showroom (1.9) and a restaurant (1.10) show the mix of styles produced in student projects at this time,[6] as well as the stylistic evolution in the late 1920s.

The AA School Principal, Howard Robertson, together with the School Secretary, Francis Yerbury, were tentatively introducing a more modern European content in addition to the existing classical American- and French-influenced Beaux-Arts curriculum. One sign of this was the introduction, in the 1929-30 AA Prospectus, of recommended readings on twentieth-century Danish, Dutch, French, and Swedish architecture, together with Mendelsohn's *Structures and Sketches* (1924), *The Life Work of the American Architect* (1925) by Lloyd Wright, and Le Corbusier's *Towards a New Architecture* (1927).

Robertson and Yerbury had visited northern Europe to view its modern architecture, and arranged excursions to Holland (1922), Denmark and Sweden (1925), Germany (1929), and to the Stockholm Exhibition (1930). We do not know whether Twentyman participated in these excursions, though his sketch books at the time do reveal travel to France and Spain (1.7). He would have certainly been exposed to, and, we shall later argue, influenced by, the work of modern Dutch and Scandinavian architects like Asplund, Dudok, and Tengbom through lectures, student projects, and visiting lecturers such as Keppler, Ahlberg, Hegemann, and Mendelsohn.[7]

Twentyman's active and long-lasting interest in northern European modernist architecture was confirmed by his

1.9 (LEFT)
Design for a car showroom, *AA Prospectus 1929-30*

1.10 (BELOW)
Design for a restaurant, *AA Prospectus 1925-6*

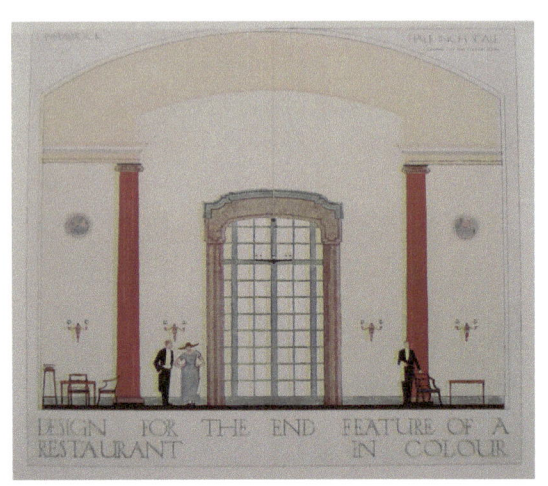

1.11 (ABOVE)
The Year 1 Term 1 mark book from the AA in 1925-6 with Richard Twentyman's entry highlighted

participation many years later in August 1946 in an AA trip to Denmark and Sweden, at a time when he was establishing his own modernist credentials (9.2). The group visited factories, housing developments, schools, and hospitals. Highlights were Lauritzen's Copenhagen Radio House (1934-45) in Denmark, and, in Sweden, Malmö's Theatre (1932-44) by Lewerentz, and Stockholm's Östberg's Town Hall (1923), and, significantly for Twentyman's later commissions, Asplund's Crematorium (1918-40).[8]

While a student at the AA, Twentyman also entered into its social life, appearing in a December 1928 five-scene Christmas 'Pentamime', reviewed in the AA Journal, performed by senior years. He also had a role in a final years' pantomime sketch in December 1929 as a 'year master' and wrote lyrics for the performance.[9]

After finishing his studies, Richard joined as a partner a local architects' firm in Wolverhampton, Henry Edward Lavender and Co, which became the practice of Ernest Clifford Lavender and Alfred Richard Twentyman in 1932. In 1939, at the outbreak of war, Richard joined the Royal Engineers and was promoted to Captain in 1941 and to temporary Major in 1943.[10]

He served in Palestine (1.13) and he may have seen and later been influenced by the 'White City' of Tel Aviv, built from the 1930s onwards in a Bauhaus International Style. His military career was interrupted in 1942 on the death of his partner, E. C. Lavender, when he returned to manage his architects' practice and recruit a new partner, Charles Geoffrey Percy (1914-63). Richard's brother Anthony joined the RAF as a Flight Lieutenant, possibly with the assistance of Air Marshall Sir Douglas Evill, his mother Grace Evill's first cousin. Anthony was taken prisoner at the fall of Singapore, and spent 1942-45 in Japanese prisoner-of-war camps in Palembang, Sumatra, and Changi, Singapore. He later made an oblique reference to this experience through a sculpture, 'Spaceframe' (1985), now on permanent display, together with a number of his other sculptures, in the grounds of Dudmaston Hall in Shropshire (1.8).

The brothers inherited their parents' creative talents. We have already mentioned their father's skill as a draughtsman and woodturner. Their mother, Grace, about whom we unfortunately know little, was a cartoonist and painter, and a friend of the artist Frances Hodgkins (1869-1947). Anthony and Richard were mutual influences on each other, Richard as an architect, and Anthony as an artist who encouraged Richard to take up watercolour, and, later, oil painting in retirement (1.6). Anthony had earlier approached John Piper to paint their family home at Bilbrook Manor, after which John and Myfwany Piper became firm friends, regularly visiting each other's homes. The commission led indirectly to the 1965 Piper stained-glass window at Twentyman's St Andrew Church in Whitmore Reans, the only occasion Twentyman used a stained-glass window in his churches.

Twentyman did not use extensive artistic decoration in his churches, but believed in the effect of a single sculptural piece placed either externally or internally as a counterpoint to his simple church designs. He commissioned several works from Don Potter, the sculptor (1902-2004), an arrangement facilitated through his brother Anthony's social and artistic friendships. Don Potter was a member of the Scouts and his skills as a sculptor were soon recognised

1.12 (ABOVE)
The Twentyman brothers' memorial stones side-by-side in Claverley Churchyard, Shropshire

by Richard Baden-Powell, the founder of the Scout Movement. Anthony Twentyman was also a Scout, and he and Don Potter met as Scout leaders in the 1920s, which led to Potter's first commission from Richard Twentyman for his church of St Martin in Wolverhampton in 1939. The architect and the sculptor worked well together and further commissions followed, described in this book.

1.13 (ABOVE)
Painting of Tiberias in Palestine by Richard Twentyman

FOUNDATIONS

1.14
Richard Twentyman (centre left) at the opening of the new wing of the Eye Infirmary in Wolverhampton 1938 with E.C. Lavender on the far left

Notes

1. J. Davies (ed.), *Bilbrook in a Bygone Age* (Codsall and Bilbrook History Society, 2018), pp.18-19 and 39-40.

2. N. Arber, *Anthony Twentyman* (Wolverhampton Art Gallery, 1990), pp.5-9.

3. M. Piper, *Anthony Twentyman*, p.11.

4. Much of the personal information about the Twentyman family has been kindly provided by relatives and friends who knew Dick and Tony Twentyman. We are very grateful for their help.

5. *The Architectural Association Journal*, (August, 1926), p.42.

6. *AA Prospectus*, 1925-26, and 1929-30.

7. J. Summerson, *The Architectural Association 1847-1947* (London: Architectural Association, 1947), p.45; and E. Darling, *Reforming Britain* (Abingdon: Routledge, 2007), p.182.

8. 'Denmark and Sweden, 1946', *The Architectural Association Journal*, 62, 706, (October, 1946), pp.35-47.

9. *AA Archives* 02 02 07 08 and 09; and *AA Journal*, January, (1929), pp.261-263.

10. *UK Army List 1944*, Alfred Richard Twentyman.

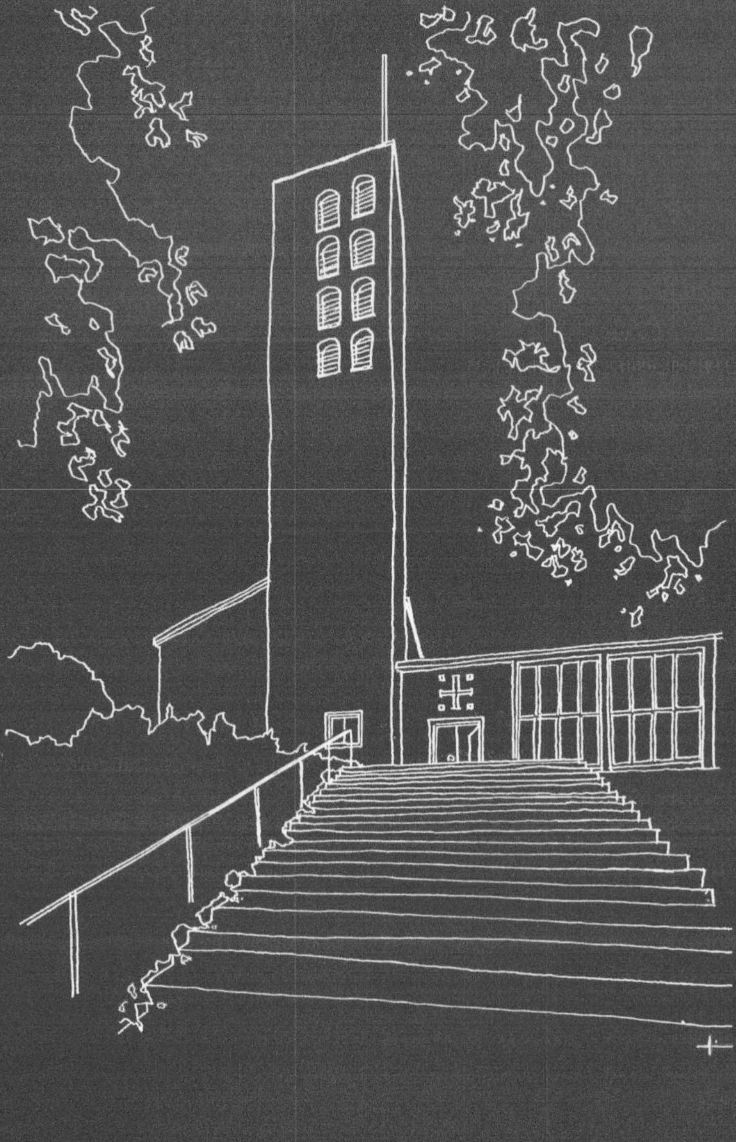

CHAPTER TWO

2
THE CHURCHES & MODERNISM

THE CHURCHES & MODERNISM

We have new wonderful materials and methods that make a new architecture possible. Are we going to be content with the frills and fripperies of the Victorian birthday cake architects, to come across rank bad taste at every turn? No, a thousand times no! We have a chance to show a new spirit in the beauty of simplicity and we must grasp it at any cost.[1]

It is telling that this quotation dates from 1945, and shows how slowly ideas of modern architecture took root in Britain, despite early examples from the 1920s in Germany, for example Bartning, Böhm, and Schwarz, as well as contributions from Dutch, Scandinavian, and Swiss architects,[2] some of whom will be mentioned later in connection with Twentyman.

By the 1930s, English ecclesiastical architecture was beginning to take note of European models.[3] The Liverpool School of Architecture under Charles Reilly's leadership from 1904-1933 produced a generation of architects such as Miller, Rowse, and Velarde, keen to develop a new English architecture, and whose work Twentyman would have certainly known.

Postwar there was an even wider acceptance that architecture should move away from Gothic models and develop new solutions not imitating the past.[4] Attitudes to modern architecture were still ambivalent among the public, however, illustrated in a 1936 Punch cartoon showing the excited new owner of a Corbusier-like modern house addressing onlookers baffled by the new design, with the words: 'Do tell me you *loathe* it'.

New materials assisted modern design. Reinforced concrete could be cast as columns, slabs, or curved vaults. It had strength and stability but was also adaptable and comparatively light. Walls could be thinner creating larger, lighter volumes, curved rooflines extended to the horizontal, and extensive glazing replaced what formerly had been supporting walls.[5] W. R. Lethaby, at All Saints, Brockhampton of 1901 (2.2), and Edward Prior at St Andrew, Roker (1907) were early pioneers of concrete, particularly in vaulting. However, Auguste Perret's Church of Notre Dame du Raincy of 1922-23 (2.1) is frequently cited as the first church to exploit the effective use of concrete to create simple expanses with slender pillars,

2.1
Notre Dame du Raincy, Île-de-France Auguste Perret 1922-3

25 RICHARD TWENTYMAN

2.2
All Saints Brockhampton-by-Ross, Herefordshire W.R. Lethaby 1901

no aisles, and large windows,[6] features in a number of Twentyman's churches, including Emmanuel, Bentley (1955-57), and St Chad, Rubery (1956-60).

Ecclesiastical responses to modernism

A church is a particular genre or 'building type'.[7] Its design is generated by specific purposes within a space used for certain social and religious activities. In this sense, church design has often followed Sullivan's original 'form follows function' statement. The publication *Church Buildings* provides detailed guidance to church designers, listing nine areas of activity and function with several sub-divisions to be integrated into the design, adapted for various denominations and their ideological and philosophical needs. The level of detail includes the dimensions recommended for a Catholic altar, in order to facilitate the various actions of a priest at the altar during a service.[8]

During the early part of the twentieth century, concerns were expressed that the traditional design of Gothic and neo-Gothic churches was not suitable for the needs of a modern church.[9] The narrow nave with side aisles and its separation from the choir, chancel, and sanctuary was no longer appropriate for religious services which now aimed to integrate rather than separate clergy and congregation.

Thomas[10] argues that the unusual volumetric design of Albi Cathedral (1282-1512) influenced 19th- and 20th-century church design, especially where large spaces were required so that congregations could see celebrants clearly. Albi, with a fortress-like appearance but without exaggerated external buttresses, had a wide central nave with pierced walkways rather than aisles. Maufe used the idea in the construction of Guildford Cathedral, the drawings for which were published in 1932. Twentyman may have been influenced by Maufe's Guildford features when he designed St Gabriel and St Martin in 1937-39, and in 1952, All Saints, Darlaston, which, like Guildford, had 'pure cubic forms, unbroken straight lines, and a lack of decorative detail'.[11] The buildings share the same focussed view from the west to the east end of the nave, and both architects created shafts of light entering obliquely from high windows to shine on the sanctuary (2.3).

THE CHURCHES & MODERNISM

2.3
Comparative plans of Albi Cathedral (c.1282)
Midi-Pyrénées and All Saints Darlaston (1952)

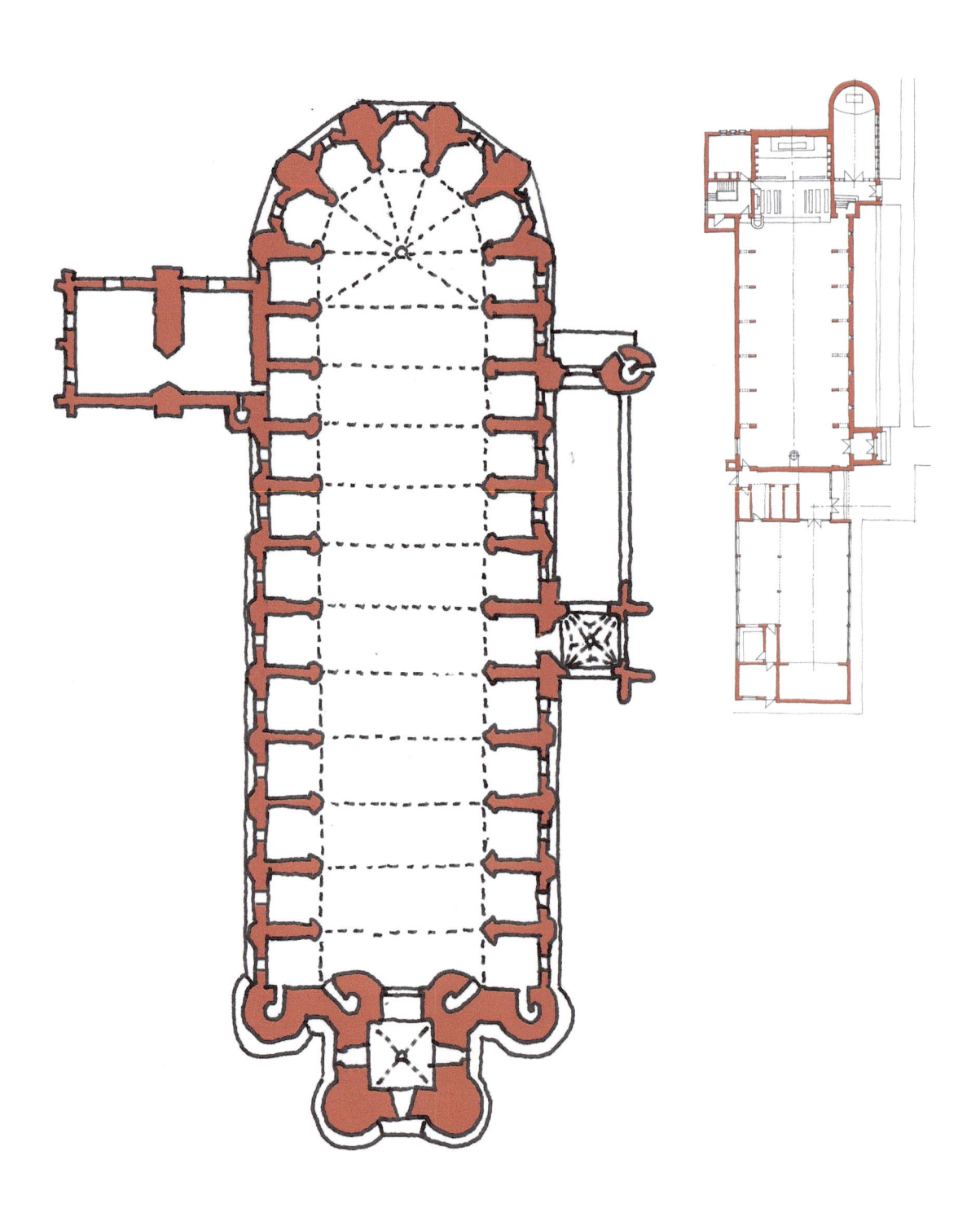

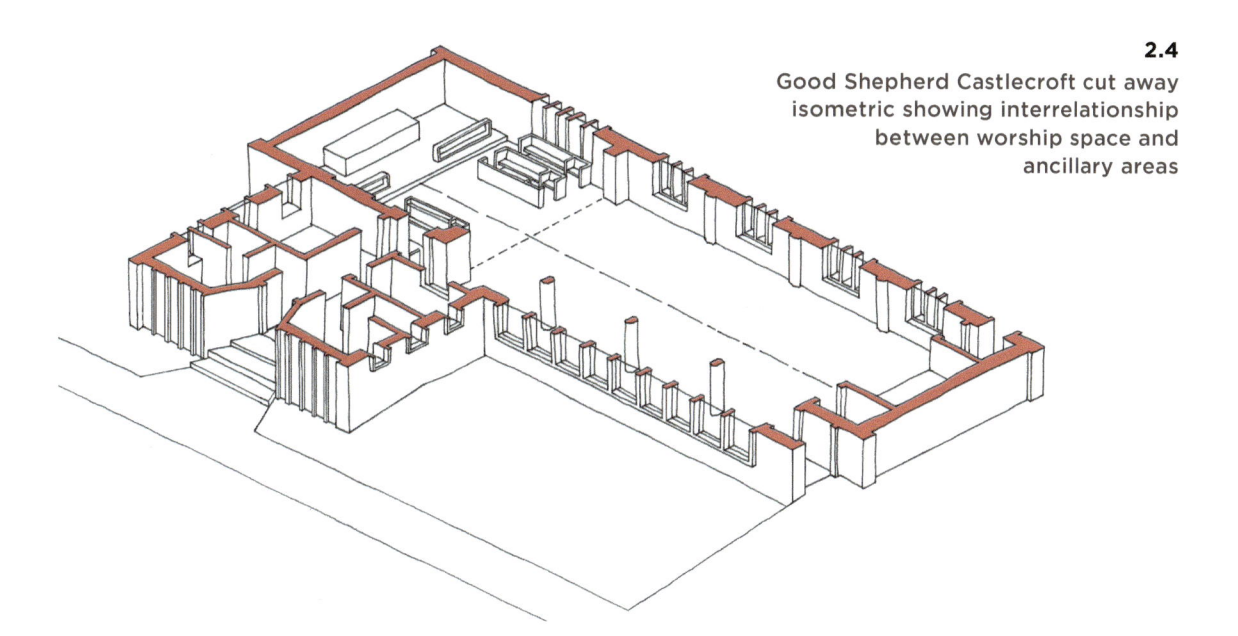

2.4
Good Shepherd Castlecroft cut away isometric showing interrelationship between worship space and ancillary areas

Mies van der Rohe suggested abandoning attempts to match form and function, instead building simple forms that could be adapted to a variety of needs over time, illustrated in his 1952 Chicago Memorial Chapel.[12] Twentyman similarly designed multipurpose postwar churches to be used both for worship and for community social purposes, creating a uni-cell separating, if required, the sanctuary from the nave with a partition, but also, if finances permitted and if the number of users was large, adding extensions according to their required function, whether as a chapel, vestry, meeting room, or kitchen. Twentyman's Church of the Good Shepherd, Castlecroft (1955) exemplifies such functional additions (2.4).

The move away from historicism towards modernism, and the adoption of a functional approach combined with the use of modern materials, together with postwar cost constraints, led to simpler church designs and the potential difficulty of reconciling modernist principles with a church's transcendental aims:

…some of our modern churches might be mistaken for factories or swimming pools… not far from where I live there is a Fire Station with its adjacent tower which might easily be mistaken for a new church.[13]

Several of Twentyman's later designs fit into this category, including St Chad, Rubery, (1956-60), one of whose parishioners still describes his church affectionately as 'the one that looks like a Fire Station'.

Though sections of the church laity and church authorities appealed for a balance between historicism and modernism, to others the lack of distinguishing features between a church and a secular building such as a factory or a fire station was not problematic. Churches should reflect a 'municipal modernism'[14] and be designed as part of the urban environment, not separate from it, using exterior materials such as brick, metal, and concrete, with internal wood furnishings, like Twentyman's postwar churches.

2.5 (RIGHT)
All Saints Darlaston in 1954

Liturgical change & church architecture

As early as 1910, Pope Pius X's liturgical views had supported less grand, 'one-room' churches,[15] and thereafter liturgical change continued to influence church architecture of all denominations, illustrated by a comment on three 1950s Coventry churches, including Twentyman's St Nicholas, Radford:

> **The impression...was one of optimism, and of the power of the Anglican and Roman, as well as the Free Churches, to go forward on the wave of the new liturgical movement as leading patrons of art and architecture.**[16]

The culmination of liturgical change was the 1962-65 Second Vatican Council (Vatican II), which was reflected in the similar liturgical attitudes of other denominations. Vatican II emphasised active community worship combining the roles of priest and congregation as co-participants rather than separating them. Such thinking led to a more interactive dialogic service with local languages replacing Latin and the priest facing the congregation. Clear sightlines became important so that all could see and partake in the service, and the altar was preferably to be placed more centrally with the congregation assembled around it.

Peter Hammond (1921-1999), an Anglican priest and architectural theorist, argued strongly for architecture to reflect a liturgy of community worship, and encouraged design experimentation with 'the square, the ellipse, the circle, and the trapezoid.'[17] Hammond was reflecting Rudolf Schwarz's (1897-1961) earlier influential views on church design. Schwarz distinguished between the traditional *Wegkirche*, literally 'way-church', (the longitudinal nave), and various varieties of the *Ringkirche*, 'ring-church', (the congregation gathered around a central altar).[18] Hammond argued that form may well follow function but unless function is based on the Liturgical Movement, and not driven by aesthetic or experiential considerations, the architecture will fail. He was critical of Coventry Cathedral:

> **The new Coventry Cathedral promises to be a spectacular example of architectural form following an inadequately conceived function...The quest for sparkling and beautiful altars at the end of long vistas is strictly irrelevant...**

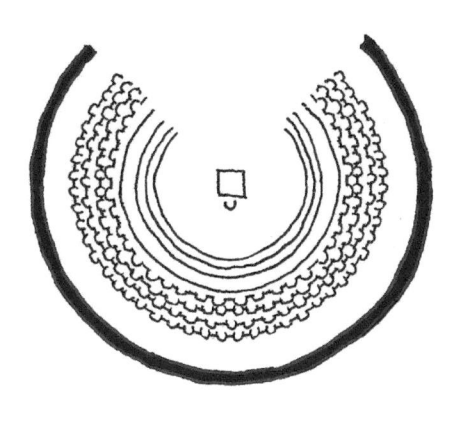

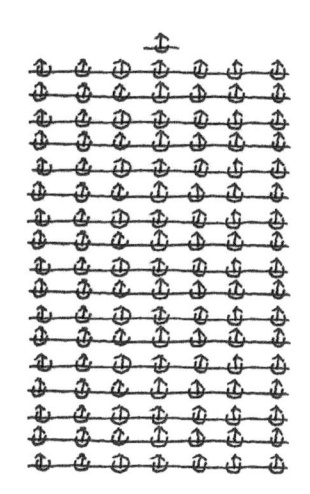

2.6 (ABOVE)
Illustrations of Ringkirche [the Open Ring] (left) and Wegkirche (right) after Schwarz 1938

> To conceive the primary function of a cathedral in terms of its effect on the casual visitor is rather like describing the Festival Hall as a building where one can have a pleasant meal with a view of the river.[19]

2.7 (BELOW)
Fronleichnamskirche Aachen Schwarz 1929-30 a monumental Wegkirche with a low, asymmetrical south aisle

The June 1962 front cover of the magazine *Private Eye* succinctly portrayed these concerns with a lone voice from the vast congregation attending the Cathedral's consecration service exclaiming: 'Alright, God, you can come in now'. Hammond also warns of the danger of 'medieval churches masquerading in contemporary fancy dress',[20] and criticizes recent churches

> which draw upon the whole rag-bag of contemporary clichés –random windows, Betonglas, skeletal bell towers, monumental crosses and the rest –but which are no more than caricatures of modern buildings.[21]

THE CHURCHES & MODERNISM

Whether Hammond would include Twentyman's churches as exemplifications of his forthright views is not clear. Twentyman's interwar churches (St Gabriel, and St Martin) have a Romanesque monumentalism but also integrate modern design and materials. They represent a natural development in ecclesiastical church design. Twentyman's postwar churches have 'skeletal bell towers and monumental crosses' but such objects have an important purpose in signalling to local communities a church's presence. Hammond praises '...unpretentious churches which combine great artistic integrity with a lucid grasp of liturgical principles'.[22]

Twentyman's churches undoubtedly show such integrity, but it may be that Twentyman does not fully meet Hammond's stringent requirements regarding liturgical function. With the exception of his last two 1965 churches (St Andrew, Whitmore Reans, and St Andrew, Runcorn), he delineates nave from chancel and sanctuary, though the division is less pronounced, and altars, although brought forward so that a celebrant can face the congregation, are not placed centrally. Such Twentyman designs were no doubt a compromise in response to local diocesan wishes and to practical requirements, since it is less convenient to partition a multipurpose church that has a centrally-placed altar, though not a compromise that Hammond might support. Giles Gilbert Scott, referring to his own practice, perhaps mirrors Twentyman's views and the development of his architectural career:

> **I had no brief either for the extreme diehard Traditionalist or the extreme Modernist...I want to see 'Modernism's' best features and characteristics retained and grafted at first on to the traditions of the past and then gradually developed.**[23]

2.8
EMMANUEL BENTLEY
The Wegkirche typology allowing a balance of modernism and traditionalism

CHURCH ART

Although proponents of the 1920s and 1930s *International Style*[24] did not welcome decoration *per se*, from the 1950s, church art was recognised as a way of continuing the modernity of the 1951 Festival of Britain, of creating a civic architecture of value to local communities, and of helping facilitate devotion,[25] as long as objects did not render a church a museum.[26] Basil Spence encouraged artistic involvement in church design[27] through his employment of several artists in his own churches in the Coventry area from 1954-57 (see Chapter 3), and in Coventry Cathedral, (1956-62), including John Hutton, John Piper, and Graham Sutherland.

A more holistic approach to design created crafted furnishings in the spirit of the Arts and Crafts movement, influenced by Pugin's belief in a totally-designed environment, demonstrated in his work designing the Palace of Westminster. Later, the philosophy of Gropius and the Bauhaus, and the concept of the *Gesamtkunstwerk*, was accepted, exemplified by Arne Jacobsen's meticulous specifications for St Catherine's College, Oxford, completed in 1962, embracing everything from the landscape setting of the College down to the detail of chairs and cutlery (2.9).

Twentyman believed in a similar approach, designing fonts, door leaves and handles, benches, choir stalls, lecterns, altar rails, and altars, in order to create a consistent design signature and preserve an artistic homogeneity. Commissioning artists such as Don Potter for specific items such as fonts and external sculptures enhanced the effect further still. Artists worked in partnership with clergy and architects, but had

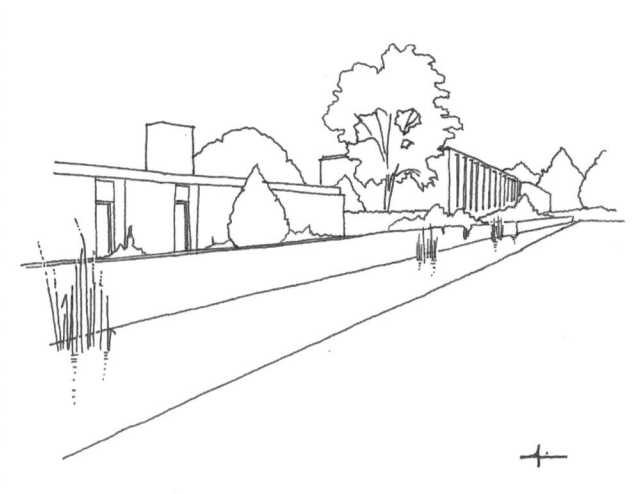

2.9 (BELOW)
St Catherine's College, Oxford
Arne Jacobsen 1962

2.10 (RIGHT)
St Chad Rubery, original watercolour perspective by Twentyman dated 1954 and exhibited at the RA in 1957

to avoid criticisms of the art being either too representational and popular, or too challenging.[28] The case of Geoffrey Clarke's sculptures for St Chad, Rubery demonstrates the point.

The Clarke Sculptures

Geoffrey Clarke (1924-2014) was known for his stained-glass windows and sculpture in Basil Spence's Coventry Cathedral, particularly his Altar Cross and Crown of Thorns. Twentyman commissioned him to design a set of reliefs for the external west wall of St Chad, Rubery.[29] (See also Chapter 5). Twentyman's letters to Clarke from 1957 to 1962 reveal the story behind the Clarke sculptures and their eventual removal.[30]

A full account is given below since it reveals the respective roles of Twentyman, Clarke, the Vicar, the Archdeacon, and the Diocesan Advisory Committee (DAC), and the complex mix of religious, aesthetic, and architectural negotiations between them.

Twentyman first writes to Geoffrey Clarke on 16 May 1957, on the recommendation of John Piper, saying he has seen examples of Clarke's past work and asking whether he would be interested in sculpting five figures on the west front of St Chad, namely the Virgin and Child, St John the Baptist, and Sts Nicholas, Chad and Stephen. He suggests incising the figures on slate panels or making them separately in bronze, or using symbols, rather than figures. By 22 May 1957, Clarke has agreed to symbols in bronze (Twentyman also mentions at this time Clarke's commission for the Diocesan Coat-of-Arms, still *in situ*). On 3 January 1958, Twentyman informs Clarke that his tender has been accepted, and encloses a list of symbols the Vicar suggests for the panels: the Lion of Judah; a 'Star' symbolising the Incarnation (which Twentyman uses extensively on his church towers); the Orb and Cross; a 'Last Things' symbol; and the Lamb and Flag. There is a long gap in the correspondence until 24 September 1959, when Clarke declares his preference for open-cast aluminium rather than bronze reliefs. On 10 November 1959, Twentyman expresses relief that the 5-foot panels are almost ready as the church is due to be consecrated on 15 December 1959.

THE CHURCHES & MODERNISM

By 18 November 1959, Clarke's drawings or photos of the reliefs have arrived, since Twentyman, somewhat puzzled, asks for a description of the symbolism used, the first indication that Clarke has deviated from the Vicar's earlier traditional religious symbols. On 2 December 1959, Twentyman asks when the reliefs will be delivered, and during the next two weeks before the 15 December consecration, the reliefs must have been put in place and then hurriedly removed at the insistence of the Archdeacon. Photograph 2.12 shows the empty niches designed to carry the sculptures. Their removal is confirmed by Twentyman on 30 March 1960, when he quotes from the St Chad's DAC resolution:

> **Whilst appreciating the desire to present a design in symbolic form suitable to a modern building, and whilst not in any sense discouraging an artist from employing a modern idiom, the committee are of the opinion that these plaques do not really convey theological truth, and are inappropriate for use in a Christian Church.**

Twentyman indicates that Clarke had given no forewarning of the changes he had made: 'Had you been able to keep to the symbols given to you in your original brief the sculptures would have been accepted', and 'The Diocese...consider that you departed from your brief without authority'. In the same letter. Twentyman suggests a compromise, that Clarke should remake the five plaques following the original symbolism, a suggestion to which the Archdeacon eventually agrees (3 August 1960), but for whatever reasons, and despite letters from Twentyman to Clarke and to the Vicar, by 1963, nothing has happened. The Vicar leaves for a new parish in 1964, and presumably the matter is dropped.

Clarke was clearly attempting to refresh religious symbolism, hence his own rejection of the more traditional symbols earlier suggested by St Chad's Vicar. His alternative abstract designs are difficult to interpret although ironically their 'modernism' may have derived from Rudolf Koch's 1930 collection of ancient and medieval symbols.[31] One of the five panels is illustrated in 2.11. The shepherd's crook below the earth's horizontal line, and the cross above it signify 'Christ's earthly and spiritual presence'.[32] Had Clarke signalled his intention to reformulate his brief, and provided the Church authorities with an explanation of the symbols, it may have been possible, with both Twentyman's and the Vicar's support, to have overcome the more conservative views prevailing at the time. Perhaps now, with a change in attitudes, the reliefs, entitled *Square World*, and which still exist,[33] might finally complete the west front of St Chad.

As an interesting footnote, the Clarke Archives contain a letter (8 July 1963) from Basil Spence Architects, politely declining Geoffrey Clarke's 'cut-price offer' of some panels, suitable for 'an external wall', presumably the rejected St Chad panels.

2.11
GEOFFREY CLARKE
Cast aluminium relief commissioned for the west front of St Chad Rubery

2.12
ST CHAD RUBERY WEST FRONT (2021)

ART IN THE TWENTYMAN CHURCHES

2.13 & 2.14 (BELOW)
Pigeon Loft Sedgley, Richard Twentyman and Spring, Anthony Twentyman, Wolverhampton Art Gallery

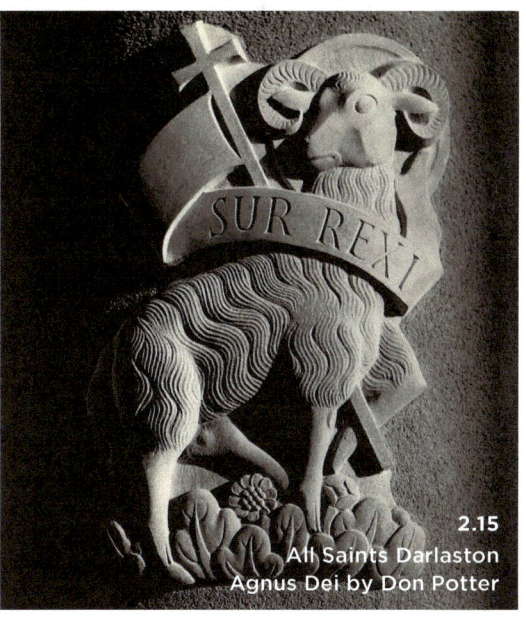

We have mentioned the influence of Richard Twentyman's family on his future career and his attitude to church art.[34] He was an artist as well as an architect and several of his paintings are in Wolverhampton Art Gallery (2.13), together with a number of the paintings and sculpture of his younger brother Anthony (2.14). As we have seen, Richard drew on Anthony's wide connections with artists of the day for his own church commissions, including Donald Potter, Eric Gill's former assistant,[35] Geoffrey Clarke, already mentioned above in connection with St Chad, and stained-glass artists John Piper (1903-1992) and Patrick Reyntiens (1925-2021).

Twentyman used art objects, including his own designed furnishings, sparingly but effectively. Don Potter's creations were an effective counterpoint to the simplicity of Twentyman's own architecture, presenting a 'balanced view of sparse ornament beautiful in its design and placed just where it is needed and nowhere else'.[36] Potter carved the figure of St Martin, a font, and a pulpit at St Martin, Wolverhampton (1937-39); at All Saints, Darlaston (1952), the stone reliefs on the main door (2.17), the *Agnus Dei* pulpit (2.15), an oak eagle lectern, and a black granite font; three sculptures at Bushbury Crematorium, Wolverhampton (1954); and a sculpture relief on the tower at St Nicholas, Radford (1954-55).[37] Finally, Piper and Reyntien's stained-glass window is a remarkable addition to St Andrew, Whitmore Reans (1965) (2.16).

2.15
All Saints Darlaston
Agnus Dei by Don Potter

THE CHURCHES & MODERNISM

2.16
ST ANDREW WHITMORE REANS
WEST WINDOW BY JOHN PIPER

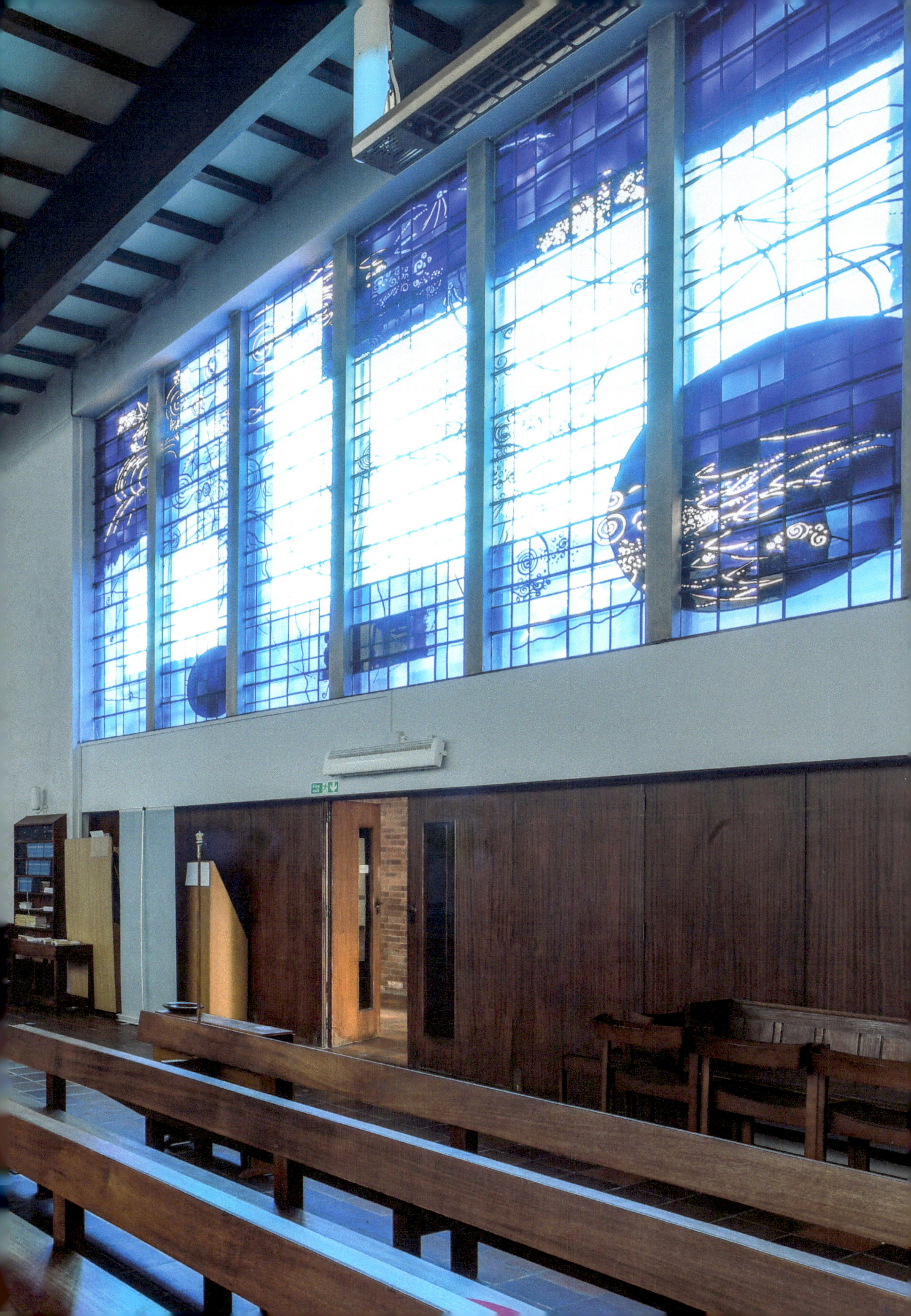

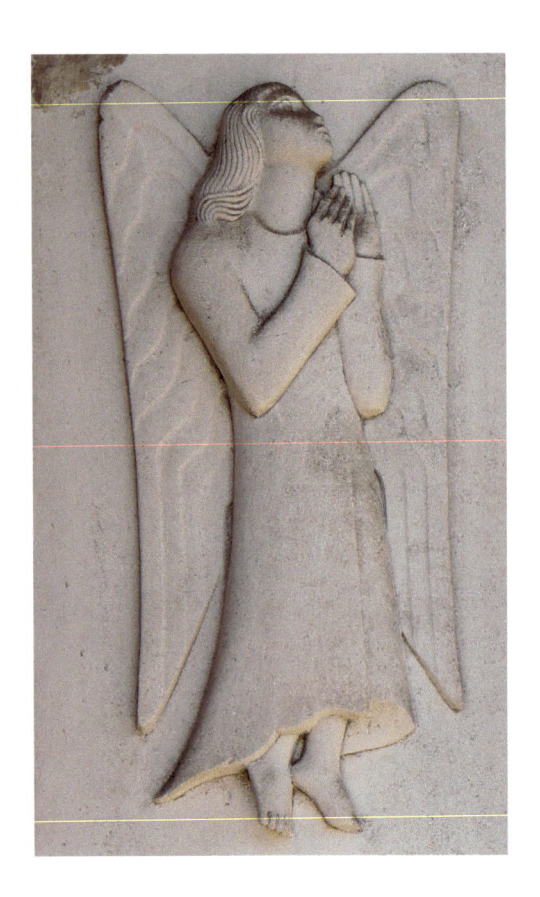

Notes

1. Letter from T. Holt, *Wolverhampton Express and Star* (31 January, 1945), quoted in P. Larkham, 'Rebuilding the Industrial Town: wartime Wolverhampton', *Urban History*, 29,3, (December, 2002) p.402.

2. G. Kidder-Smith, *The New Churches of Europe* (London: Architectural Press, 1964).

3. N. Bullock, *Building the Postwar World* (London: Routledge, 2002).

4. N. Pevsner, 'The Modern Movement in Britain', reprinted in S. Charlton and A. Powers (eds.), *British Modern Architecture and Design in the 1930s* (London: Twentieth Century Society, 8, 2007), pp.17-38.

5. A. Christ-Janer and M. Foley, *Modern Church Architecture* (New York: McGraw-Hill 1962), pp.4-10.

6. C. Osborne, *American Catholics and the Church of Tomorrow* (Chicago: University of Chicago Press, 2018), p.96.

7. N. Pevsner, *A History of Building Types* (London: Thames and Hudson, 1986).

8. *Church Buildings* (London: Architectural Press, 1967), p.373.

9. Osborne, *American Catholics*, p.186.

10. J. Thomas, 'The Influence of Albi Cathedral', *The Journal of Architecture,* 3,2, (1998), pp.85-105.

11. Thomas, 'Albi Cathedral', p.105.

12. Christ-Janer and Foley, *Modern Church Architecture*, p.185.

2.17 (ABOVE)
All Saints Darlaston main entrance by Don Potter

13 Bishop Beck of Salford quoted in R. Proctor, *Building the Modern Church* (Farnham: Ashgate, 2014), p.69.

14 R. Proctor, *Building the Modern Church* (Farnham: Ashgate, 2014), p.69.

15 Kidder-Smith, *The New Churches of Europe*, p.11.

16 'New Churches', *The Architects' Journal*, 20 March, (1958), p.423.

17 P. Hammond, 'A Liturgical Brief', *The Architectural Review*, 1 April, (1958), p.242.

18 R. Schwarz, *The Church Incarnate* (Chicago: Regnery, 1958), a translation of *Vom Bau der Kirche* (Würzburg: Werkbund Verlag, 1938).

19 Hammond, 'Liturgical Brief', p.244.

20 Hammond, 'Liturgical Brief', p.255.

21 P. Hammond, (ed.), *Towards a Church Architecture* (London: Architectural Press, 1962), p.25.

22 Hammond, 'Liturgical Brief', p.244.

23 G. Stamp, 'Battersea Power Station', *The Twentieth Century Society Journal*, 1, (1981), p.4.

24 W. Curtis, *Modern Architecture since 1900* (London: Phaidon, 2006), pp.257-74.

25 Proctor, *Building the Modern Church*, p.75.

26 E. Maufe, *Modern Church Architecture* (London: ICBS, 1938), p.7.

27 L. Campbell, *Coventry Cathedral: Art and Architecture in postwar Britain*, (Oxford: OUP, 1996).

28 Proctor, *Building the Modern Church*, p.111.

29 C. Turner, 'Square World', *Art and Christianity*, 81, Spring (2015), pp.2-5.

30 *The Archive of Geoffrey Clarke*, (St Chad, Rubery), Henry Moore Institute and Leeds Museums & Galleries.

31 J. LeGrove, 'Fragile Visions: Reading and Re-reading the Work of Geoffrey Clarke', in R. Arya, (ed.), *Contemplations of the Spiritual in Art*, (Oxford: Peter Lang, 2013), pp.151-72.

32 Le Grove, 'Fragile Visions', p.164.

33 At the time of writing, the panels can be viewed at *The Lightbox*, Woking.

34 Biographical information on the Twentyman family is taken from: *Graces Guide* (online), https://www.gracesguide.co.uk/Harold_Edward_Twentyman; N. Arber, 'J.A. Twentyman', *Pembroke College Record* (Oxford: Witney Press, 1989), pp.27-29; *Wolverhampton Record Office Archives*, Ref. D/TWM/4 and D/TWM/30.

35 'Donald Potter', *Mapping the Practice and Profession of Sculpture in Britain and Ireland 1851-1951* (University of Glasgow History of Art online database, 2011).

36 G. Stamp, 'Battersea Power Station', p.7. The views expressed are those of Giles Gilbert Scott (1880-1960), but they encapsulate Twentyman's use of ornament.

37 V. Light, *Don Potter: an inspiring century* (Brook: Canterton Books, 2002), p.164.

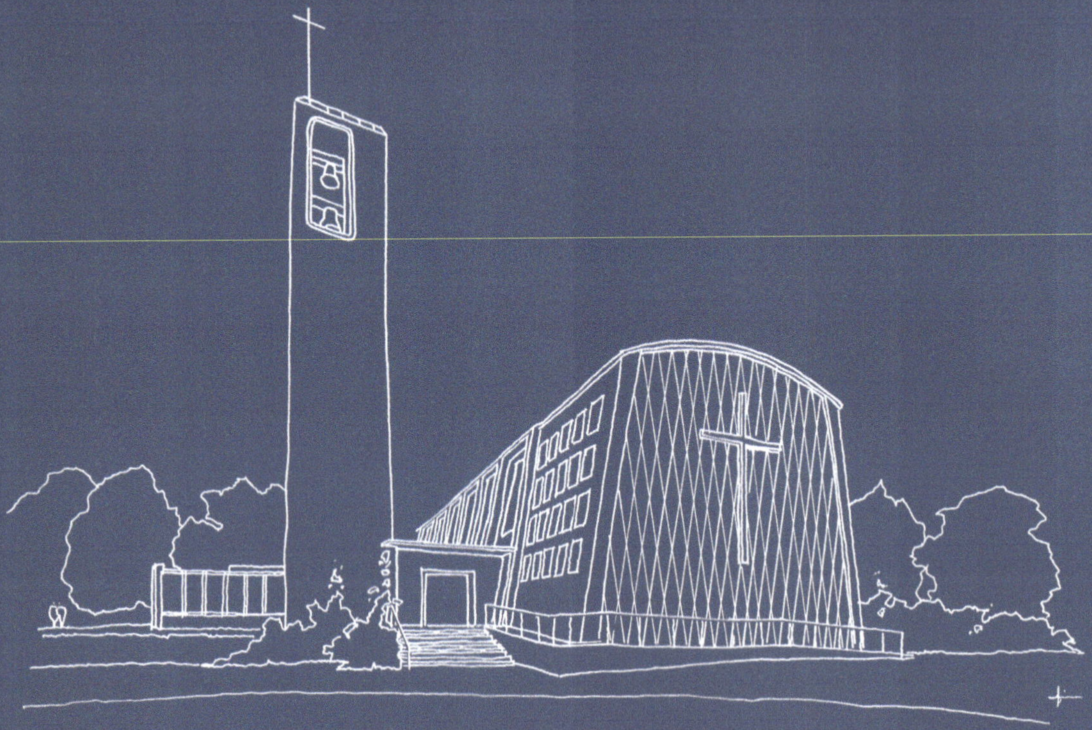

CHAPTER THREE

3
RECONSTRUCTION & EXPANSION

RECONSTRUCTION & EXPANSION

From the 1930s to the 1970s, social, political, and economic events led to extensive housing developments in the West Midlands suburbs.[1] These in turn led to pressure on local dioceses for new churches as a civic community resource, either to replace existing but inadequate churches or those destroyed in WWII,[2] a demand which Twentyman was uniquely wellplaced to supply.

St Nicholas, Radford, and All Saints, Darlaston were destroyed by bombing in 1940 and 1942 respectively, and replaced by new Twentyman churches in 1954-55 and 1952, funded by local contributions and the War Damage Commission.

Municipal housing had started in Darlaston in 1920 and by 1965 3,500 new council houses had been built, many for those working in local engineering firms like the F. H. Lloyd steelworks in Wednesbury and Rubery Owen in Darlaston.[3] During the war, such firms were fully employed providing essential armaments including tanks, aircraft parts, and shells. The Atlas Works, owned by GKN, was spread over an area of 20 acres and employed 3000 people by the end of the war, and F. H. Lloyd had the largest foundry in Europe. In Walsall, served by Twentyman's St Gabriel and Emmanuel churches, 2,417 homes were built between 1925 and 1930, including 'homes fit for heroes'[4], to provide council homes and replace slum dwellings. By 1965 Walsall Council owned 18,500 homes.[5]

Wolverhampton Borough, including Twentyman's St Martin and St Andrew churches, with an expanding population and employment in large engineering companies, had 41,000 houses by September 1940. Like Darlaston and Walsall, it suffered from dense urbanisation, poor quality housing, and derelict land.[6]

DIOCESAN INVOLVEMENT

Prompted by the Church Commissioners, the Diocesan Bishops of Birmingham, Coventry, and Lichfield, all dioceses in which Twentyman churches were built, realised that growing suburban populations and expansion in housing provision required a parallel community development in church and church hall provision if the Church was to fulfil its social purpose, and if new residents were not to become totally secularised. They 'saw it as essential that new churches should be built in new areas.'[7] E. W. Barnes, Bishop of Birmingham from 1924-1953, built fifteen multipurpose churches between 1928 and 1939.[8] Twentyman's St Chad, Rubery (1956-60), serving the Rednal Housing Estate bordering the huge Longbridge car plant, was one of six churches built in response to the *Circles Without Centres* Bishop's Appeal of 1953-58, initiated by Barnes' successor Leonard Wilson (Bishop from 1953-69).[9] The Circles were the new estates, with churches providing the necessary core Centres for the communities.

Coventry had started to develop a New Churches Scheme under Bishops Carr and Haigh in the 1930s.[10] This continued under Neville Gorton, Bishop from 1943-52, keen to satisfy growing social demands through church building. He commissioned Basil Spence, who in 1951 had won the competition to build Coventry Cathedral, to design three churches, now Grade II listed, serving

3.1
The ruins of the former All Saints
Darlaston 1871 (G.E.Street) after
bomb damage in July 1942

3.2
Sir Basil Spence's churches in Coventry
Tile Hill, Bell Green and Willenhall

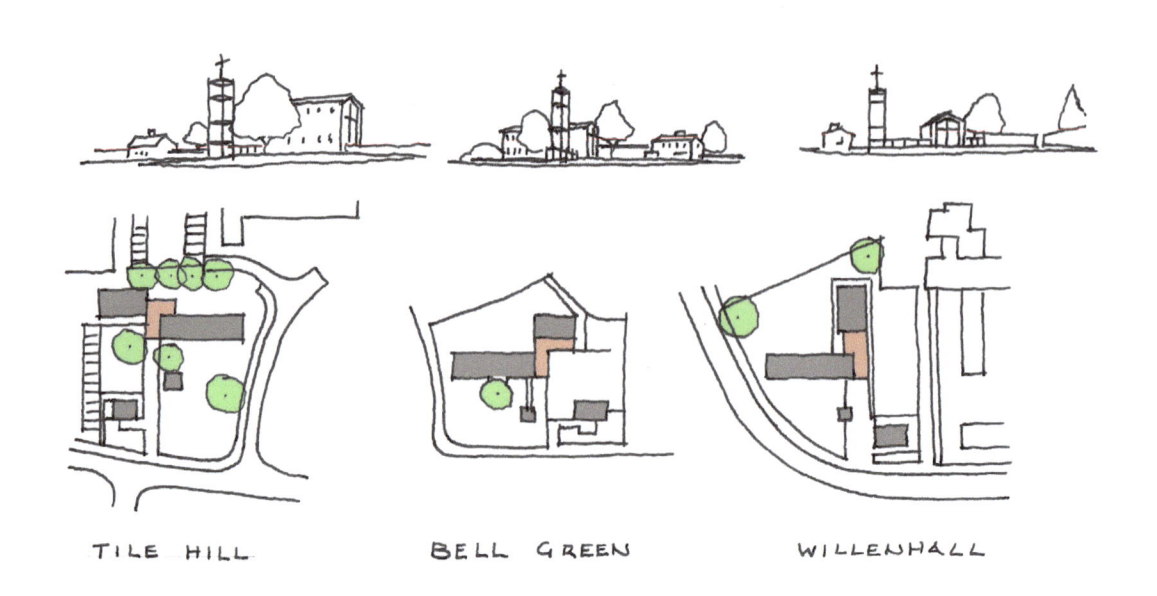

TILE HILL BELL GREEN WILLENHALL

three Coventry housing estates, with a total budget of £50,000, funded by the War Damage Commission. They were St Oswald, Tile Hill, St John the Divine, Willenhall, and St Chad, Bell Green/Wood End.

They were built to a design common to all three churches from 1954-57 by Wimpey and Co. with no-fines concrete, an inexpensive system used at the time in housing developments enabling rapid construction.[11] The three churches' simple box-like appearance was relieved by effective use of natural lighting through a judicious mix of large windows and small but carefully-placed glazed apertures, much like Twentyman's lighting in his 1950s churches, and by Spence's commissioning of artists like Ralph Beyer, Gerald Holtom, and Carroll Sims to provide single striking sculptures and works of art.

Stretton Reeve, Bishop of Lichfield Diocese from 1953-74, having raised £1,000,000 in the late 1950s and early 1960s, launched a further £1,000,000 7-year fund-raising Bishop's Campaign for new church construction in 1966. The campaign had a target of £250,000 asked of a thousand West Midlands private firms, the remaining £750,000 to come from Church Commissioners, diocesan funds, and parishioners. Construction plans included twelve churches, and, with an emphasis on community needs, nineteen church halls and nine dual-purpose buildings.[12]

3.3 & 3.4
All Saints Darlaston under construction, mid 1950s

The Bishop justified the past and present campaigns, since there were now, as a result of population movement and growth,

huge new housing estates…(where) young married people with children were to be found in their thousands, and it was the prime duty of the Church to be where the people were.[13]

RECONSTRUCTION & EXPANSION

3.5
ST NICHOLAS RADFORD
The reredos in African mahogony & walnut

Notes

1. J. Boughton, *Municipal Dreams* (London: Verso, 2019).

2. N. Bullock, *Building the Post-War World* (London: Routledge, 2002).

3. B. Parker, *'The Inter-War Years', A History of Darlaston*. (Online). http://www.history-website.co.uk/articles/Darlaston/interwar.htm.

4. M. Swenarton, *The Politics and Architecture of Early State Housing in Britain* (London: Routledge, 2016).

5. J. Boughton, *Municipal Dreams – Council Housing in Walsall, Parts 11 and 111*, December 2017/January 2018. (Online). https://municipaldreams.wordpress.com/2017/12/12/walsall_council_housing.

6. P. Larkham, 'Rebuilding the Industrial Town: Wolverhampton', *Urban History*, 29.3, (2002), p.392.

7. M. Gilman, *A Study of Churches Built for the Use of Congregations of the Church of England between 1945 and 1970*, Ph.D. thesis, University of Sheffield, (2000), p.25.

8. M. Gilman, *A Study of Churches*, p.189.

9. C. Phillips, *Being Church* (sic) *in Longbridge: Practical Theology of Local Churches in a Post-Industrial Community*, Doctor of Applied Theological Studies thesis, University of Birmingham (2015), p.81.

10. 'Coventry Churches', *British History Online*, https://www.british-history.ac.uk/vch/warks.

11. D. Walker, *English Religious Architecture of the 50s* (2008). (Online). https://warwick.ac.uk/fac/arthistory/research/projects/basilspence/essays/religiousarchitecture.

12. *Lichfield Mercury*, 6 May, 1966. Stafford Record Office, ref. B/A/26/11/2/2.

13. *Uttoxeter Advertiser*, 18 May 1966. Stafford Record Office, ref B/A/26/11/2/2. Aidan Ridyard's father also recalled being a curate in such a parish in the 1960s with ten weddings every Saturday in summer.

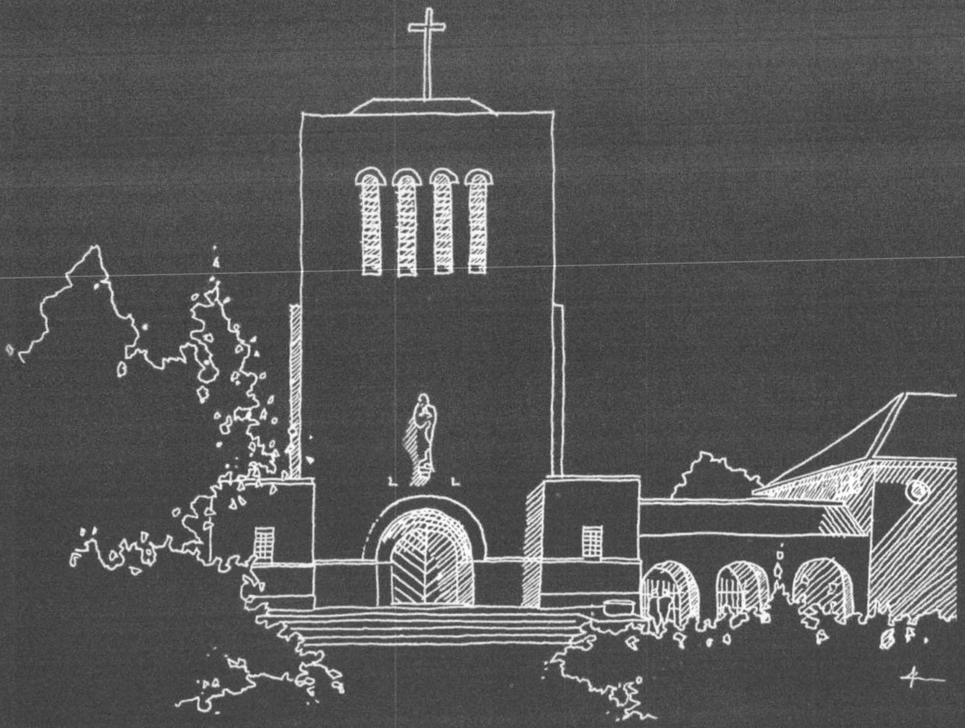

CHAPTER FOUR

4

INTERWAR CHURCHES 1937-9

4.1 (RIGHT)
St Georg, Stuttgart by Hugo Schlösser 1920-30

4.2 (OPPOSITE TOP)
St Gabriel, Fullbrook, Walsall south facade 1937-39

INTERWAR CHURCHES

Identifying specific architectural influences on Twentyman is not easy, since the archives do not provide evidence of Twentyman's views on this subject, with one exception. In an article on crematoria, Twentyman expresses his general views on architecture. Buildings, he writes:

> should be designed to follow the basic principles of good architecture...The practical requirements, rather than any preconceived idea of the appearance , should be the main factor dictating the form, and, now that we have a live, contemporary style, it would... be unreasonable to use any past one...The architect...should...do his best to design a building, which, while avoiding any shams, should also avoid any excessive dramatization...Sculpture either inside or outside a building can improve it, but sentimentality or slickness should ...be avoided. Austerity can be avoided by using wood and intelligent use of colour...dramatic effects are out of place.[1]

These comments, published in 1955, reveal Twentyman's adherence to the idea of form following practical functions, his support of new architectural styles, rather than past models, and his belief in the appropriate use of sculpture, wood, and colour to complement design simplicity. We saw earlier that Twentyman's training at the London Architectural Association would have exposed him to modernist architectural ideas,[2] and made him aware of examples of both secular and church architecture from Britain and continental Europe. McNally's 1947 book on English churches[3] includes St Gabriel and St Martin, and also features many 1930s churches built in a similar style including those designed by Martin-Smith, Miller, Kenyon, and Cachemaille-Day, especially the latter's 1939 St Barnabas church in Tuffley (4.3) with its monumental style and narrow elongated windows. Maufe's 1948 review of European church architecture[4] includes examples of German and Swiss Expressionism and Nordic monumentalism, with designs by Bartning, Böhm, Höger, Metzger, Moser, Schlösser, (4.1), Schwarz, Tengbom, and Webber, some going back to the 1920s.

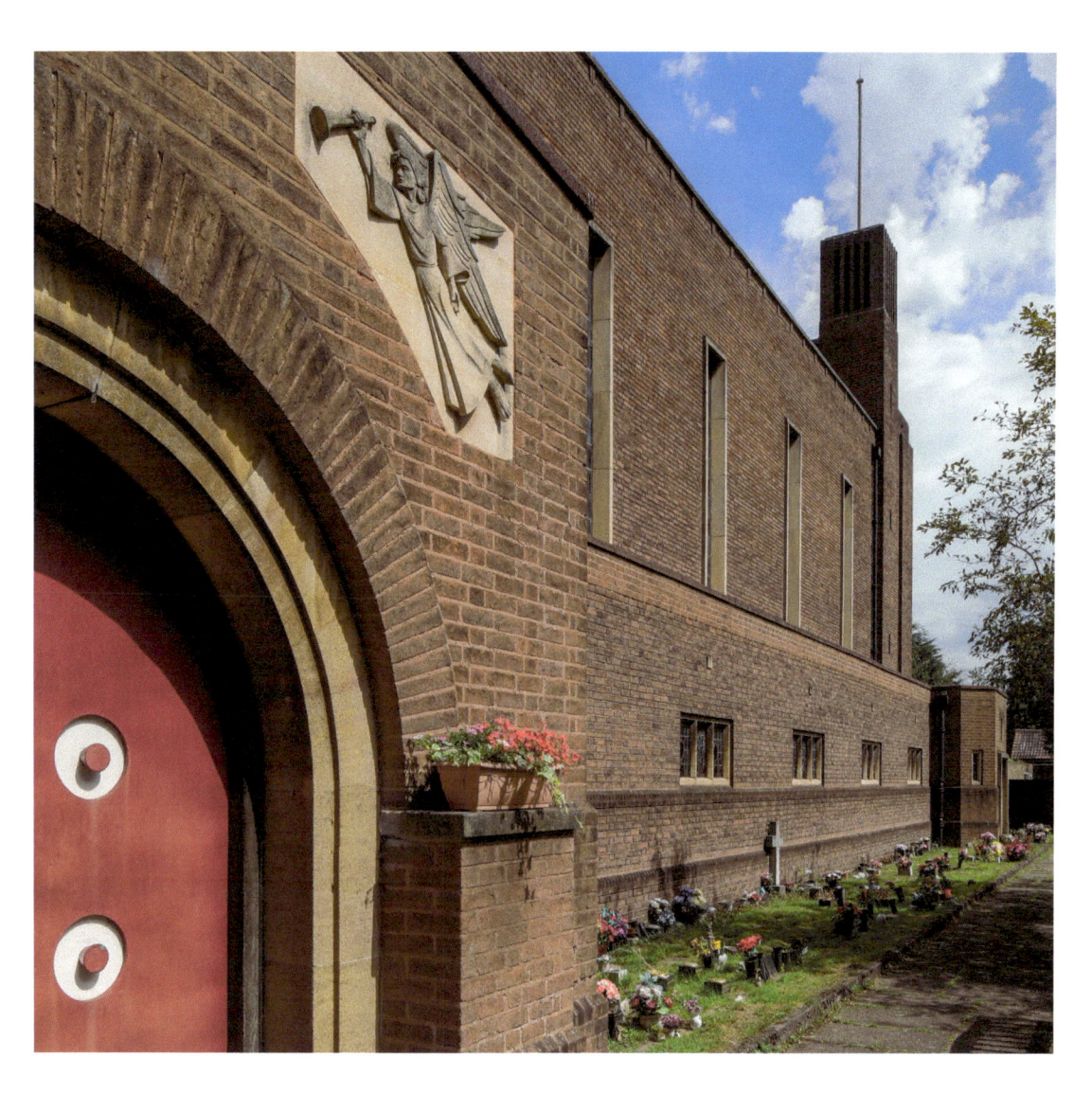

4.3 (RIGHT)
St Barnabas, Tuffley, Gloucestershire
by Nugent Cachemaille-Day 1939

INTERWAR CHURCHES 1937-9

ST GABRIEL

FULLBROOK, WALSALL

Twentyman's first church is clearly a fortress-like monument in brick, (see 4.4), stylistically similar to its 'sister' church, St Martin, Wolverhampton (see below). Externally it is reminiscent of the spare classical language of several secular buildings of the time, for example, Giles Gilbert Scott's Cambridge University Library (1931-34), and Herbert Rowse's monumental ventilation towers in Liverpool (1931-34).[5] Twentyman is likely also to have been influenced by a more local building, Lyons and Israel's Wolverhampton Civic Hall (1934). In a letter written several years later in 1979, Lawrence Israel acknowledges the debt British architects of the time owed to earlier Scandinavian architecture:

> **The 30s was a transitional period and architects were influenced by the Scandinavians and Dutch. The buildings which had a considerable impact were Dudok's Hilversum Town Hall in Holland, and in Stockholm Gunnar Asplund's Crematorium, Ragner Östberg's Town Hall and Ivor Tengbon's Concert Hall.[6]**

Several London Town Halls had monumental designs in this style,[7] which was becoming the norm for public commissions during the period, influenced by the examples given by Israel above as well as Asplund's Stockholm City Library (1927).[8]

St Gabriel is orientated parallel to the street frontage, and is therefore approached perpendicular to its west to east axis. The exterior presents a series of unadorned cubist brick blocks of simple design rising at the east end to the tower inserted in a keep-like structure, resembling Velarde's St Gabriel, Blackburn (1932-33) and his Expressionist-influenced St Monica, Bootle (1933-36).[9]

4.4
ST GABRIEL, FULLBROOK
SOUTH FACADE

4.5
ST GABRIEL, FULLBROOK
CROSSING & TOWER FROM THE
SOUTH

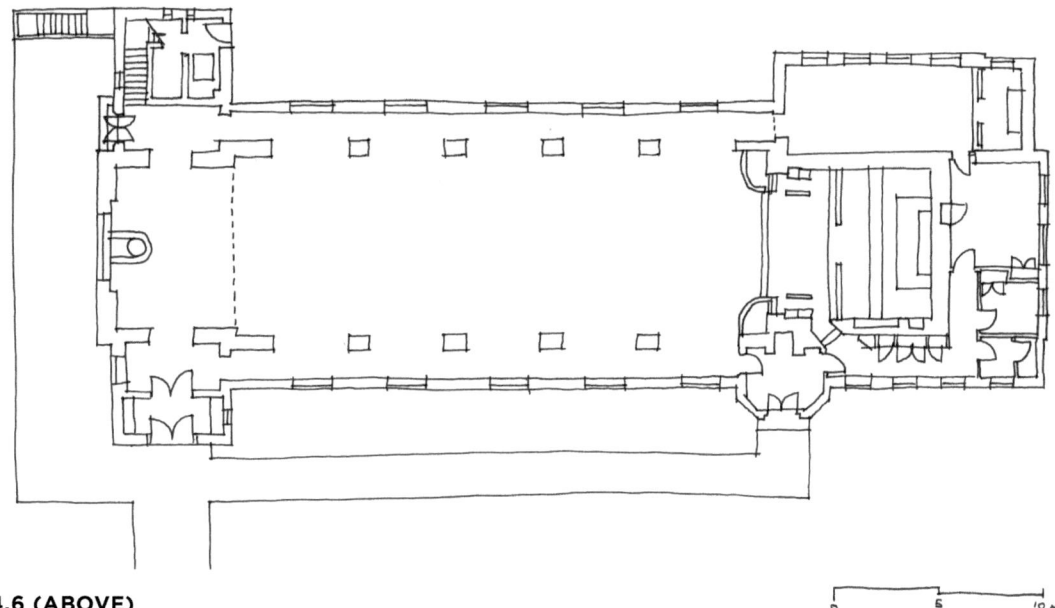

4.6 (ABOVE)
The linear plan of St Gabriel is approached perpendicular to its axis from the south-west, entering below the western gallery. Originally aligned with the font, the circulation pattern rotates east as the central axis intersects with the approach

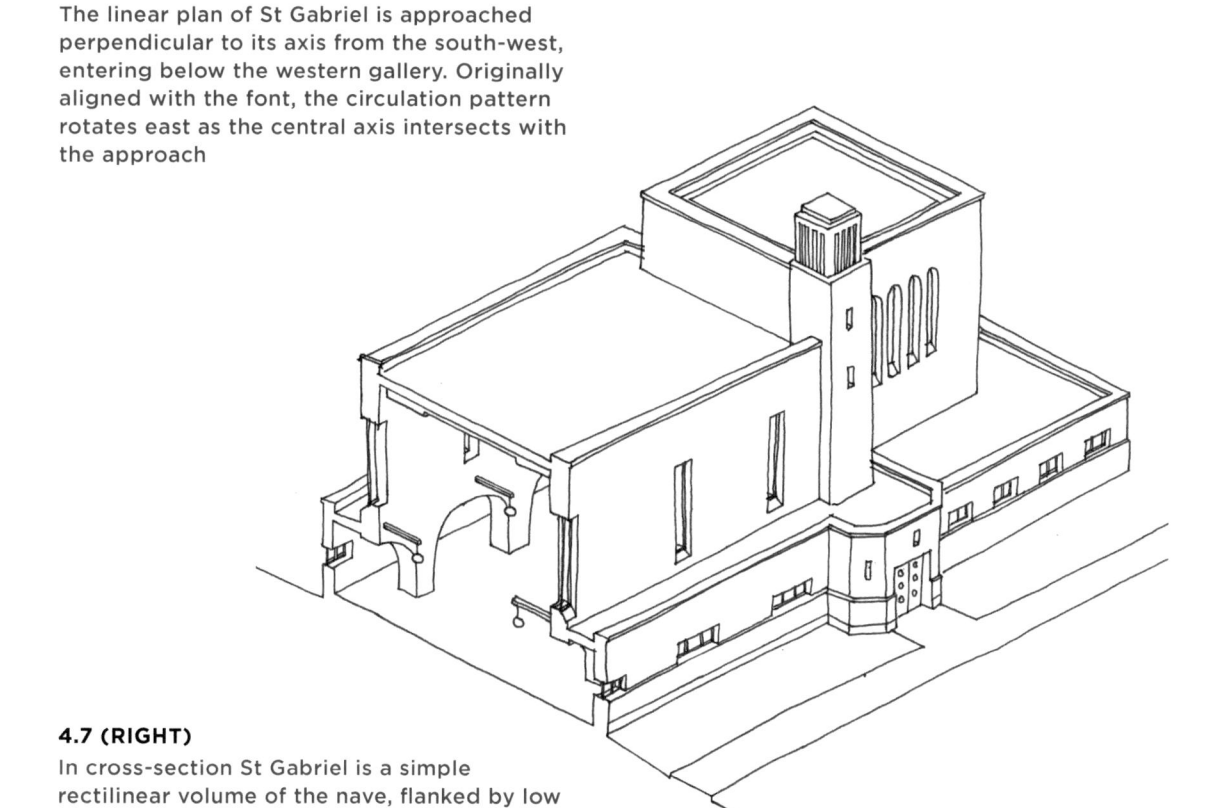

4.7 (RIGHT)
In cross-section St Gabriel is a simple rectilinear volume of the nave, flanked by low aisles which continue as a form around the east end forming vestries and a Lady Chapel

INTERWAR CHURCHES 1937-9

4.8 (BELOW)
St Gabriel, Fullbrook
the nave looking east with
repositioned font in south aisle

4.9 (RIGHT)
St Gabriel, Fullbrook
the sanctuary and the
lantern above it

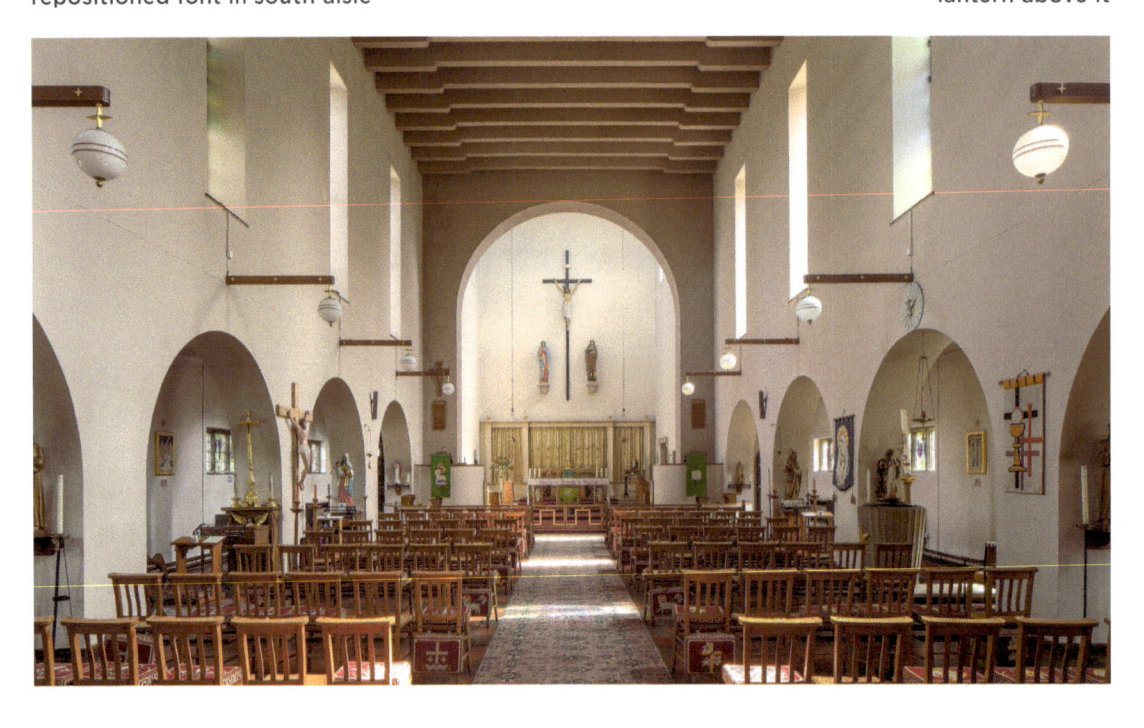

Light is provided by tall, narrow, rectangular windows at high level, above the smaller Arts and Crafts-influenced passageway windows (4.4). Externally, the church begins a theme which evolves in Twentyman's work, linking the new vicarage to the church (and later church halls) as part of a broader composition, a design developed by Basil Spence in his Coventry churches. At St Gabriel, this is organised as a continuation of the church's southern street frontage increasing the feeling of length and presence to the street.There is a traditional choir and organ gallery at the west end, where the main entrance accesses the church from the south. This brings visitors into a lowered volume below the gallery, subtly allowing them to pause and reorient themselves before the axis shifts to the east on the central axis of the space. This directional shift recurs in the composition of the postwar churches at Darlaston and Bentley.

A sightline to the sanctuary is provided by the wide nave with low arches each side inserted in the walls to provide passageways rather than aisles. These create a defined rhythm of bays, both externally and internally, where arches connect the passageways to the nave, with the language supplemented internally by projecting brackets, from which round pendant lamps are suspended.

The separation of the chancel and sanctuary from the nave is achieved by means of a high simple arch which frames the further view of the altar, with a later reredos and originally a simple black marble cross above it.

INTERWAR CHURCHES 1937-9

4.10 (BELOW)
The Lady Chapel north of the sanctuary

Painted concrete roof beams, articulated by an elongation at their ends, traverse the nave. Period fittings include a tapered fluted font, now moved from the west end to the middle of the south passageway, and a modernistic pulpit and lectern. Chairs rather than benches can be easily rearranged.

Certain features are present that will recur in Twentyman churches: passageways rather than aisles; the unobstructed view of the altar; the fluted font and detailing on the doors; plain exterior precast concrete crosses at west and/or east ends; and an overall plan to include a separate Lady Chapel, vestry, and community rooms.

Such aspects reveal Twentyman's interest in modernism, a concern for simple aesthetic design, and an awareness of modern liturgical requirements, but also his sensitivity to tradition, producing a compromise between Peter Hammond's fundamentalist requirements and Edward Maufe's more spiritual concerns,[10] a difference to which we will return.

4.11 (BELOW)
The cantilevered lighting brackets in the nave, with the four-pointed star motif

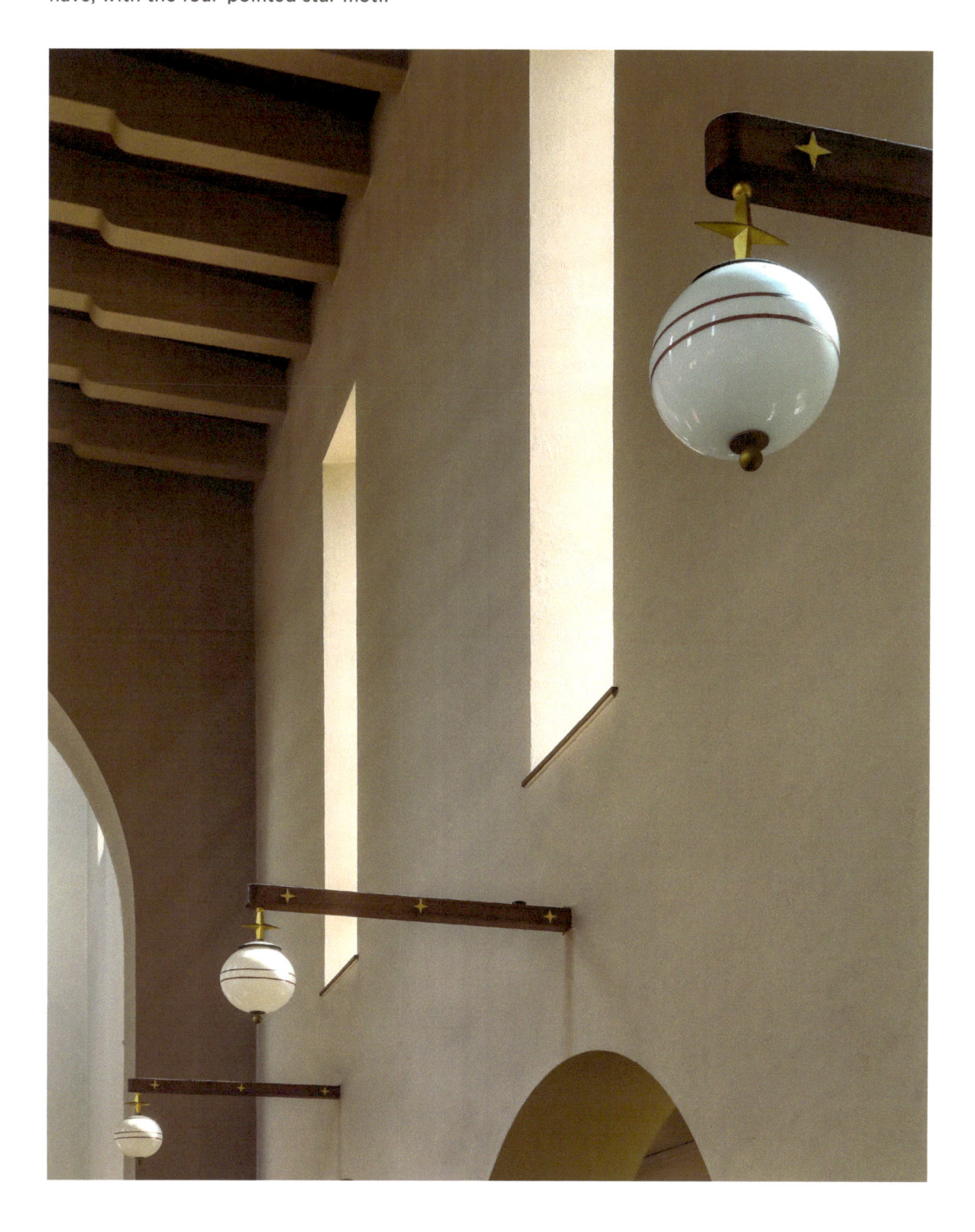

INTERWAR CHURCHES 1937-9

4.12 (BELOW)
St Gabriel, Fullbrook isometric studies of plan form and massing

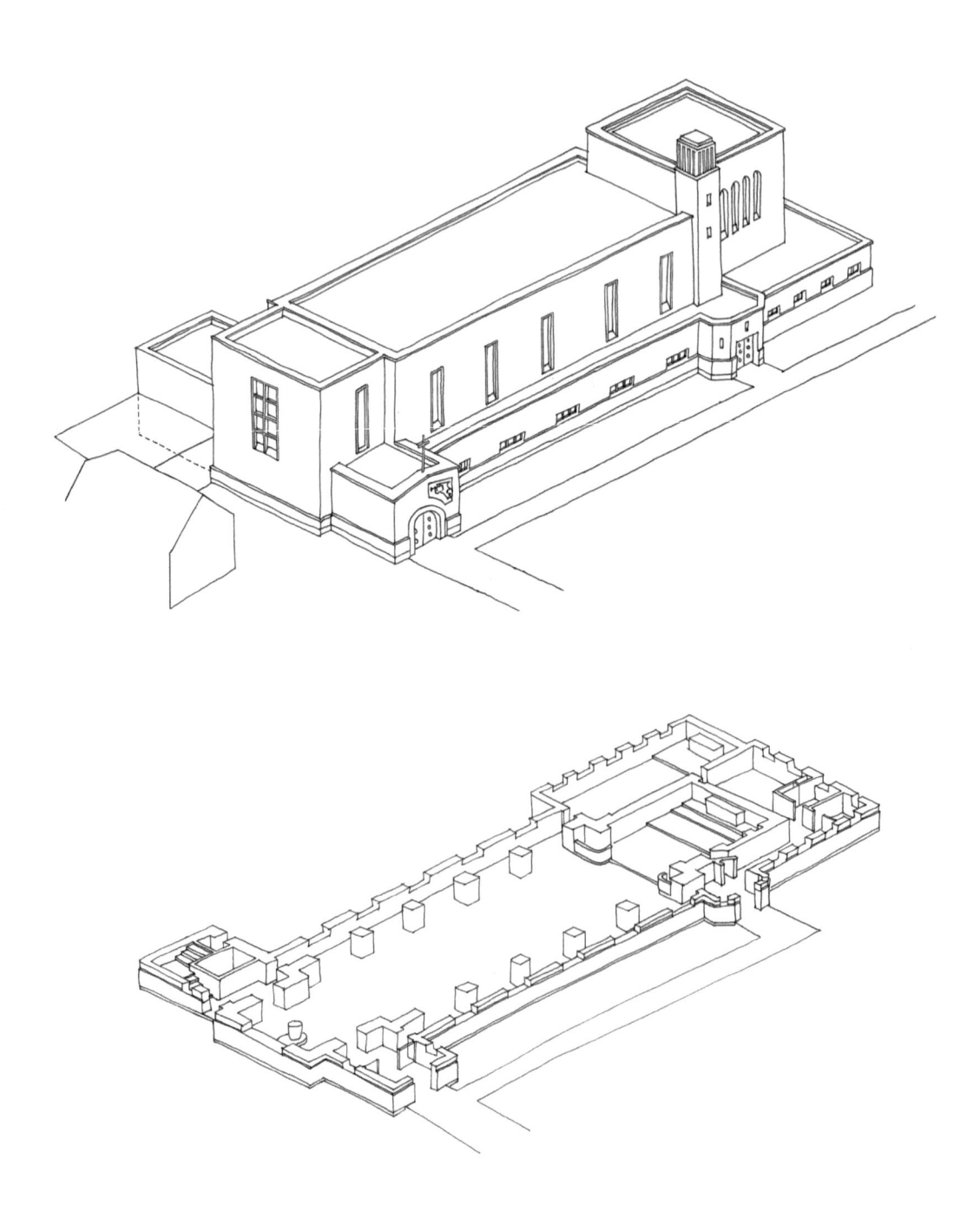

4.13 (BELOW)
St Martin of Tours, Parkfields isometric studies of plan form and massing

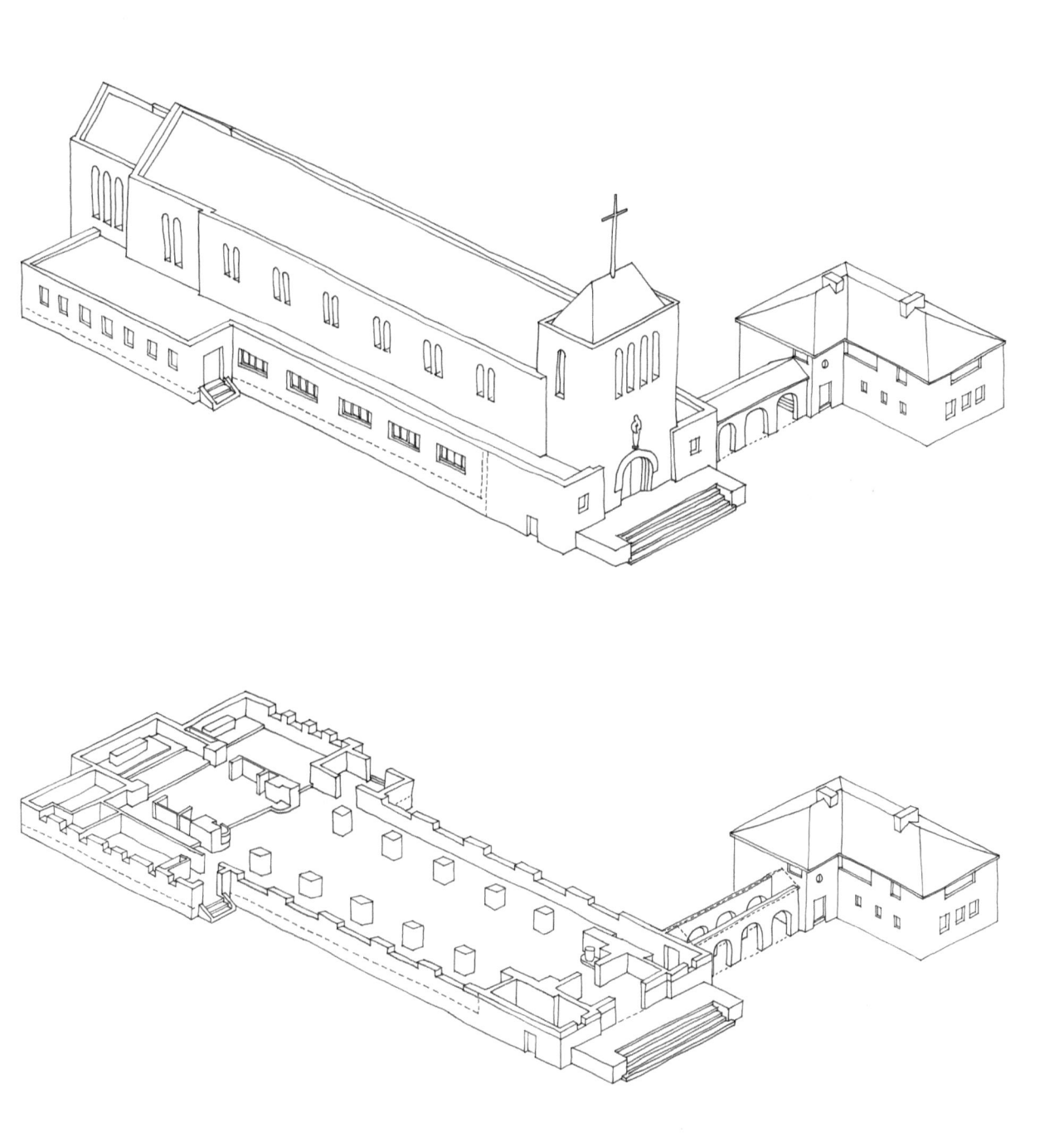

4.14
ST MARTIN OF TOURS, FROM THE WEST WITH
THE ARCADED SCREENS LINKING IT TO THE
VICARAGE, AS A SINGLE COMPOSITION

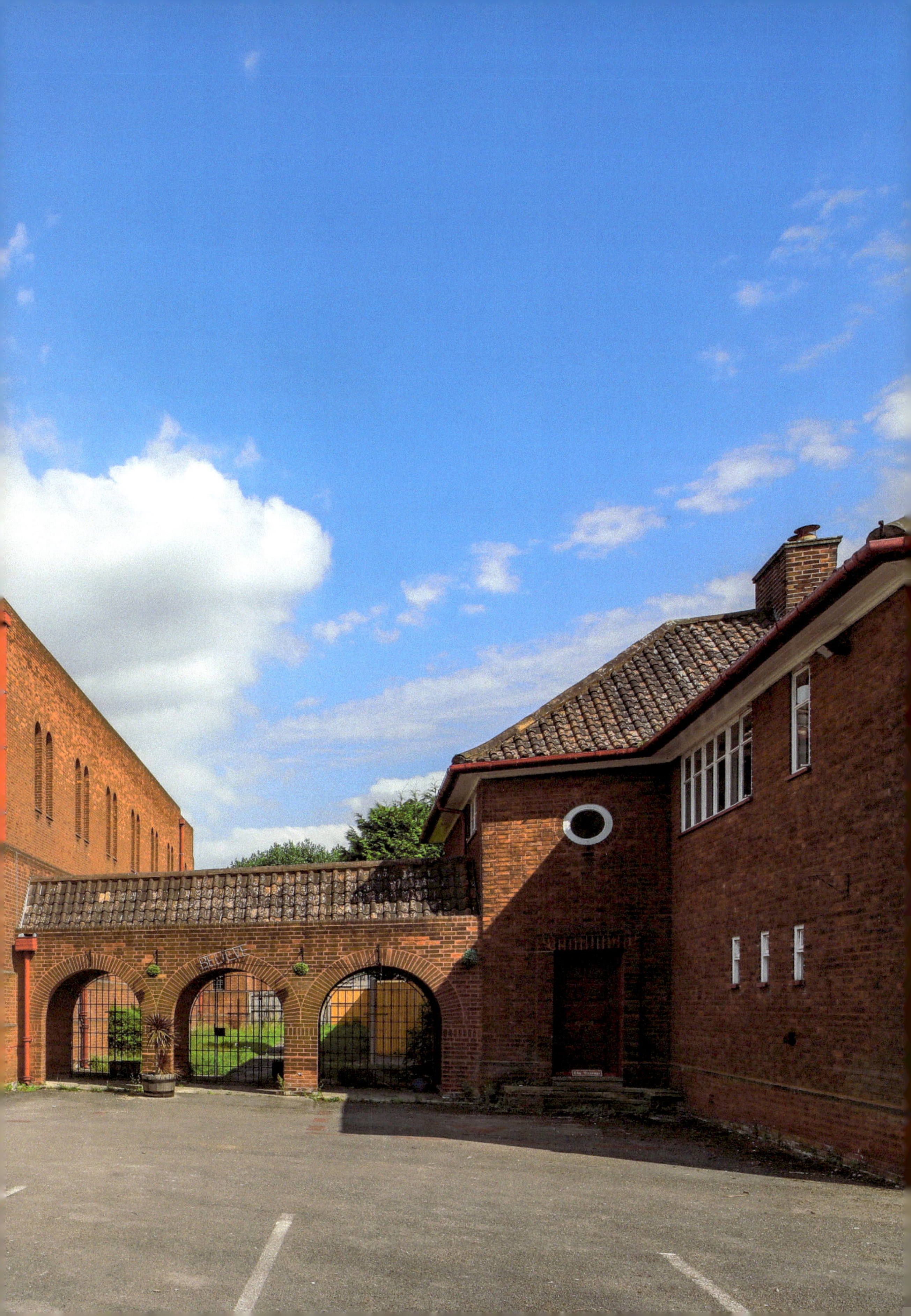

ST MARTIN OF TOURS

PARKFIELDS, WOLVERHAMPTON

Twentyman was already becoming known as a church architect by 1939. His designs for St Martin had won a 1938 architectural competition judged by Sir Charles Nicholson. A letter of recommendation from the Lichfield Diocesan Trust dated 21st October 1938 was fulsome in its praise and mentions Twentyman's involvement in St Martin:

> **…(Lavender and Twentyman) are easily the leading firm of Architects…and have a very wide experience…at the moment they are Architects to the new Rough Hills Church and Vicarage** (i.e. St Martin –authors' note) **…I do not think you can do better.** [11]

Wolverhampton was expanding in the early twentieth century, ultimately merging with the towns of the Black Country to form the wider conurbation after the war. The population was 133,190 in 1931 and 147,000 by 1942, with employment provided in mechanical engineering, commerce, and finance.

As we saw in earlier chapters, there were problems of dense urbanisation, generally poor quality housing, and derelict land. The provision of council housing was seen as one solution to these problems, and the Rough Hills and Parkfields estates, south of central Wolverhampton, were developed on the site of former collieries and mines.

4.15
ST MARTIN OF TOURS
WEST FACADE

INTERWAR CHURCHES 1937-9

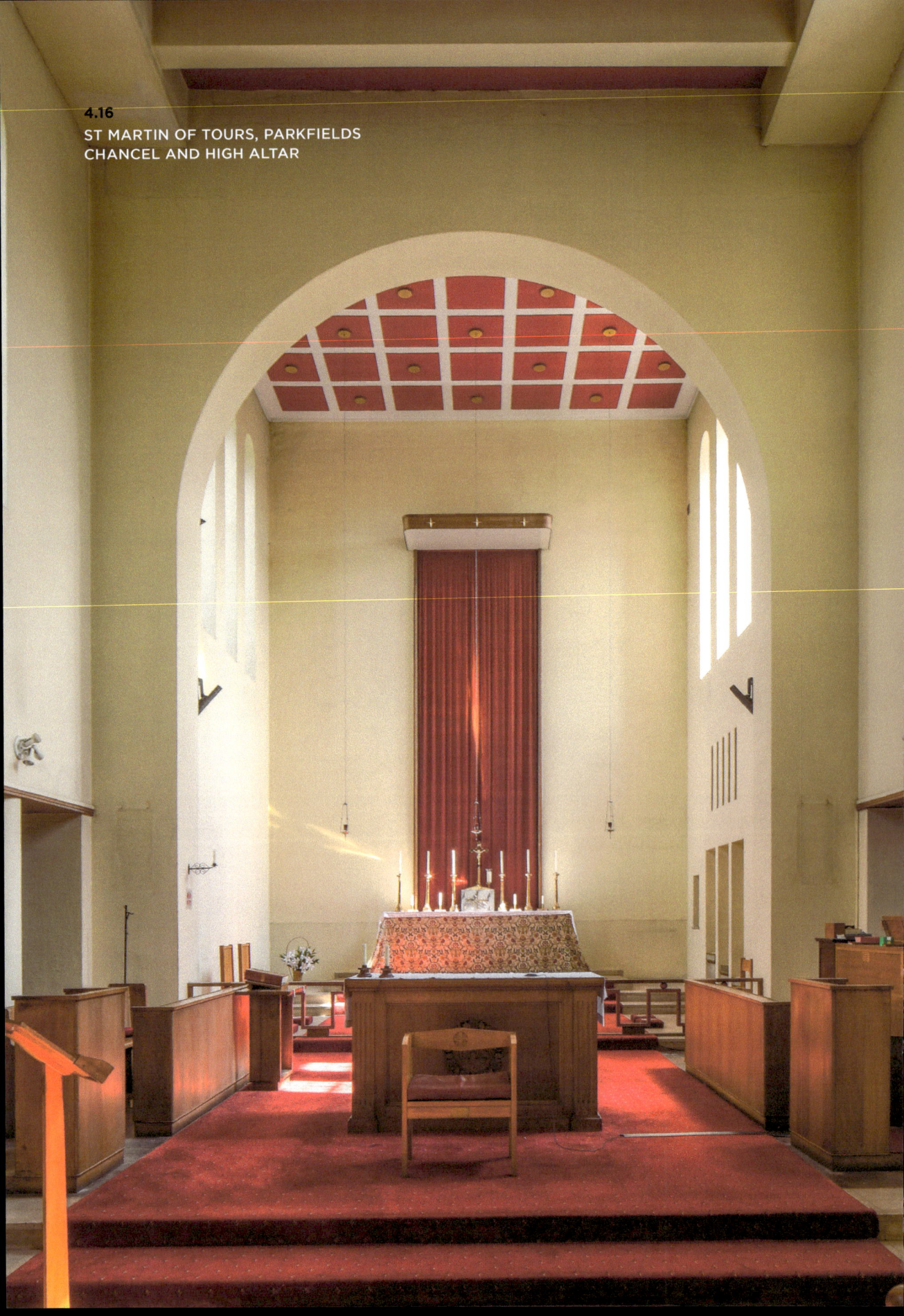

4.16
ST MARTIN OF TOURS, PARKFIELDS
CHANCEL AND HIGH ALTAR

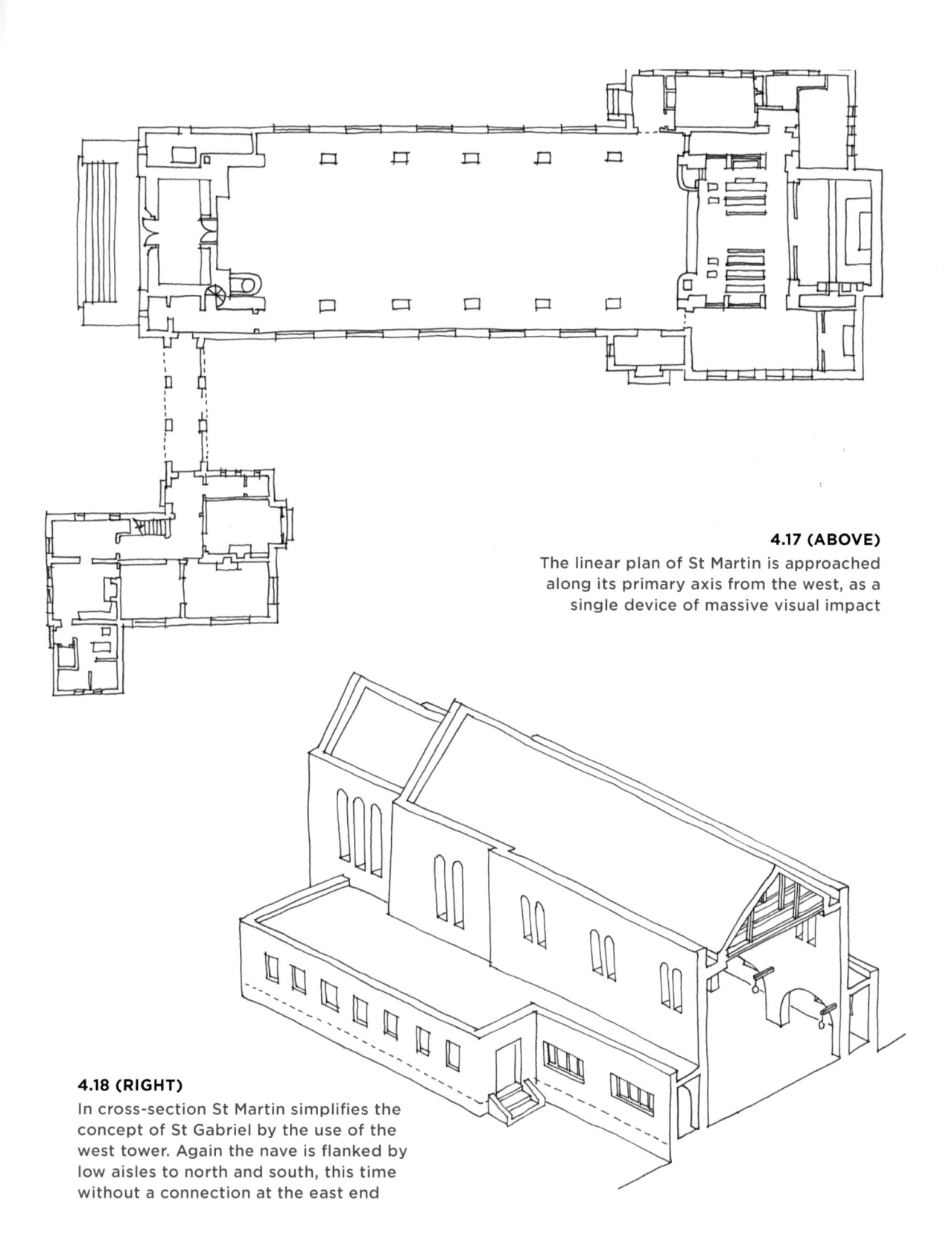

4.17 (ABOVE)
The linear plan of St Martin is approached along its primary axis from the west, as a single device of massive visual impact

4.18 (RIGHT)
In cross-section St Martin simplifies the concept of St Gabriel by the use of the west tower. Again the nave is flanked by low aisles to north and south, this time without a connection at the east end

INTERWAR CHURCHES 1937-9

4.19 (BELOW)
St Martin, Parkfields the nave looking east, the cantilevered lighting brackets as at St Gabriel with replacement fittings

St Martin, built with funding from a local Tettenhall family, the Marson bequest, was a response to housing expansion and the need to offer religious and social services to the workers and families living on these new estates.

A 1910 Ordnance Survey (OS) map (4.20) shows the future location of St Martin in the midst of the former Cockshutts and Rough Hills collieries and mines, with little residential building except that spreading from Blakenhall to the west. A 1930 OS map (4.21) illustrates the subsequent expansion of housing in the area around St Martin's future location, partly motivated by slum clearance schemes in Wolverhampton. By 1931 over 5000 council houses had been built in Wolverhampton Borough, of which the Rough Hills and Parkfields estates were a part.[12] A 1946 aerial photograph shows the church serving the estates (4.22). Such council housing developments continued after WWII until the 1950s and justified the location of St Martin in the midst of them.

The church's site was challenging. Formerly a slag heap with mine workings beneath, still typical of the area, it required a deep, reinforced concrete foundation raft to bridge onto more stable clay at an additional cost of £1500, some 10% of the construction budget. St Martin is stylistically similar to its 'sister' church of St Gabriel, Walsall, described above, and built around the same time, in that it is an 'impressively blocky'[13] rectangular brick building, although the arrangement is different, and the stripped-back classicism of Fullbrook has become distinctly neo-Romanesque

4.20
1910 OS plan of Parkfields showing site of St Martin

4.21
1930 OS plan of Parkfields showing site of St Martin

4.22
Aerial photograph of Parkfields in 1946

INTERWAR CHURCHES 1937-9

4.23 (BELOW)
The Lady Chapel a significant departure from the comparable space at St Gabriel

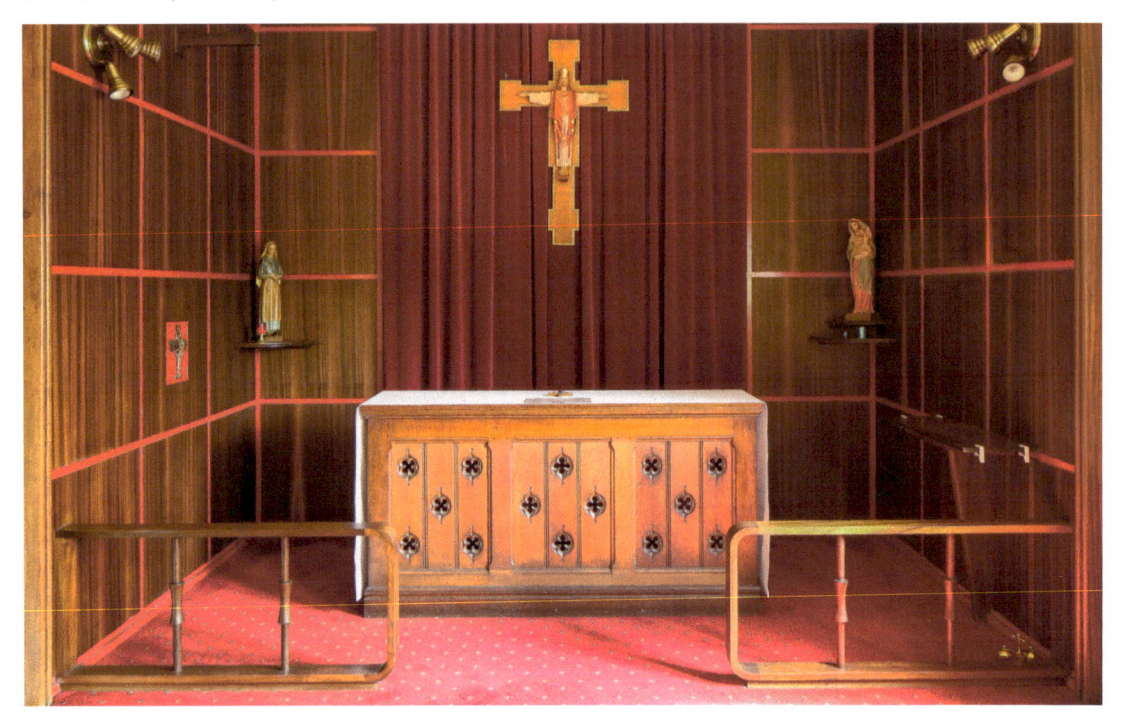

at Parkfields (4.12 & 4.13). It cost around £15450, including fittings.[14] St Martin is orientated perpendicular to the street frontage, roughly east-west, and was designed to seat 515, including seating in the choir and chapel. It is linear in composition with a subtle cross-axis to the south connecting with the adjacent vicarage as at St Gabriel, and near the existing parish hall further to the south-east.

The vicarage, a substantial 5-bedroom brick house, is connected to the church's south-west side entrance by a pantile-covered brick cloister of three double arch bays. The arches complement the large round-headed west entrance, still used on special occasions such as weddings, set in an austere, Norman-style, rectangular tower and belfry, reflecting the neo-Romanesque influence of the architecture, placed on axis at the west end. Wide stone steps lead up to the main entrance, accessed through a large red door, with a characteristic Twentyman ribbed motif. The upper part of the tower is pierced with four, long, thin, round-arched bell openings. Don Potter's three-ton, solitary, stone figure of St Martin with his broken sword seen against the massive unadorned west wall, has a striking effect (4.15). It demonstrates effectively an austere version of Mies van der Rohe's phrase 'less is more', recalling the impact of Georg Kolbe's 1929 sculpture in Mies' minimalist Barcelona Pavilion[15] (see 4.25).

Externally, the fortress-like design is continued on the north and south facades, with pairs of tall, clear-glazed, narrow, rounded, arched lights in steel frames on

4.24 (BELOW)
Detail of altar rail in Lady Chapel. Walls are in black walnut veneer with purple inlay

each side of the nave at clerestory level, a double set of rounded lights taller than the nave windows in the chancel, vestries to the north, and a chapel to the south. A set of paired triple lights in the sanctuary provides the light that Twentyman regarded as an important 'material' in his churches, using deep reveals to conceal the source while flooding the space with light. Outside at aisle level of the nave, are five north and south sets of 4-light brick mullioned windows. At the external east end is a simple raised brick cross, a detail which would become a recurrent Twentyman feature.

The interior (4.19) has a traditional layout with separation of the chancel from the nave with a step leading to oak choir stalls, and a plain round arch with altar rails and steps to the altar separating the chancel from the sanctuary. A tall curtain with a canopy is behind the altar, creating a focal point when viewed from the west end of the nave (4.16). Colours, at the time of writing quite vibrant, were originally muted.[16] The sanctuary ceiling was light pink on pale grey wood squares; the chancel and nave ceiling was grey with painted grey-blue beams on a north-south axis; nave walls were putty-coloured.

One of the architectural features signalling a break from tradition, used also at St Gabriel, is the replacement of traditional aisles by passageways punctuated by six low rounded arches either side of the nave, an idea which evolves over time in later Twentyman churches. The narrow vestigial aisles create more space for a wider nave so that all can see the altar. Each arch originally had a suspended lamp orb above it, attached on the end of a projecting timber beam. The lamps have been replaced by clusters of three hanging lamps on each beam, although the originals remain on site in storage.

4.25 (LEFT)
Mies van der Rohe Barcelona Pavilion 1929

4.26 (RIGHT)
St Martin of Tours by Don Potter above the west door

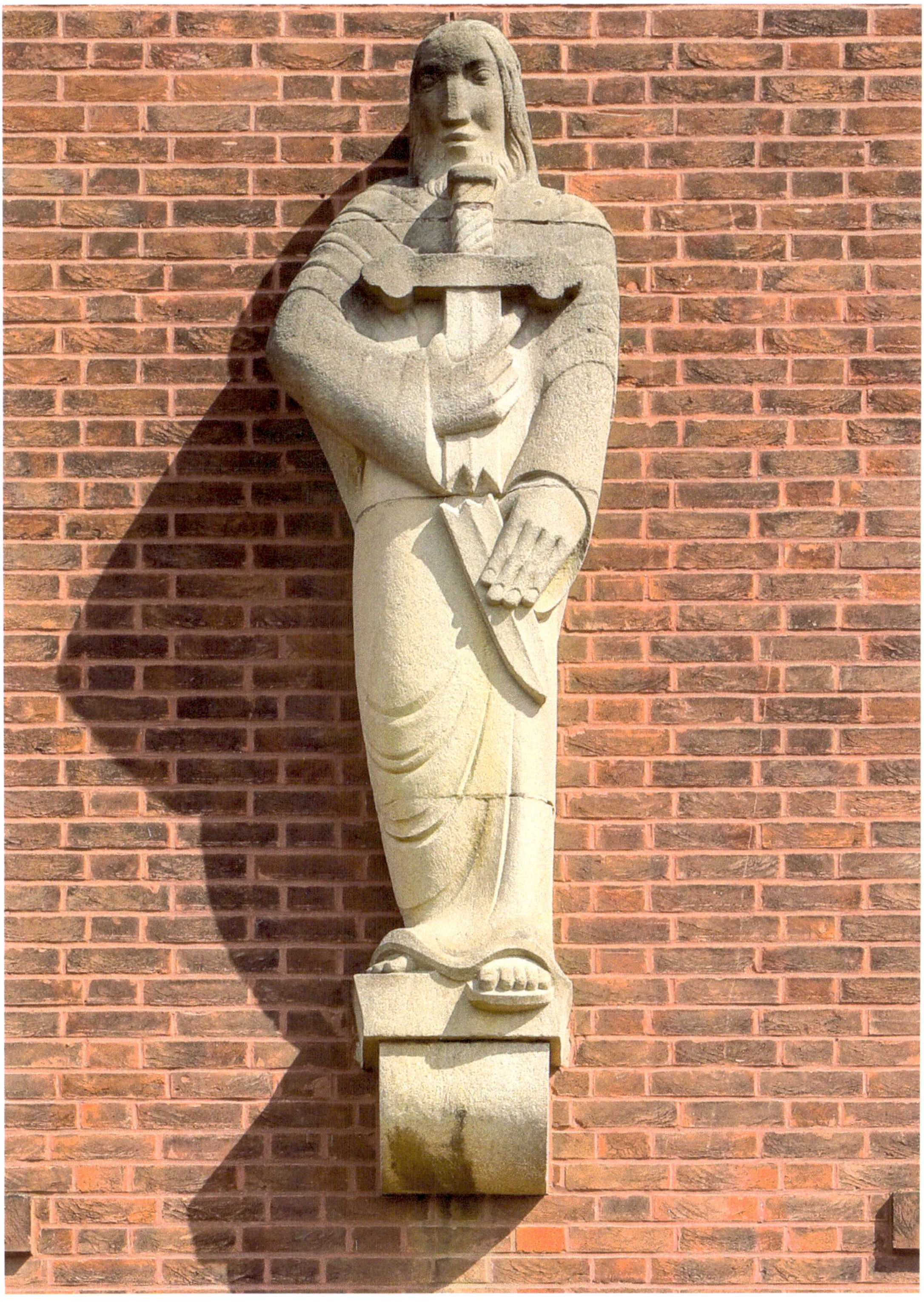

ST MARTIN, TWENTYMAN AND CHURCH ART

The figure of St Martin was Don Potter's first commission from Twentyman and Potter's first sculpture after his association with Eric Gill. Other works by Potter are inside the church. There is a tall, round, tub font at the south-west end in Clipsham stone with sculpted figures of celebratory saints, and an elm cover surmounted by a remarkable figure of a baby with crossed legs being held in a raised hand. A similar ebony sculpture by E. Bainbridge Copnall portraying Christ's Baptism is in Bernard Miller's St Columba (1932) in Anfield, Liverpool, and the Liverpool School of Architecture, where Miller trained, may have influenced Twentyman's own work.

On the square-panelled, rounded oak pulpit, Potter carved an *Agnus Dei*. Potter and Twentyman worked together well and other commissions followed, including at All Saints, Darlaston, as we shall see below.

The issue of church decoration and furnishing has always been the subject of much debate and disagreement.[17] Anson sums up the situation between 1920 and 1940:

> ...Fashions were seldom stable or uniform. On the one hand there were imitation Gothic or Baroque altars, pulpits...etc.; on the other streamlined furniture which would have looked equally at home in, say,...the new Shakespeare Memorial Theatre at Stratford-on-Avon, or in any typical cinema...'[18]

Judging from Twentyman's use of decoration and furnishing at St Martin and in his later churches, Twentyman was in sympathy with Anson's second more modernist categorisation, while still adopting a restrained approach.

Twentyman and his clients would have been aware of arguments about church design prompted by changes in the liturgy of both Protestant and Roman Catholic faiths, set in motion by Pope Pius X in 1910. The changes emphasized community involvement in services and greater interaction between celebrant and congregation.[19] At one extreme, writers such as Peter Hammond stressed the importance of defining the activities taking place and the functions arising from them, rather than starting from a more spiritual standpoint and creating an emotional response in participants, which he referred to as 'a craving for visual effect'.[20] Architects like Edward Maufe were more sympathetic to a transcendental approach:

> **The religious mind seeks the infinite...there should be a certain mystery – there should be spaces in which the imagination can play...**[21]

Hammond was critical of Maufe's views and almost parodies his own approach in *Towards a Church Architecture*:

> **...we should be heading towards rather plain brick boxes with no tricks.**[22]

St Martin and Twentyman's subsequent church designs provide a balanced response to these arguments. Twentyman was concerned with functionalism but also with the psychological aesthetic effects on congregations, demonstrated in his developing mastery of the use of concealed light. He was also pragmatic and realised the necessity of listening to his ecclesiastical clients who showed a preference for modern approaches without revolutionary design.

Pevsner was somewhat harsh in his judgement of St Martin:

> **1939 is just a little late for all this; if it were 1933, it would be remarkable – at least in England.**[23]

This misses the point that it is a provincial building by a provincial architect developing a successful West Midlands practice. Within the region therefore, it is significant and deserves greater recognition. One of Twentyman's greatest talents was an outward-looking approach to architecture, building on the emerging 'English' tradition of the interwar period, with an increasing appreciation of developments in thinking elsewhere in Europe during the postwar period. This personal journey as an architect is vividly illustrated in the evolution of Twentyman's church designs over his 36-year activity.

4.27 (ABOVE)
The gilded bas-relief eagle on the reading desk at St Gabriel

INTERWAR CHURCHES 1937-9

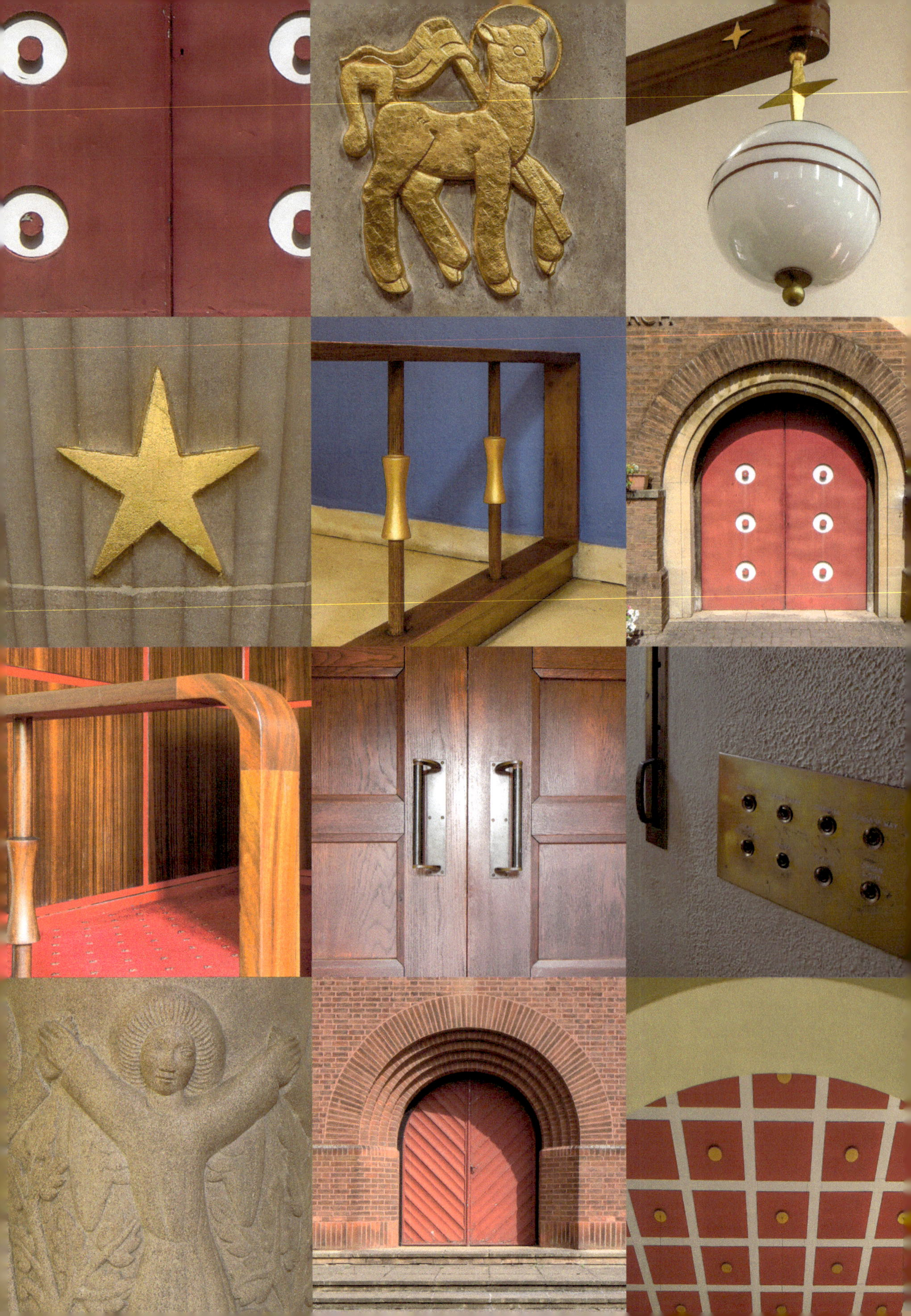

Notes

1. R. Twentyman, 'The Design and Layout of Crematoria', *Royal Sanitary Institute Journal*, July (1955), p.504.

2. N. Bullock, *Building the Postwar World* (London: Routledge, 2002), p.71.

3. R. McNally, *Fifty Modern Churches* (London: ICBS, 1947).

4. E. Maufe, *Modern Church Architecture* (London: ICBS, 1948).

5. I. Jackson et al., *Herbert Rowse* (Swindon: Historic England, 2019), C20 Architects Series.

6. L. Israel, Letter about Wolverhampton Civic Centre, 1979, (Online). http://www.yourwolvescivic.co.uk/history/plans-and-drawings.html.

7. *London's Town Halls*, (Swindon: English Heritage, 1999).

8. P. Larkham, 'Rise of the English Civic Centre in English Urban Form and Design', *Urban Design*, 9, 1, (2004), p.11.

9. D. Wilkinson, and A. Crompton, *F. X. Velarde* (Liverpool: Liverpool University Press, 2020), C20 Architects Series.

10. E. Maufe, *Modern Church Architecture* (London: ICBS, 1948), pp.6-7.

11. Letter to Reverend Roach, Shrewsbury, Shropshire Record Office Archives, ref. P253/K/1/11.

12. D. Mills, *Rough Hills*, Wolverhampton (Cirencester: Mereo Books, 2017), p.197.

13. N. Pevsner, *Staffordshire* (Harmondsworth: Penguin, 1975), p.322.

14. McNally, *Fifty Modern Churches*, p.30.

15. R. Weston, *Key Buildings of the 20th Century* (London: Norton, 2010), p.58.

16. *Architect and Building News*, 18 August 1939, pp.181-84.

17. A. Powers, 'Art and Artefacts', in S.Charlton, E. Harwood, and C. Price (eds.), *100 Churches 100 Years* (London: Batsford, for Twentieth Century Society, 2019), pp.157-61.

18. P. Anson, *Fashions in Church Furnishings* (London: Faith Press, 1960), p.339.

19. E. Harwood, 'Liturgy and Architecture', in *The Twentieth Century Church*, Journal of the C20 society, no. 3, 1998, pp.49-74.

20. P. Hammond, *Towards a Church Architecture* (London: Architectural Press, 1962), p.28.

21. Maufe, *Church Architecture*, p.6. See also J. Dunmur, *Edward Maufe* (Manchester: Moyhill Publishing, 2019).

22. Hammond, *Towards a Church Architecture*, p.10.

23. Pevsner, *Staffordshire*, p.322.

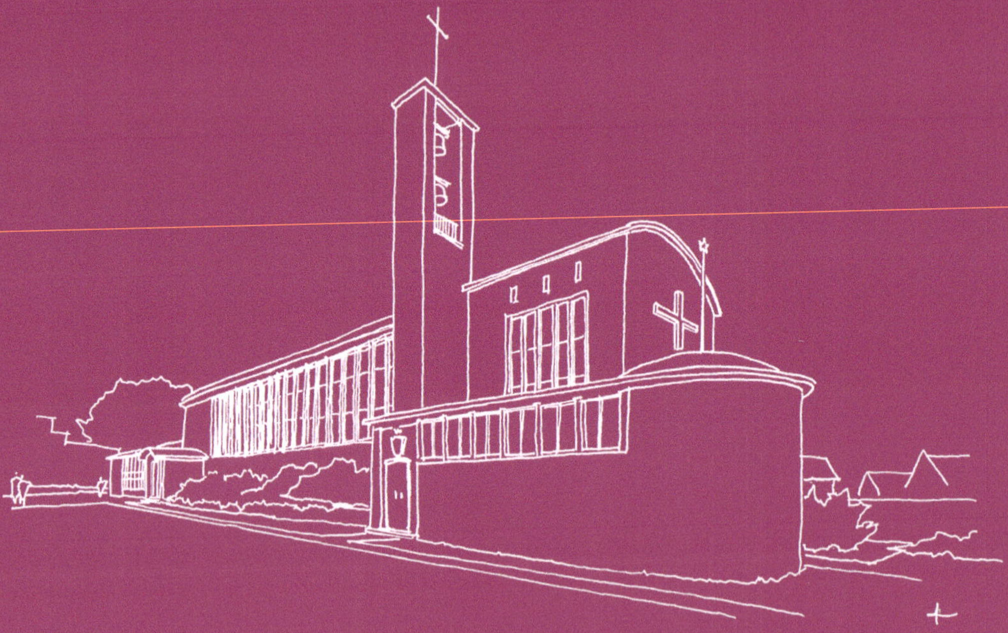

CHAPTER FIVE

5
A CHANGE IN STYLE THE 1950s

5.1 (RIGHT)
Hickman & Mould ice-cream factory, Wolverhampton 1934

5.2 (FAR RIGHT)
Clock House Chambers, Wolverhampton 1938

A CHANGE IN STYLE

In this chapter, we describe five churches designed by Twentyman during the period 1952 to 1960. We shall see that they represent a considerable shift in style from the two interwar churches, St Gabriel and St Martin, discussed in the previous chapter. The first church Twentyman designed after St Gabriel and St Martin, All Saints, Darlaston (1952) signals an evolution from the neo-Romanesque to the more radical approach to church design which Twentyman develops through the 1950s.

The design differences between the churches are such that some have wondered whether, at St Gabriel and St Martin, Twentyman was implementing the ideas of his architect partner Ernest Lavender, and whether All Saints, rather than St Gabriel or St Martin, therefore represents Twentyman's first original church building.[1] No doubt a rebalancing of interests was occurring within the practice from Ernest Lavender, who died in 1942, to the new senior partner, Richard Twentyman, and Twentyman, as a relatively new partner in the practice, may have worked closely with Lavender when designing St Gabriel and St Martin. There is no evidence, however, that St Gabriel and St Martin are not Twentyman churches. Both, together with All Saints, are in the list of Twentyman churches compiled by his retired practice partner, John Hares.[2] Moreover, in the thirteen intervening years between St Gabriel/St Martin, and All Saints, a period which included World War II, there had been a gradual move in Europe, America, and in Britain, including provincial England, towards a new vernacular of modernism, continuing the innovations presented by the 1951 Festival of Britain.

Materials were in short supply, postwar restrictions on building materials being lifted only after 1954, adding to pressures to reduce construction costs. A church architecture developed of simpler structures with slender pillars, modified aisles, and large areas of glazing, creating more space and light. In Britain, there was less concern that religious and secular buildings should be distinguished from one another, at least externally, supported by a comment from Hammond:

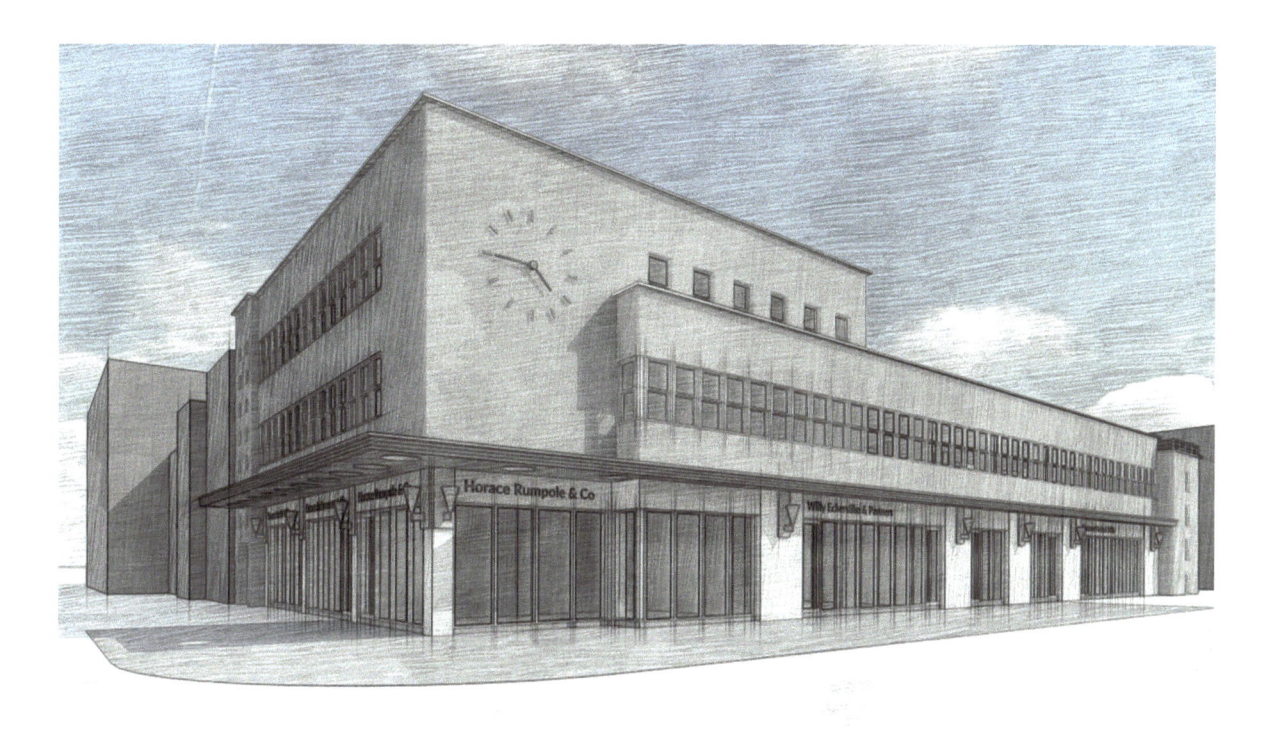

> **...there is no reason why the technology and materials of churches should be in any way different from normal building, in fact they have to be the same (the ideation of the commonplace and so on).**[3]

Twentyman was designing residential and commercial buildings in a more modern idiom during the interwar period, drawing on ideas in Le Corbusier's *Vers Une Architecture*, published in 1923 and translated into English in 1927. Clock Chambers (1938), for example, the former Gas Showrooms in Wolverhampton, has pilotis, a flat roof, ribbon windows, and a simple Portland stone box structure (5.2). Hickman and Mould's Wolverhampton ice-cream factory built in 1934, and a house built for a Mr Illes in 1933 in Wrottesley Road, Tettenhall[4] share a similar design language. Twentyman must have decided that an overt modernism was not appropriate for church architecture in the 1930s, but by the 1950s attitudes and conditions had changed, the result being the design of Twentyman's 1950s churches. It is likely, then, that St Gabriel and St Martin, forward-looking but also representing a definite glance back at tradition, and All Saints are all designed by Twentyman, but demonstrate an evolution of his church architecture consistent with interwar and postwar shifts in cultural attitudes and social contexts.

ALL SAINTS
DARLASTON 1952

There were two major motivations for the construction of All Saints, Darlaston. The original Gothic Revival church, designed by G E Street during 1871-72, and containing stained glass by Burne-Jones, was destroyed by bombing on 31 July 1942. A replacement church was therefore required, and particularly in response to population expansion in the West Midlands and in the Darlaston area served by All Saints.[5] All Saints' building costs of £36,000 were funded from diocesan sources, as well as from local business and parishioners' contributions. As early as August 1942, the church council had formed a restoration committee and made plans for the rebuilding of the church. They raised £10,000 towards the new church, and received £28,320 from the War Damage Commission.

The bomb that destroyed the original church created a crater 50 feet deep and 40 feet across, and the Twentyman church was built directly on this site. Concrete piles were sunk 12 feet below floor level, and, over the bomb crater itself, they were sunk a further 8 to 12 feet.[6] Like St Martin, it is a large church designed to seat over 300, and shows the transition to a simpler, lighter language of structure and fabric. The reinforced concrete brick-faced structure has a curved barrel-vaulted copper roof over the nave, providing maximum height for the size of the church.

Externally on the south elevation, six, small, square-headed lancet windows mark the rhythm of the six internal nave bays. Above the lancets, the facade begins to dissolve into a grid of steel-framed windows

5.3
ALL SAINTS FROM SOUTH-EAST

5.4
ALL SAINTS TOWER & LADY
CHAPEL FROM SOUTH-WEST

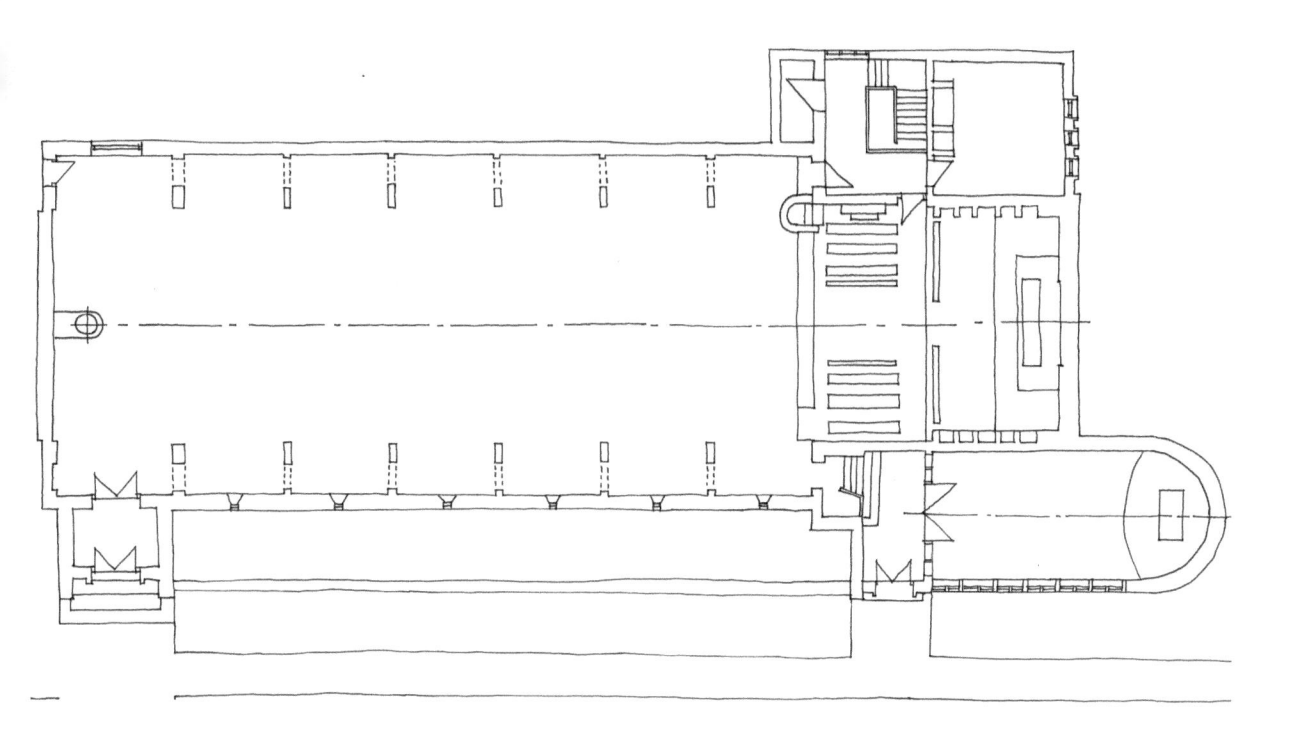

5.5 (ABOVE)
All Saints is approached perpendicular to its main axis from the south-west (as at Fullbrook) using the length of the south facade to maximise its impact

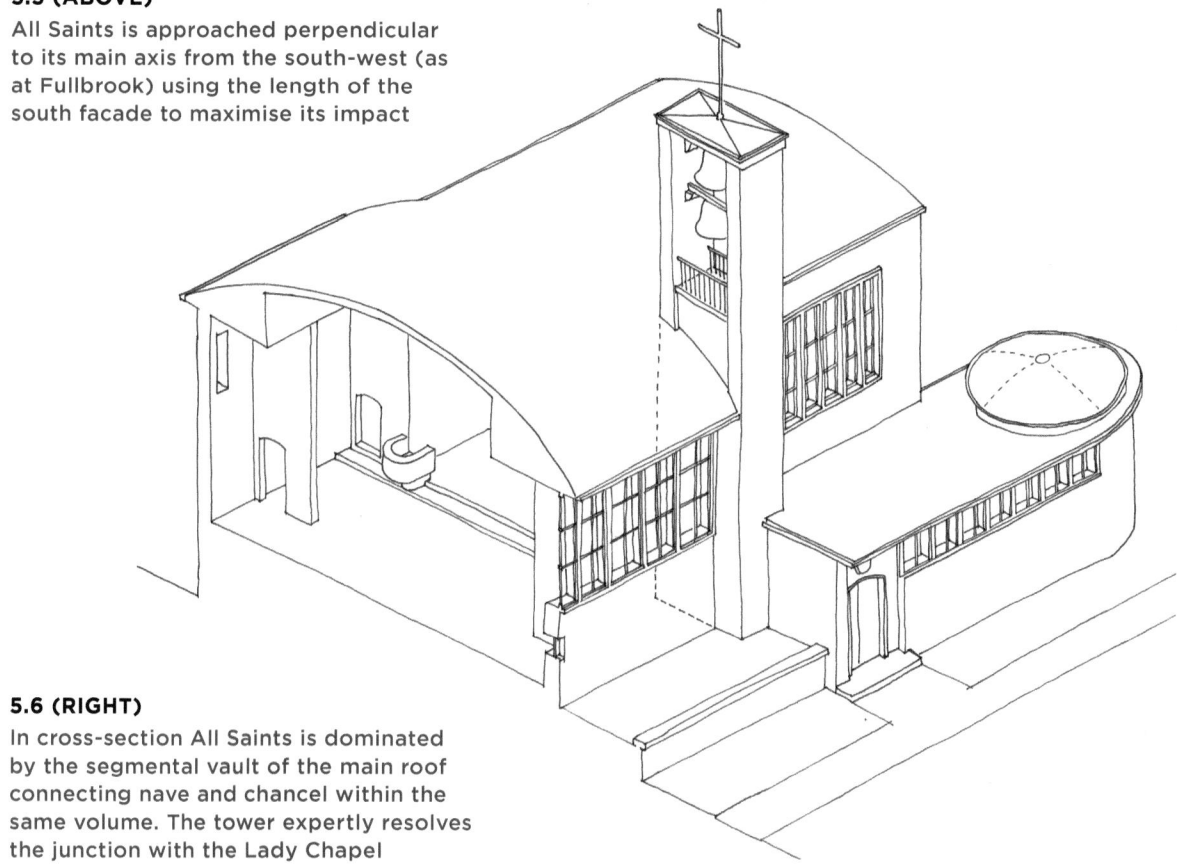

5.6 (RIGHT)
In cross-section All Saints is dominated by the segmental vault of the main roof connecting nave and chancel within the same volume. The tower expertly resolves the junction with the Lady Chapel

A CHANGE IN STYLE THE 1950s

5.7 (BELOW)
All Saints showing the link block connecting the nave with the later church hall

5.8 (RIGHT)
All Saints the south-west portal with sculpture by Don Potter

between deep stone mullions, creating a much lighter aspect compared to St Martin. The south elevation is dominated by the row of eighteen tall windows each with six rectangular lights reaching to eaves level. The expanse of windows stretches from the south-west porch externally down the south elevation of the nave terminated by the projecting side of the bell tower.

To the east of the tower the width of the vault narrows to a recessed choir with five tall mullioned windows, each of three lights matching the nave windows. Below the windows, the Lady Chapel projects southwards and eastwards beyond the east wall of the sanctuary with six small two-light windows on the upper wall and an apsidal east end. Here, Twentyman's customary Sussex bond quickens into a regular Flemish bond to cope with the curvature, a technique he uses on the circular tool house at Bushbury Crematorium. The Chapel has a domed copper roof topped by a mast and five-pointed star, another recurrent motif.

The north elevation has six bays, with a tall window in the first western bay only, and five two-light windows high on the walls of the eastern bays. The north wall of the sanctuary has five tall windows matching those on the south side. There is a large Latin cross in relief at the external east end of the church, a Twentyman feature, and a circular oculus window high up on the west end. The slender tower is constructed of two concrete planes faced in brickwork. It has a large opening high on its west and east sides in which two church bells are hung on show above each other. The tower

A CHANGE IN STYLE THE 1950s

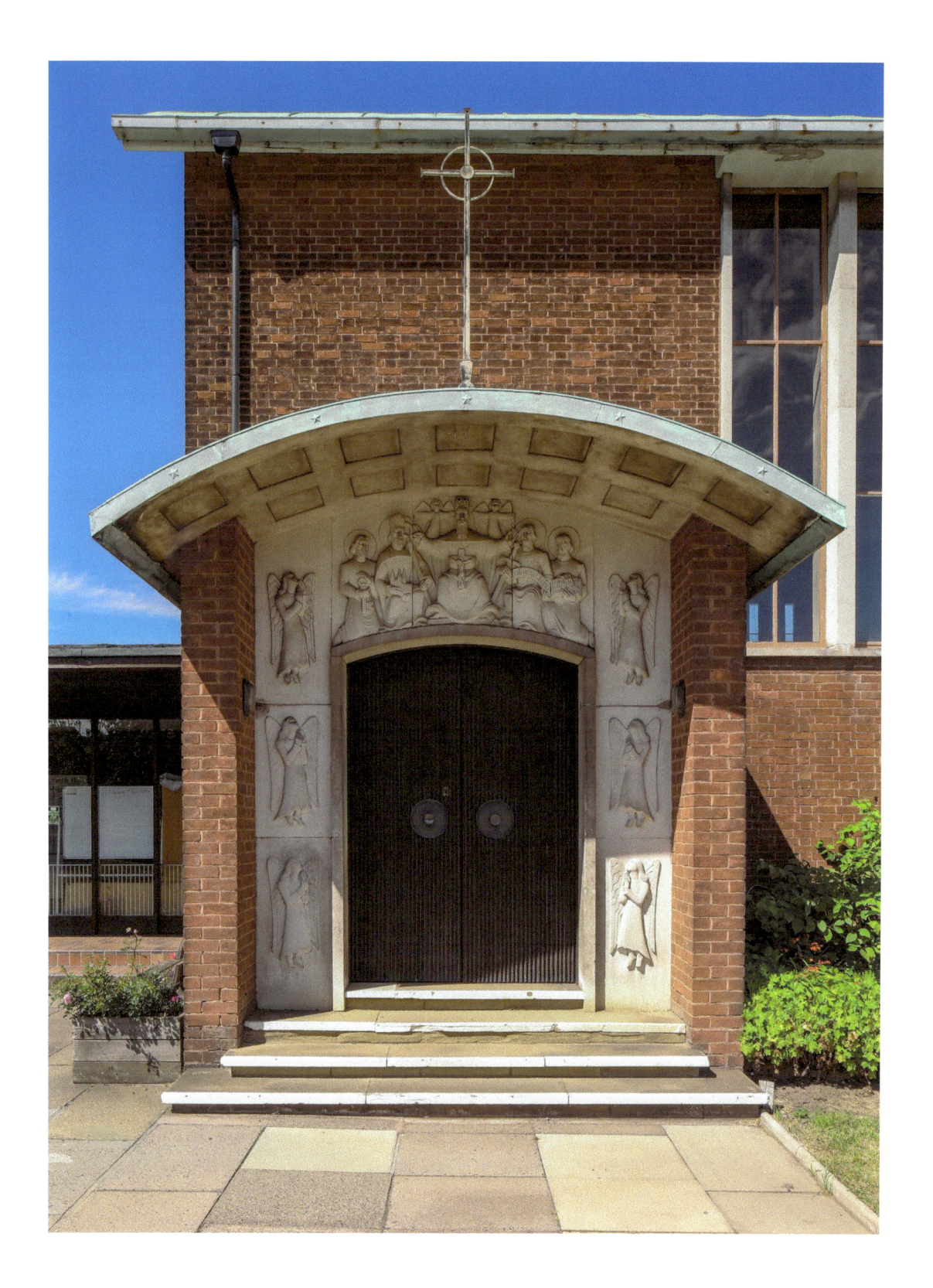

could not be more different from St Martin's keep-like structure, and functions more as a visual modernist landmark connecting to its surrounding residential and commercial community.

There are two south entrances to the church, one main projecting porch on the south-west corner leading into the west end of the nave, the other providing an alternative entry into the Lady Chapel at a reduced level, reflecting the slight slope across the site, west to east. The west porch consists of a rectangular double doorway with a segmental curved copper roof recalling the main curved roof. The wooden doors are fluted with round bronze door knobs set in circular plates, a signature Twentyman motif. Framing the entrance, carved *in situ* out of the Portland stone surround, is the sculpture by Don Potter, his second commission from Twentyman. Three angels are sculpted either side of the portal, and the frieze above the door portrays the central figure of Christ with outstretched arms and the four principal Evangelists, Matthew, Peter, John, and James on either side (5.8).

Potter created three further works for Twentyman at All Saints, all three functional objects necessary for performance of the liturgy but also striking in their design, an echo of William Morris' dictum of creating objects that should be both useful and beautiful. The font, placed centrally at the west end, is made of a black granite incised with gilded lattice work and a sycamore cover with engraved fishes. The simple curved concrete pulpit with an unusual blue-green mosaic base has an *Agnus Dei* carved in a stone panel, similar to that in St Martin.

The carved oak lectern is surmounted by an impressively stern Eagle of St John the Evangelist (5.10). All four creations reflect Twentyman's view that any decoration should be used sparingly but purposefully and should avoid over-dramatic effects. It is a matter of opinion whether Twentyman would have approved later additions to All Saints. There are stained-glass panels at the west end added in the 1960s, and the original blue-grey dorsal curtain hanging centrally at the east end was replaced in the 1970s by a tapestry, then the third largest in the country, designed by Stephen Lee and woven by parishioners in the vicarage lounge over a period of two years.

The interior view from the west to the east end is similar to St Martin in that the nave is divided from the choir by steps, and the choir from the sanctuary by shallow steps and altar rails (5.9). However, there is no archway as at St Martin so the demarcation is less pronounced, as the nave is simply narrowed by the organ loft and tower to north and south respectively. The impression of openness and space is a revelation, especially since the high curved sanctuary ceiling can be seen from the nave, and the full-length north and south windows illuminate the chancel with typically deep reveals masking the light source (5.11). Together with the nave windows, they flood the interior with light, a consistent design feature of Twentyman's churches in the 1950s.

The other notable difference between St Martin and All Saints is the design of the aisles. At St Martin the row of rounded archways face the body of the nave creating low arcades each side, reminiscent

5.9
ALL SAINTS CHANCEL WITH THE STEPHEN LEE TAPESTRY

5.10 (BELOW)
All Saints the lectern carved in English oak by Don Potter

5.11 (BELOW)
All Saints the nave looking west showing the aisles formed within the cross-walls

of the traditional aisles in a basilica plan. All Saints has a subtly different design. A series of concrete cross-wall partitions from floor to ceiling level act as internal north/south buttresses to create the six nave bays. These partitions are pierced with low slightly curved wood-lined archways so that a continuous narrow passageway is created, running west to east along both sides of the nave, as vestigial aisles. The partitions have the effect of shielding the congregation and celebrant from glare from the large south windows, achieving a similar softening effect to that of the deep concrete mullions in the north and south sanctuary windows. Influences from earlier European architects are apparent. Karl Moser, for example, in his Church of St Anthony, Basle (1927)[7] strove to produce interiors that would be spacious and light but produced at an economic cost, characteristics of Twentyman's own postwar churches. Rudolf Schwarz's 1930 Corpus Christi Church, Aachen[8] has the minimalist box-like lines with light sources from high windows favoured by Twentyman. Höger's 1933 church on Hohenzollernplatz, Berlin[9] has a series of internally buttressed nave bays, each with tall windows, the buttresses pierced to create low passage aisles, recalling those at Velarde's St Gabriel, Blackburn (1932-33) and at All Saints.

The high altar was originally against the east wall but was stripped down and moved nearer the congregation when the tapestry was installed in 1974, so that the vicar at that time would have been able to face the congregation from behind the altar,

5.12 (RIGHT)
All Saints plan showing later addition of church hall to the west of the original building (1956)

rather than have his back to them, consistent with the new liturgy.[10] The original altar would have been similar to that in the chapel with Alpha and Omega symbols on ribbed timber. The altar and all the oak furniture including the benches were designed by Twentyman in the typical fluted style found in all his churches. The concrete nave ceiling has a ribbed effect running west to east, emphasizing the perspective, and the aisle ceilings and other soffits are of oak-faced plywood. The choir is of curved plaster originally painted blue-grey with a series of recessed coffers. The east wall is of polished travertine slabs, into which the tapestry is recessed to create a flush finish, within a niche where the original dorsal curtain was hung. A large church hall west of the church was also designed by Twentyman. Opened in 1956, it is accessed through a glazed link separating it visually from the west end of the church, although adding to its impact from the street, creating a south-facing frontage nearly 70m long.

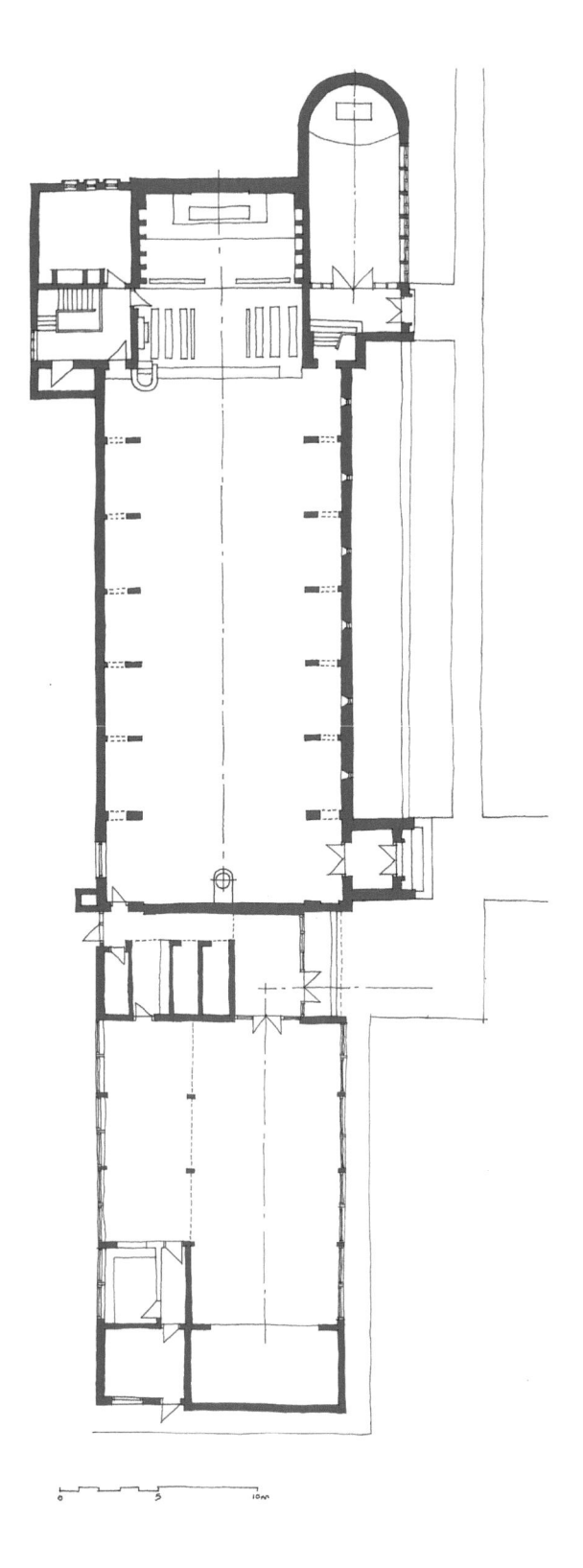

5.13 (BELOW)
All Saints, Darlaston isometric studies of plan form and massing

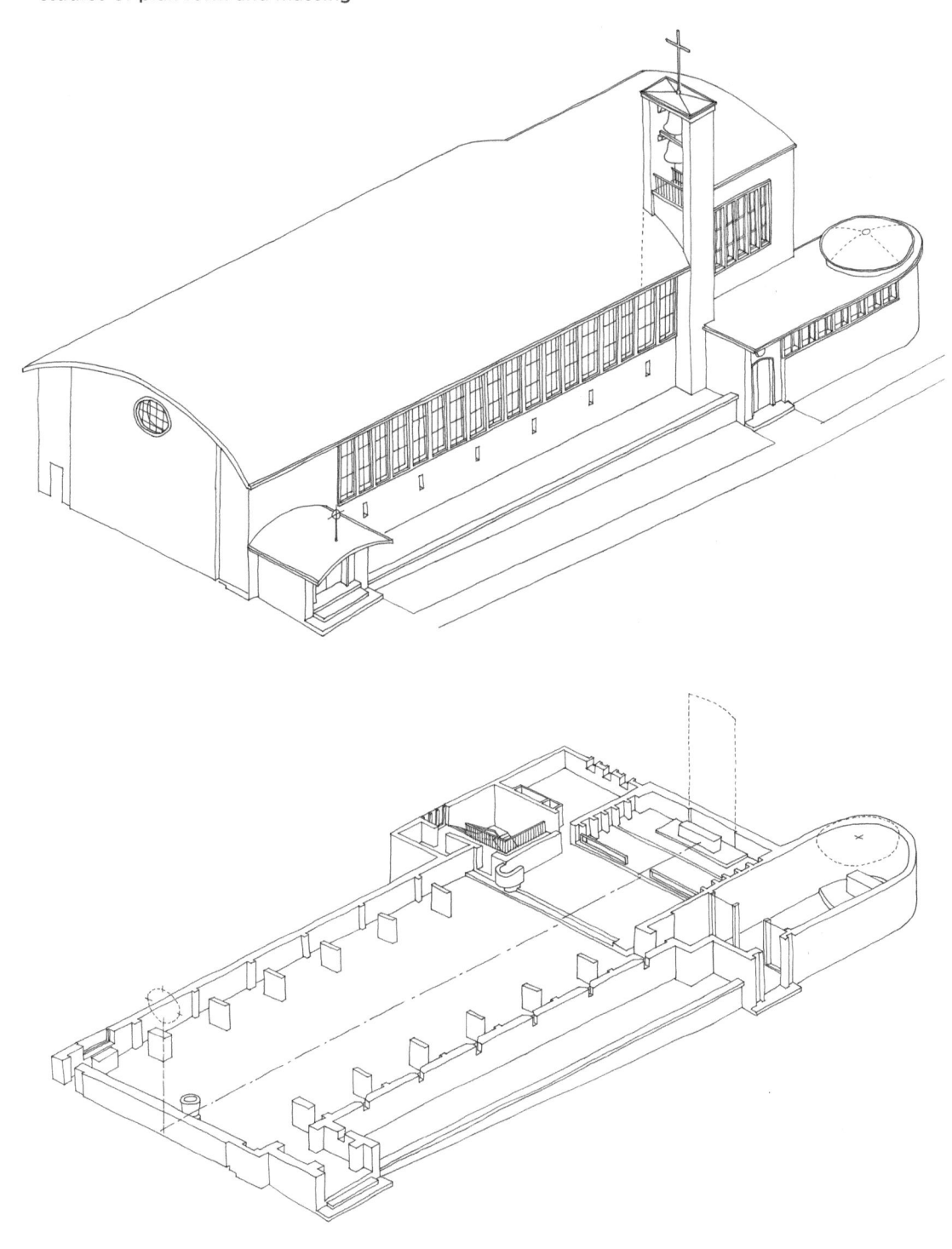

A CHANGE IN STYLE THE 1950s

5.14
ALL SAINTS THE SOUTH FACADE

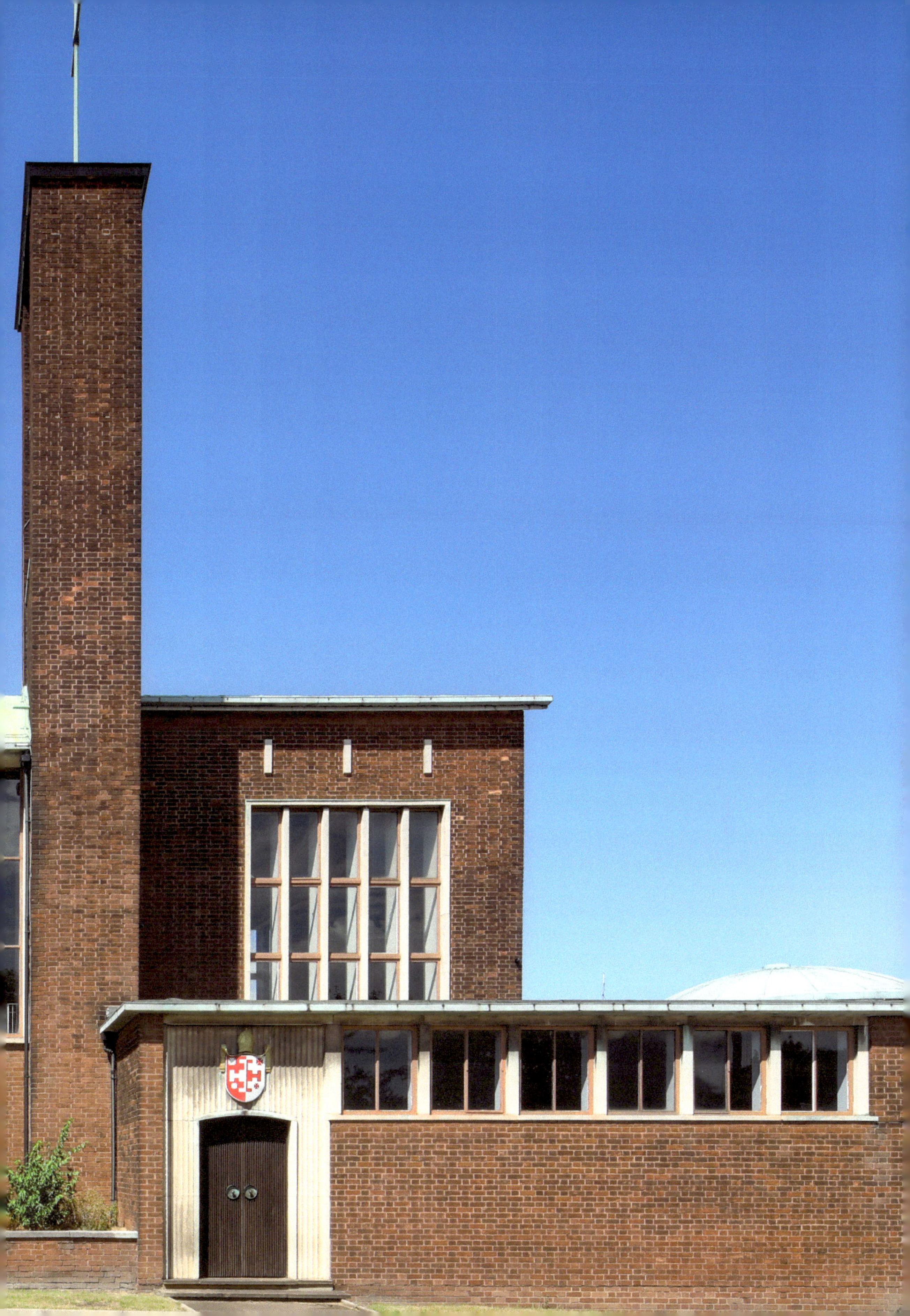

THE GOOD SHEPHERD

CASTLECROFT, WOLVERHAMPTON 1955

The Church of the Good Shepherd, though small, reveals much about Twentyman's approach to practical design. A series of simple box-like structures with different functions are brought together to create a unified building. A long rectangular structure with a pitched roof forms the core meeting place, either for church services or social events. A further more elevated structure creates the sanctuary (5.15) to the liturgical east while a small stage is recessed at the opposite end of the shared nave which can be configured to face east or west. Each can be closed off from the main space depending on the required function.

This dual-purpose church/hall typology was becoming popular at this time as can be seen in the evolution of McNally's 1947 publication *Fifty Modern Churches* into his 1956 *Sixty Post-War Churches*, sub-titled *Churches, Church Centres, and Dual-Purpose Churches*.

Additional structures are added according to need. Here the south-west entrance leads into a lowered passageway running along the south side of the shared nave linking with further spaces (a kitchen, vestry, and meeting room), projecting south at right angles to the main building. This was originally the axis of the main entrance, unusually choreographing the user into the nave at the east (chancel) end, perhaps betraying a slight bias towards the secular in planning terms.

5.15
THE GOOD SHEPHERD
CASTLECROFT FROM SOUTH-EAST
(LOOKING *LITURGICALLY* EAST)

5.16
THE GOOD SHEPHERD EXTERNAL
FACADE OF CHANCEL

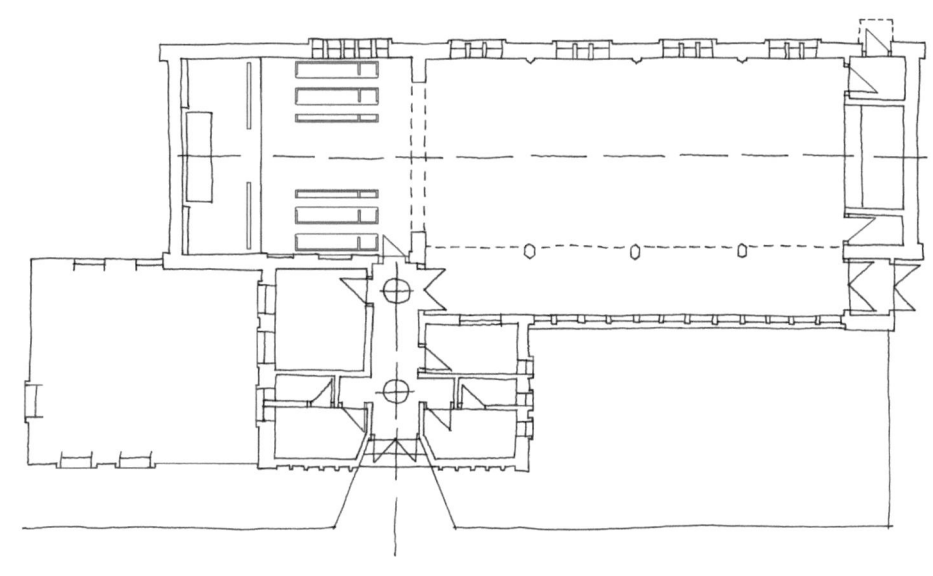

5.17 (ABOVE)
The deceptively simple plan of The Good Shepherd illustrates the dual purpose nave with the lowered cloister to the south connecting with the lower entrance wing

5.18 (ABOVE)
The cross-section shows the clear volumetric articulation of the formal spaces from their supporting functions in the south wing

A CHANGE IN STYLE THE 1950s

5.19 (BELOW)
The Good Shepherd interior looking east, a vertical rollershutter can separate the spaces

5.20 (RIGHT)
The Good Shepherd chancel and south clerestory formed from twelve windows

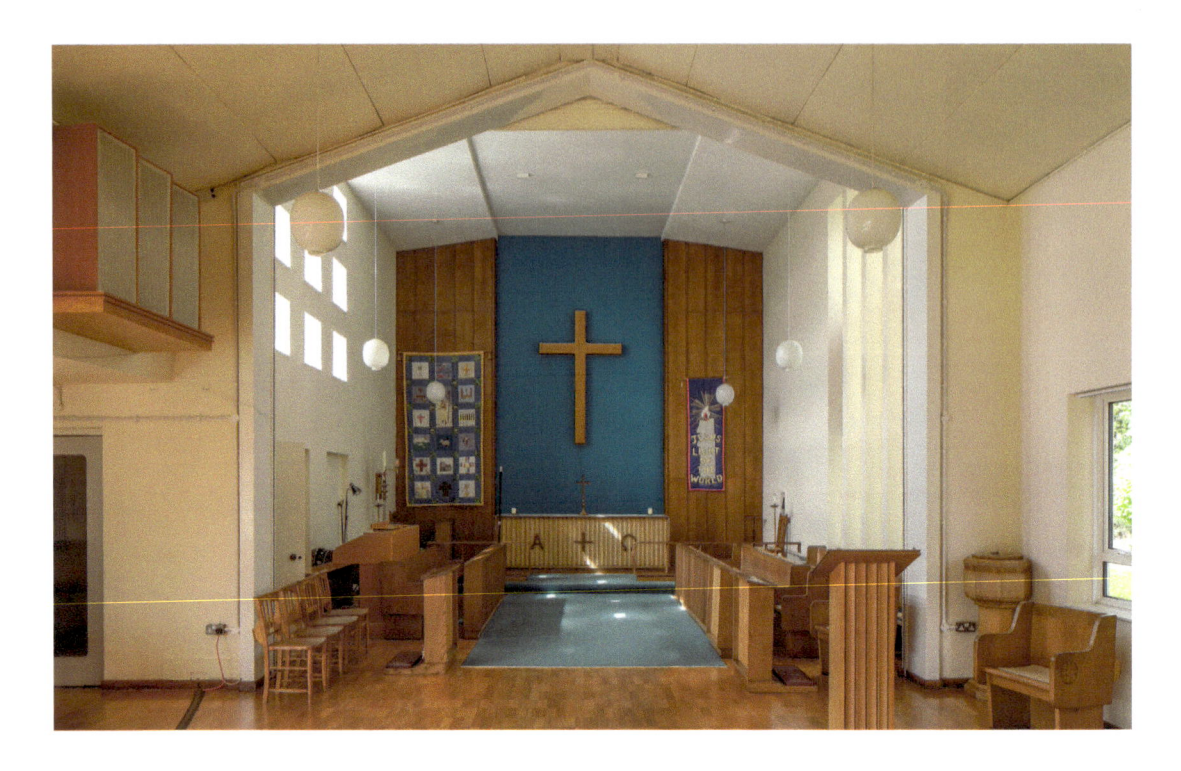

Currently this is no longer the entrance to the building, despite the continuing mixture of activities accommodated. Considerable thought is again given to the provision of natural light. The north side of the main body has nine long metal-framed windows set in deep concrete mullions, and three sets of horizontally arranged south-facing windows within the lowered aisle, implying the side of a cloister.

On the north side of the chancel is a floor-to-ceiling panel of fifteen lights, echoed by three rows of four small square windows high on the south side which create shafts of light illuminating the sanctuary (5.20), similar to Twentyman's St Nicholas, Radford, and echoing similar rectangular openings in Schwarz's 1930 Corpus Christi Church in Aachen. Other external features characteristic of Twentyman's work include a precast concrete Greek cross on the plain rendered west wall, and a Latin cross on the east wall.

Twentyman took particular care over the design of his doors, and Castlecroft's entrance doors have his familiar fluted wooden doors with circular metal door knobs in metal pattress plates.

A CHANGE IN STYLE THE 1950s

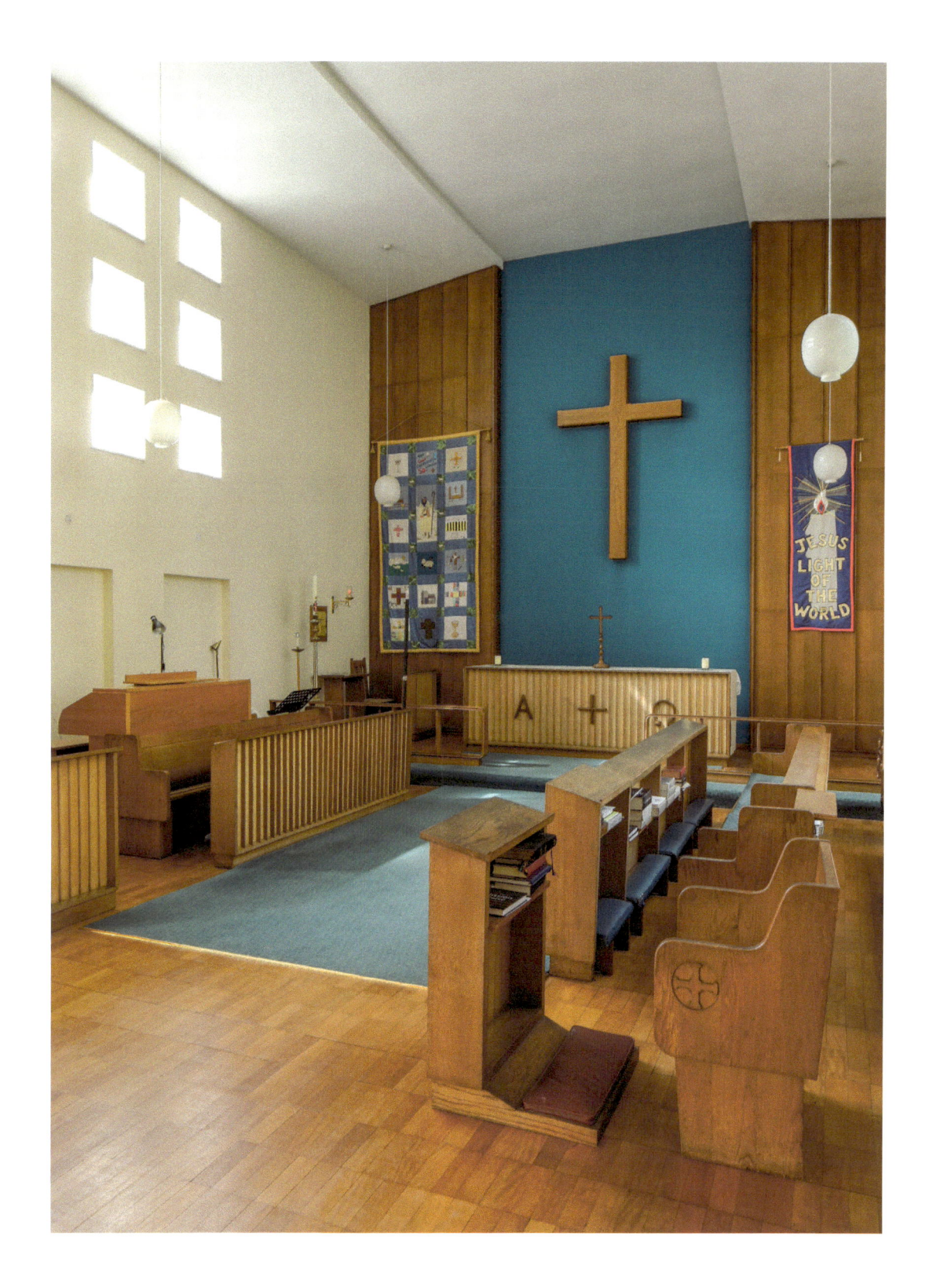

5.21 (BELOW)
The Good Shepherd the altar and chancel rail

5.22 (BOTTOM)
The Good Shepherd the south wing and entrance

5.23 (BELOW)
The Good Shepherd, Castlecroft
isometric studies of plan form and massing

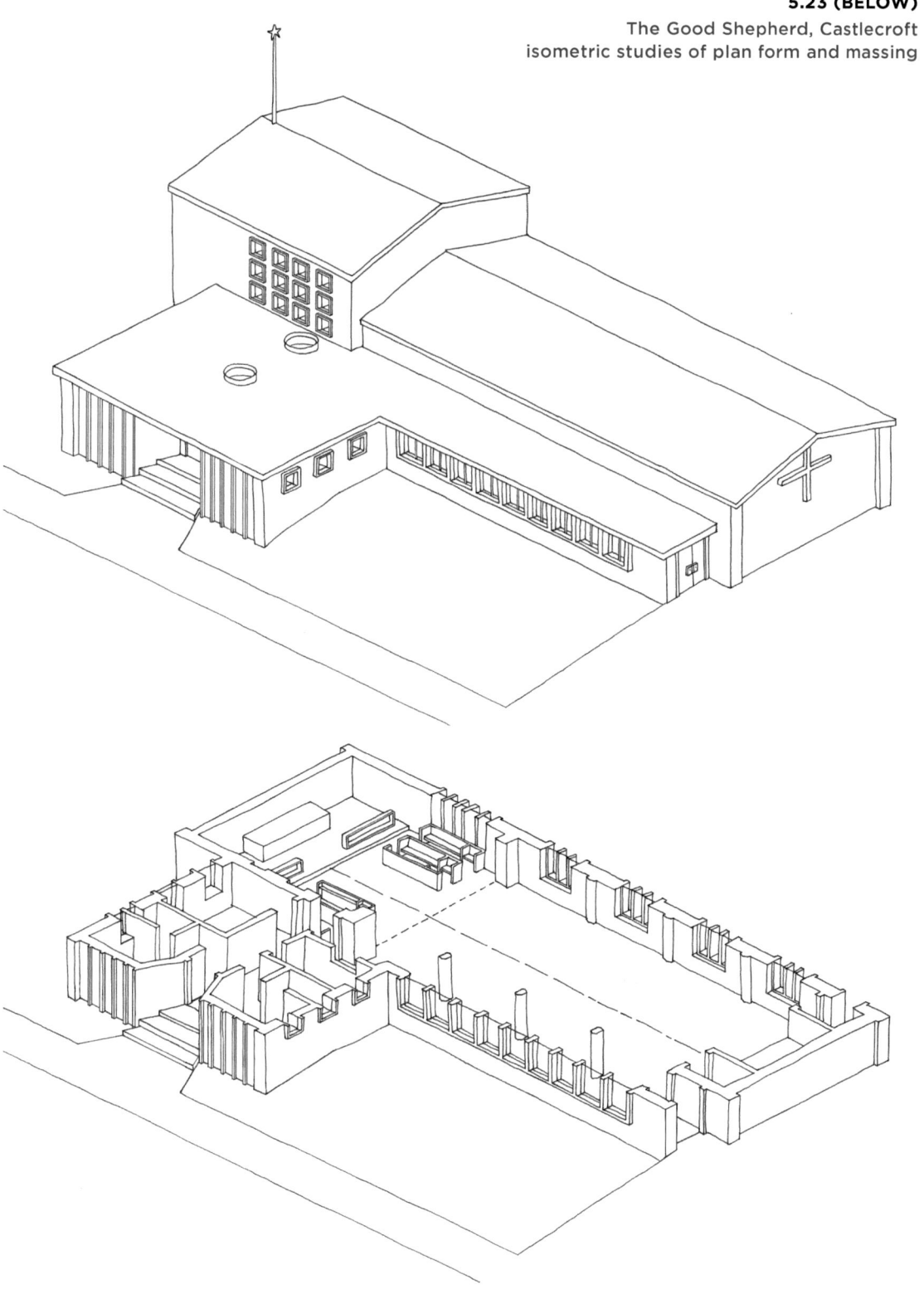

A CHANGE IN STYLE THE 1950s

ST NICHOLAS

RADFORD, COVENTRY
1954-5

The population of Radford increased in the early part of the twentieth century from 5,000 to 20,000 in 1927 with expanding industries and houses provided to meet the demand. Like All Saints, Darlaston, the original church was destroyed by bombing in 1940, but parishioner, diocesan, and War Damage funds helped towards a new church. Photos show the old church in 1937, and the new building that replaced it.

At the time of writing, the church is unfortunately closed, and problems with concrete and asbestos degradation are likely to lead to its eventual demolition, despite local campaigns for its preservation. It is not entirely surprising that people were 'mystified by the external appearance of the church',[11] since the inward leaning walls, 10 degrees from the vertical, which internally added to an impression of exaggerated height, give it, with the curved roof, the appearance of a hangar.[12]

Externally, with its high sides and rounded roof, it bears a resemblance to Peter Behrens' 1909 AEG turbine factory in Berlin. *The Architects' Journal* regarded the sloping walls as 'aesthetically unsatisfactory', though praised the east wall behind the altar,[13] veneered in walnut with diamond-shaped panels and light provided by the several side windows. The yellow brick-faced walls and copper-covered roof are of reinforced concrete, designed with remarkable refinement, the main roof vault being only 4" thick at the centre. The elegant tower, similar in design to All Saints,

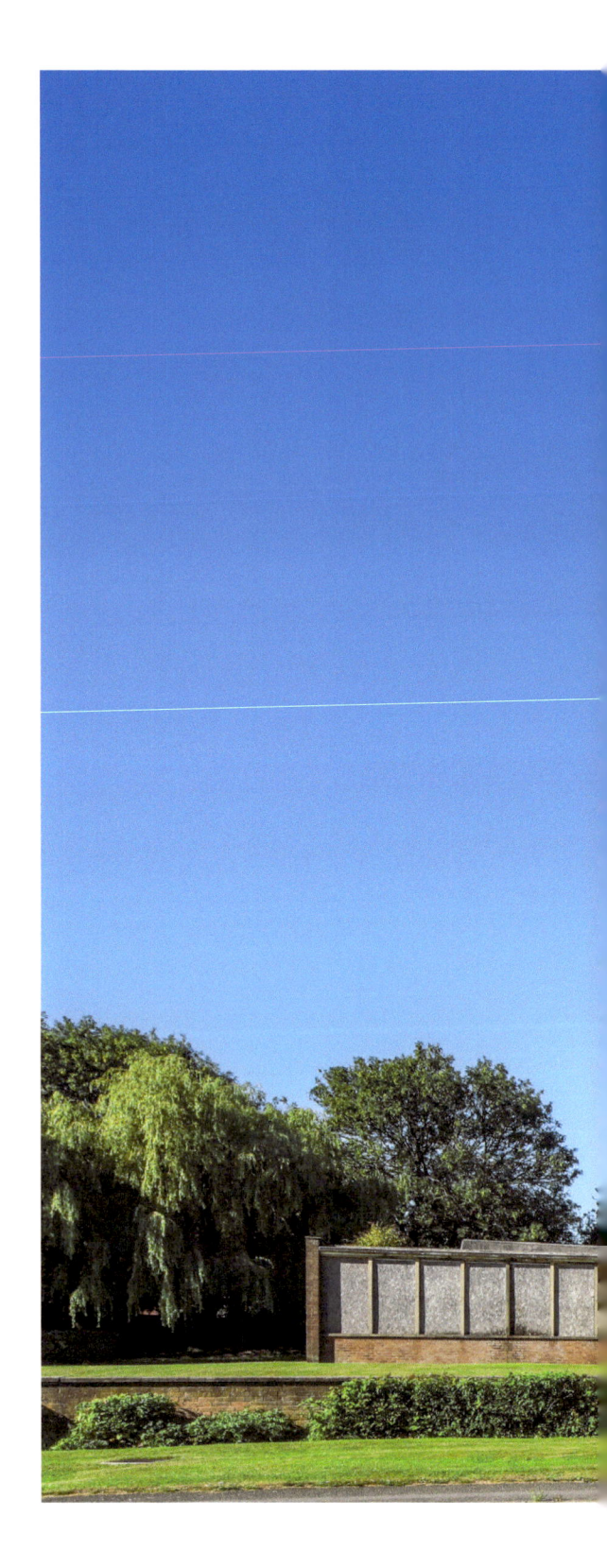

5.24
**ST NICHOLAS, RADFORD
FROM SOUTH-EAST**

5.25 (BOTTOM)
St Nicholas the altar and chancel
photographed soon after completion

5.26 (BELOW)
St Nicholas *Informes de la
construcción* dated January 1957

Darlaston, is solid brick with two bells and a sculptured relief of St Nicholas by Don Potter. It introduces a slight entasis, and creates a powerful image when viewed from the lower main road to the east, seen in a contemporary photograph published in the Spanish journal *Informes de la Construcción* in 1957[14] (5.26). The exterior east end is stone-faced with diamond patterns matching the interior wall and a large cross (5.25).

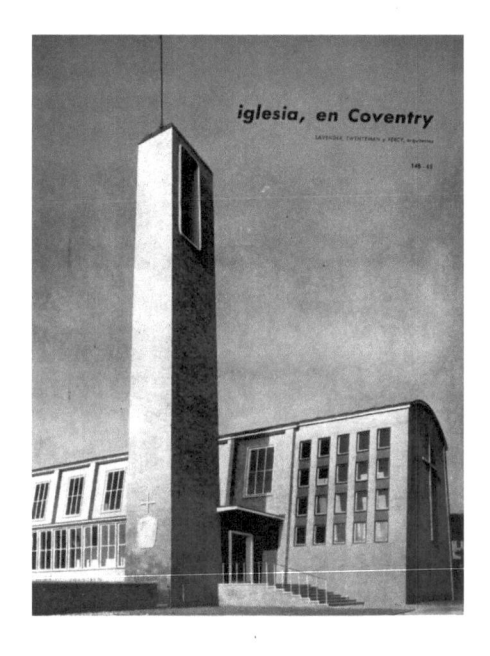

5.27
ST NICHOLAS, RADFORD
TOWER & EAST ENTRANCE

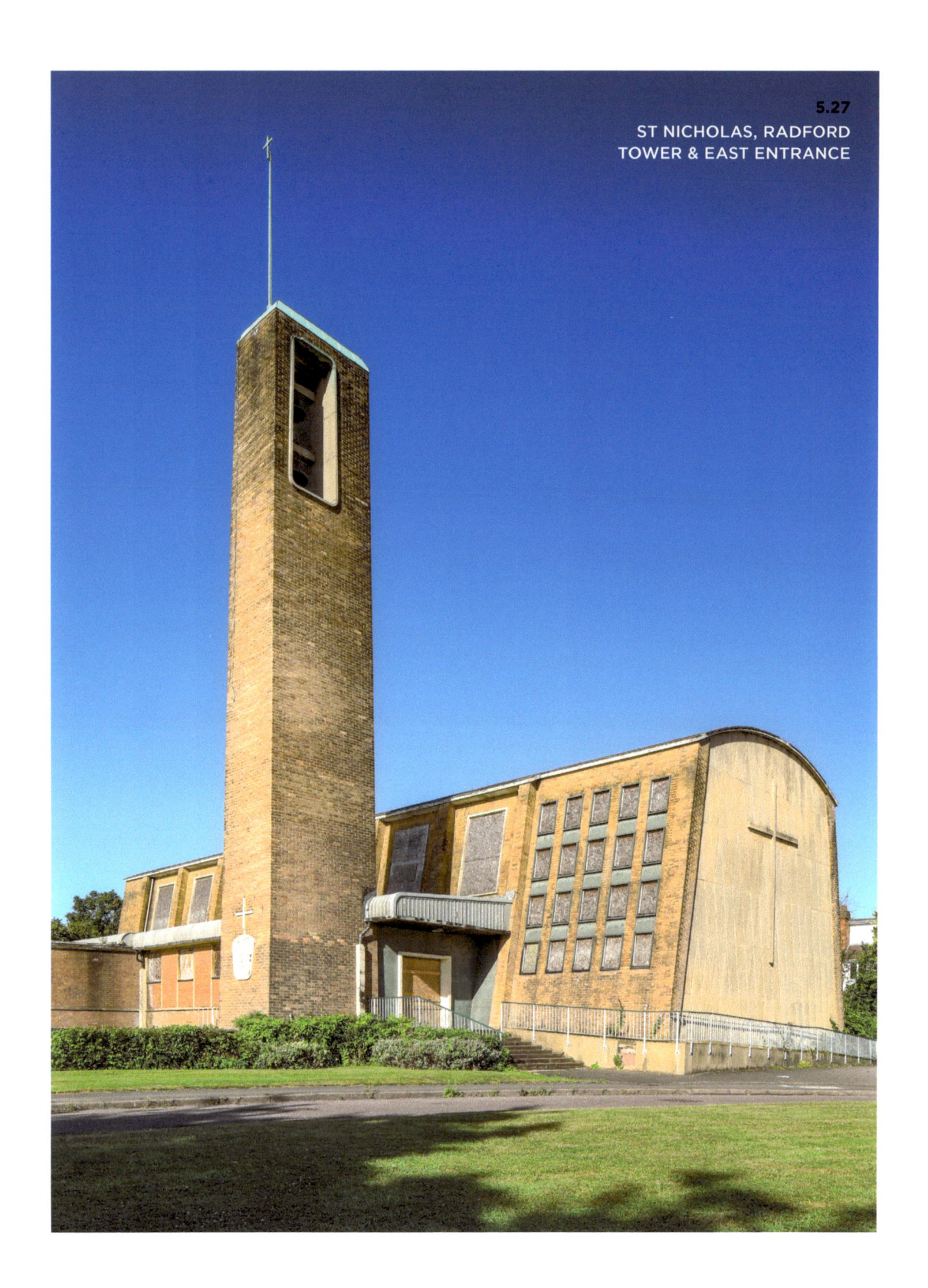

5.28 (BELOW)
St Nicholas south facade with hall in the foreground

The ceiling is of African walnut boards, and floors are of stone and green slate. Further locally-archived photographs reveal a wide rectangular nave with internal solid buttresses and no aisles, providing an uninterrupted view of the altar, and chancel and sanctuary are more integrated with the nave than in earlier Twentyman churches. Entrance to the church brings worshippers into the chancel east end of the church, rather than the more usual west end.

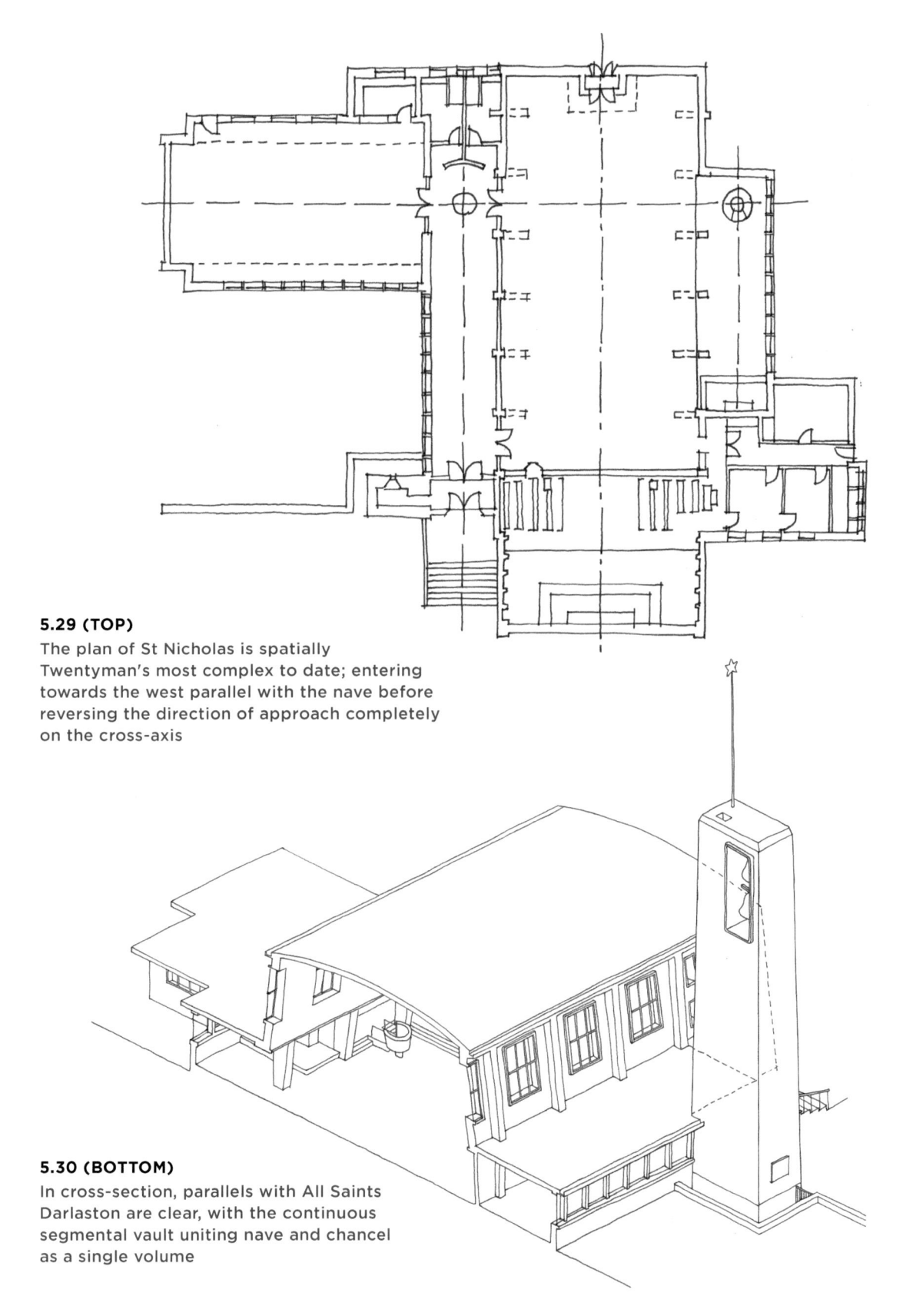

5.29 (TOP)
The plan of St Nicholas is spatially Twentyman's most complex to date; entering towards the west parallel with the nave before reversing the direction of approach completely on the cross-axis

5.30 (BOTTOM)
In cross-section, parallels with All Saints Darlaston are clear, with the continuous segmental vault uniting nave and chancel as a single volume

A CHANGE IN STYLE THE 1950s

5.31 (BELOW)
St Nicholas south side of chancel showing battered wall construction, photographed prior to the church's closure

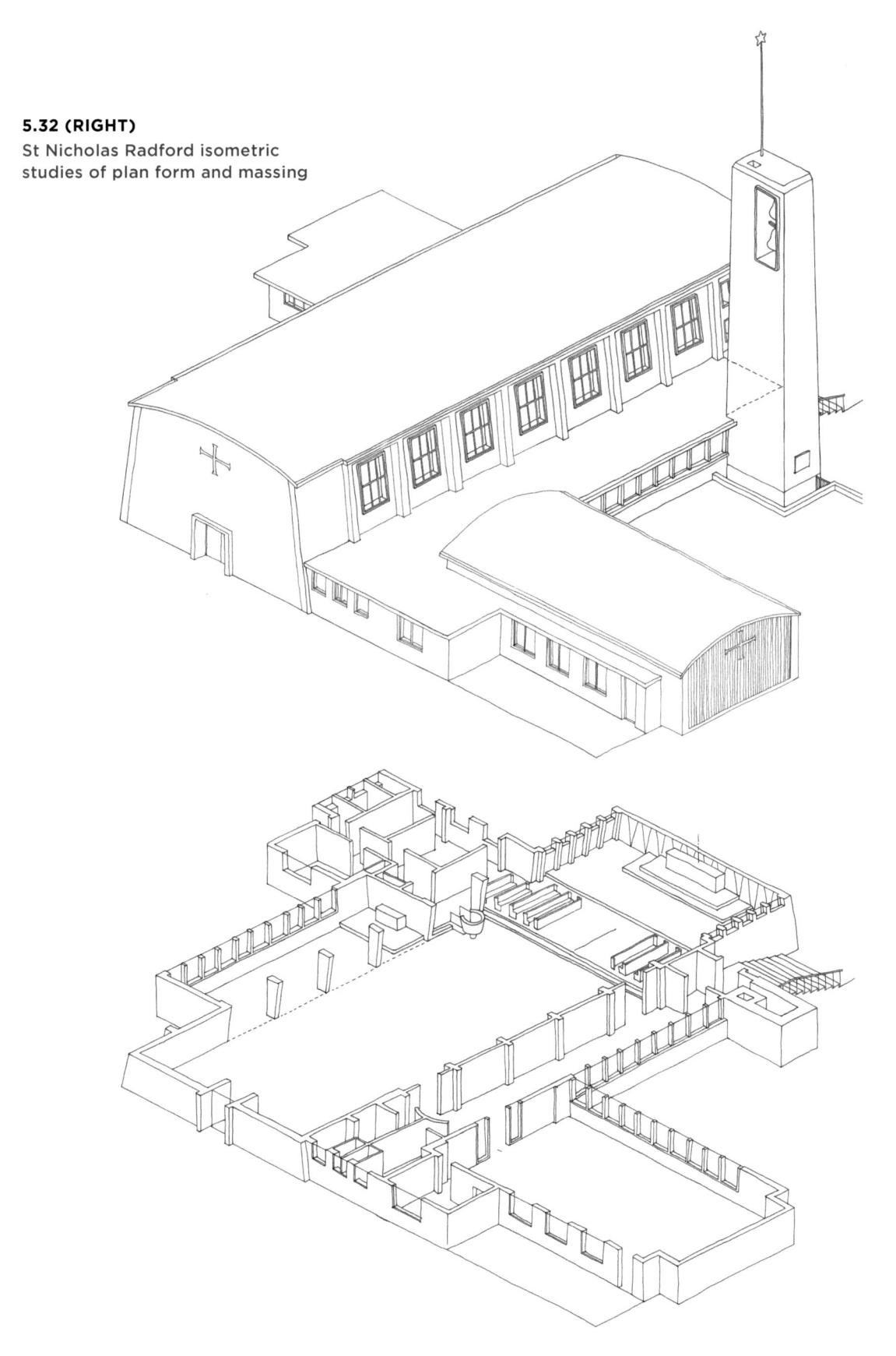

5.32 (RIGHT)
St Nicholas Radford isometric studies of plan form and massing

A CHANGE IN STYLE THE 1950s

5.33
ST NICHOLAS RADFORD
EAST ELEVATION WATERCOLOUR
DATED AUGUST 1951

NORTH EAST ELEVATION

ONE INCH TO EIGHT FEET

EMMANUEL CHURCH

BENTLEY 1955-7

Emmanuel Church, Bentley was the only Twentyman church funded by personal benefactors. The Owen family built it in memory of Alfred Ernest Owen (1869-1929), the founder of Rubery Owen, a large engineering company, which in the 1950s employed 5,000 workers on its Darlaston site, and 17,000 workers internationally.[15] It replaced an existing Welfare Hall converted into a church for worship each Sunday,[16] and was built on the site of an old Manor House, Bentley Hall, demolished around 1929 because of subsidence caused by coal mining.

Its imposing setting is approached by a long flight of steps on an open landscaped hill overlooking local housing estates, in Twentyman's time a newly developed area the church was originally built to serve. It is the only Twentyman church, apart from his two crematorium chapels, not located directly in the midst of housing and thoroughfares but part of a landscaped setting.

The church has a capacity of 325 and cost £35,000 to build. It is of reinforced concrete, faced with hand-made buff bricks in Sussex bond. Roofs, gutters, and downpipes were originally made of copper. The main body of the church has six sets of tall mullioned windows on the south wall, with window slits set above them as a clerestory, and a set of long lights flanking the sanctuary, a Twentyman theme in the postwar churches (5.34).

5.34
EMMANUEL CHURCH BENTLEY
SOUTH FACADE

5.35
EMMANUEL CHURCH TOWER &
HALL FROM SOUTH-WEST

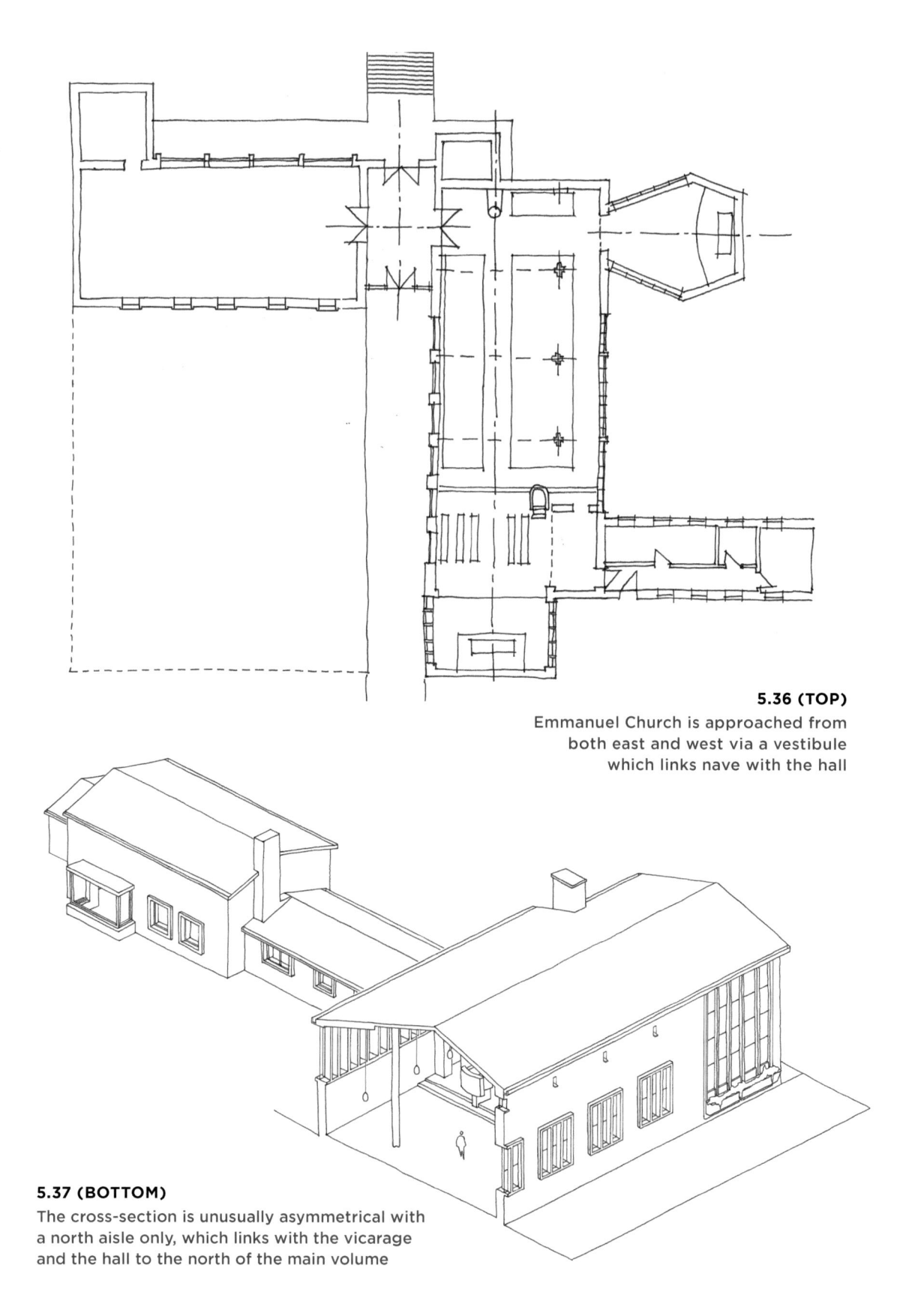

5.36 (TOP)
Emmanuel Church is approached from both east and west via a vestibule which links nave with the hall

5.37 (BOTTOM)
The cross-section is unusually asymmetrical with a north aisle only, which links with the vicarage and the hall to the north of the main volume

A CHANGE IN STYLE THE 1950s

5.38 (BELOW)
Emmanuel Church the vestigial cloister formed with the hall to the south

5.39 (RIGHT)
Emmanuel Church the west portal at the top of the wide flight of steps

Twentyman was now controlling the use of natural light with an increasing skill and ambition. The overall effect of the nave was dependent on creating a soft glare-free light. His aim was further to refine this into a progression from a low intensity at the west end towards high intensity at the east,[17] culminating in a chancel flooded with natural light. As with all of Twentyman's churches this was achieved by modulating the proportions of windows, and the depth of their reveals. Thin, deep mullions help to create softness, with higher intensities achieved with taller windows in the sanctuary. Glare is reduced with deep reveals and the differentiation of scale between the lower windows on the south side of the nave, compared to the taller north-facing ones in the aisle.

A CHANGE IN STYLE THE 1950s

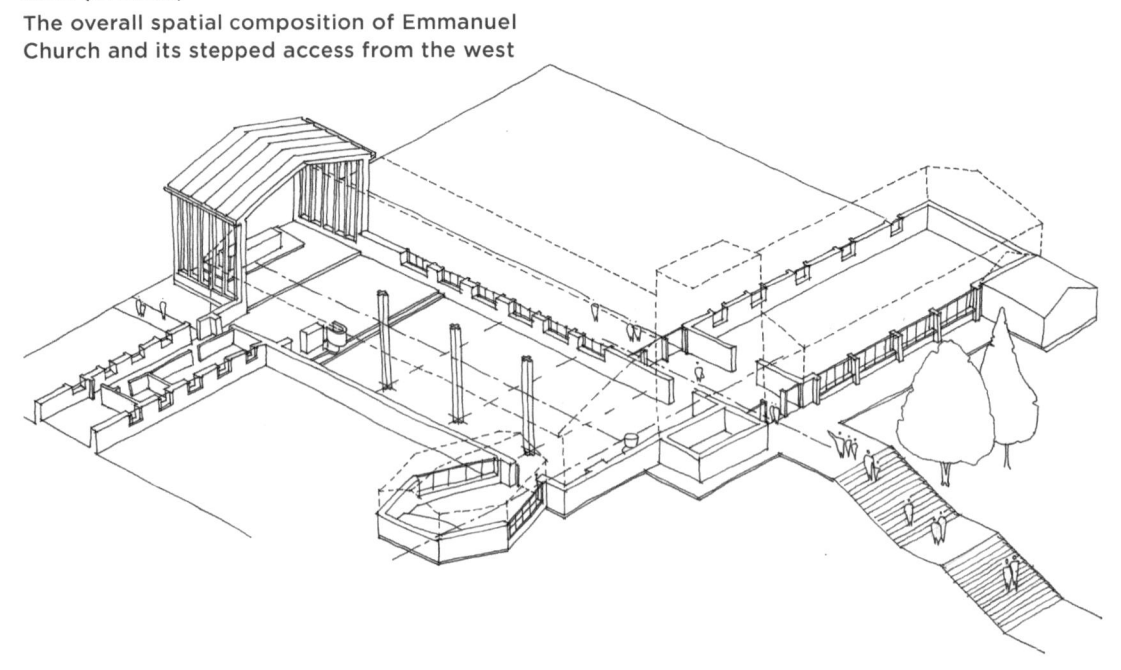

5.40 (BELOW)
The overall spatial composition of Emmanuel Church and its stepped access from the west

There are three 12-inch diameter cruciform concrete quatrefoil columns, painted purple, separating the nave from the north aisle to support the larger north span of the reinforced concrete roof, not required on the south side, creating an asymmetric volume.

The L-shaped composition is completed by the hall which projects south at right angles to the church, the two forms united by a double-sided entrance vestibule. This device, which is an evolution of that developed at Radford, presents a full height glazed screen towards the eastern court, while a more defensive brick facade with solid doors faces towards the grand flight of steps which link the church with its community below. As at Radford, this point of spatial transition is again marked with the impressive 70ft tower to the west, containing four bells behind paired, off-set, louvered, belfry openings.

5.41
EMMANUEL CHURCH CHANCEL

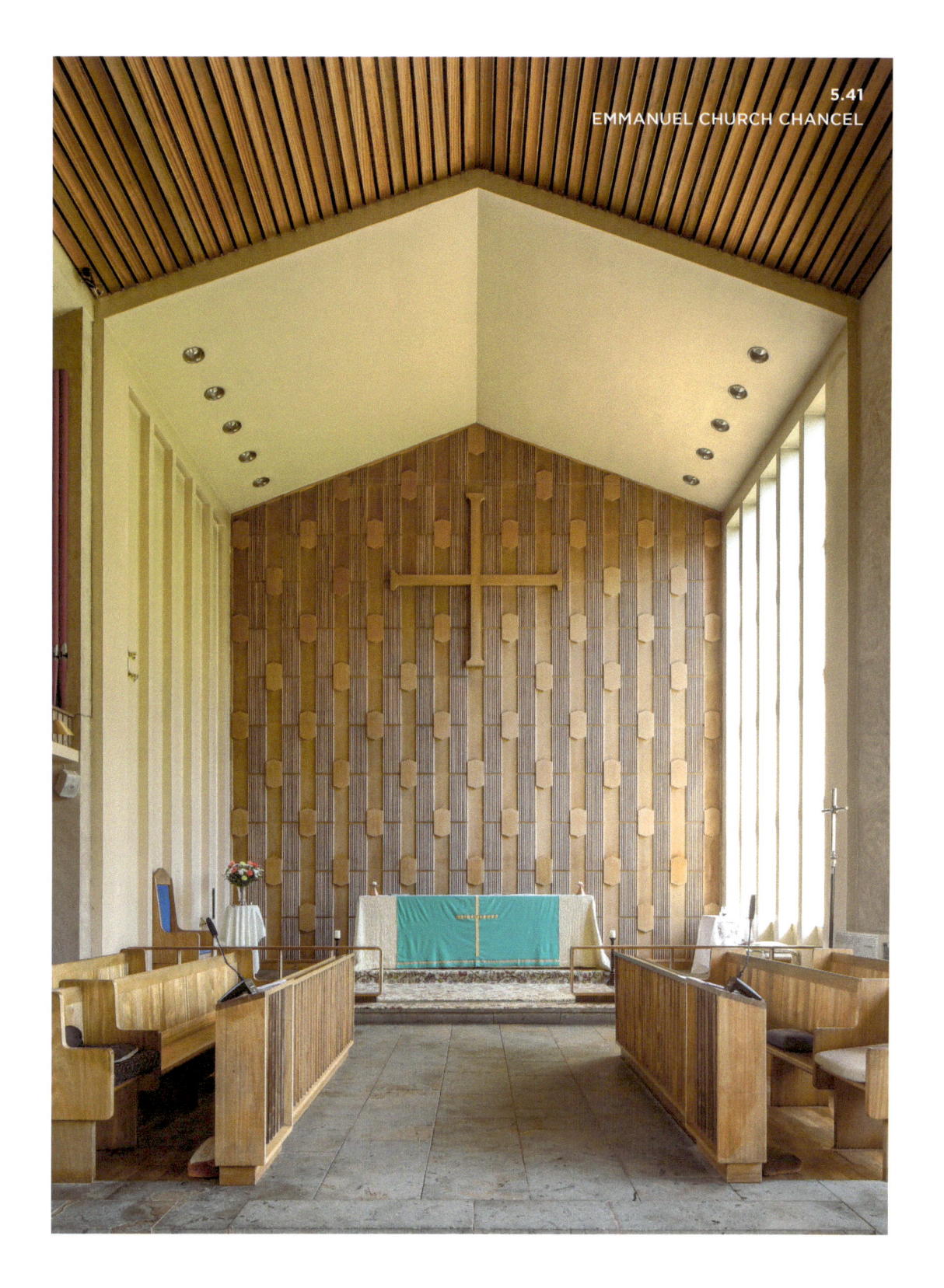

5.42 (BELOW)
Emmanuel Church nave with quatrefoil concrete columns

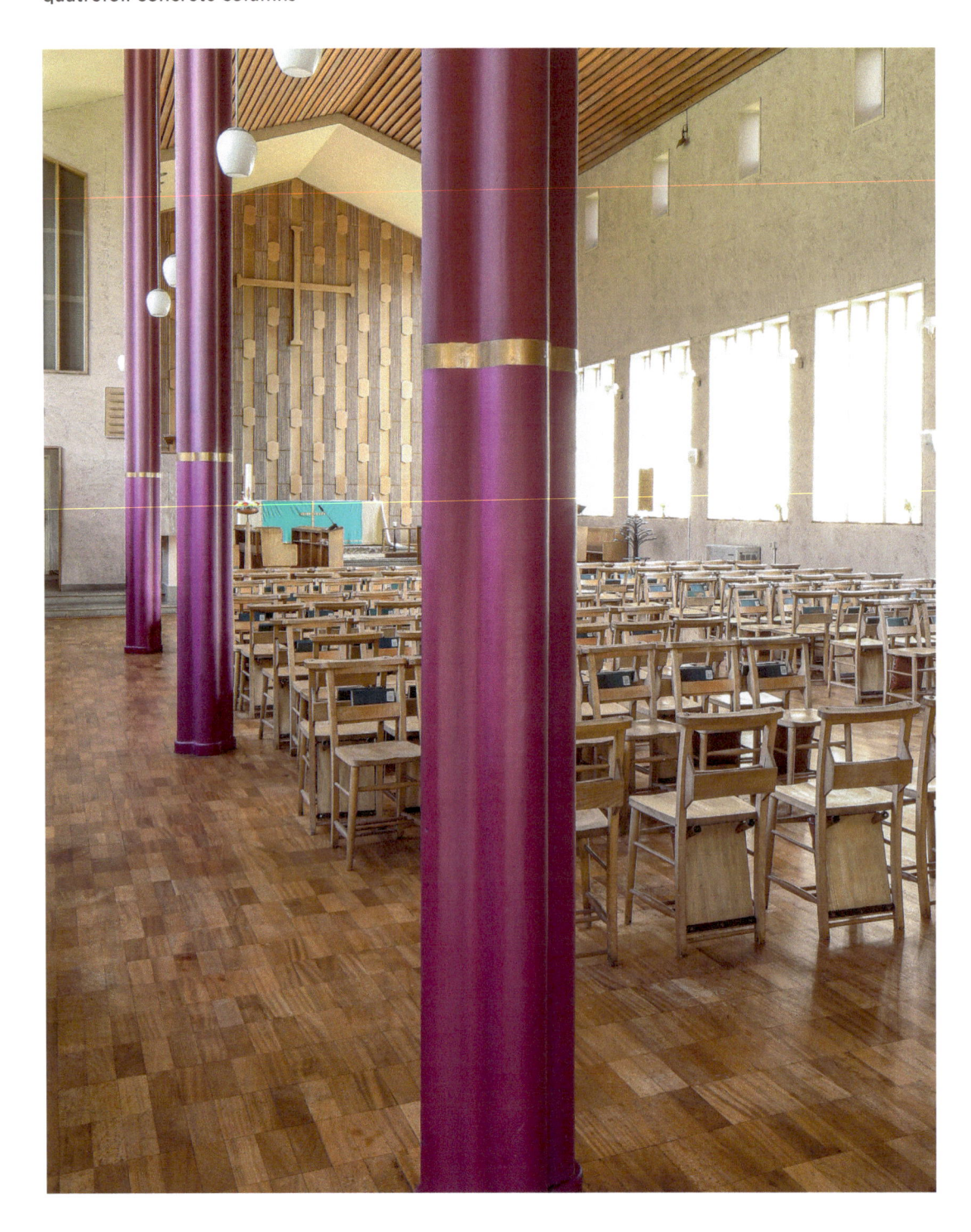

5.43 (BELOW)
Emmanuel Church nave with modulation of daylight from west to east

A projecting hexagonal Lady Chapel is set opposite the vestibule on the north-west corner, balancing a service wing linked to the attached vicarage at the north-east corner. This creates a second implied cloister to the north of the church (albeit so visually compromised by the landscape that it is difficult to perceive on the ground).

As an overall composition, Bentley is Twentyman's grandest and most expansive, creating a complex series of linked buildings occupying their dramatic hill-top site like a medieval citadel towering above the townsfolk below. It is an effect the tall and austere campanile only adds to, bringing a distinctly Tuscan feel to this corner of the Black Country.

5.44 (BELOW)
Emmanuel Church isometric study showing massing and composition of interconnecting forms

The hierachy of form is carefully modulated, with the clear organisational focus on the nave and tower. To the south, the scale drops to the hall, and still further to its service wing at the very south-west corner of the site. The scale of the hall does however retain enough presence to define the L-shaped court to the south-east corner of the site, an effect which is further emphasised by zones of trees and planting completing the vestigial cloister.

To the north, the extended slope of the north aisle roof lowers the eaves to meet the connecting northern wings at either end of the main nave/chancel block.

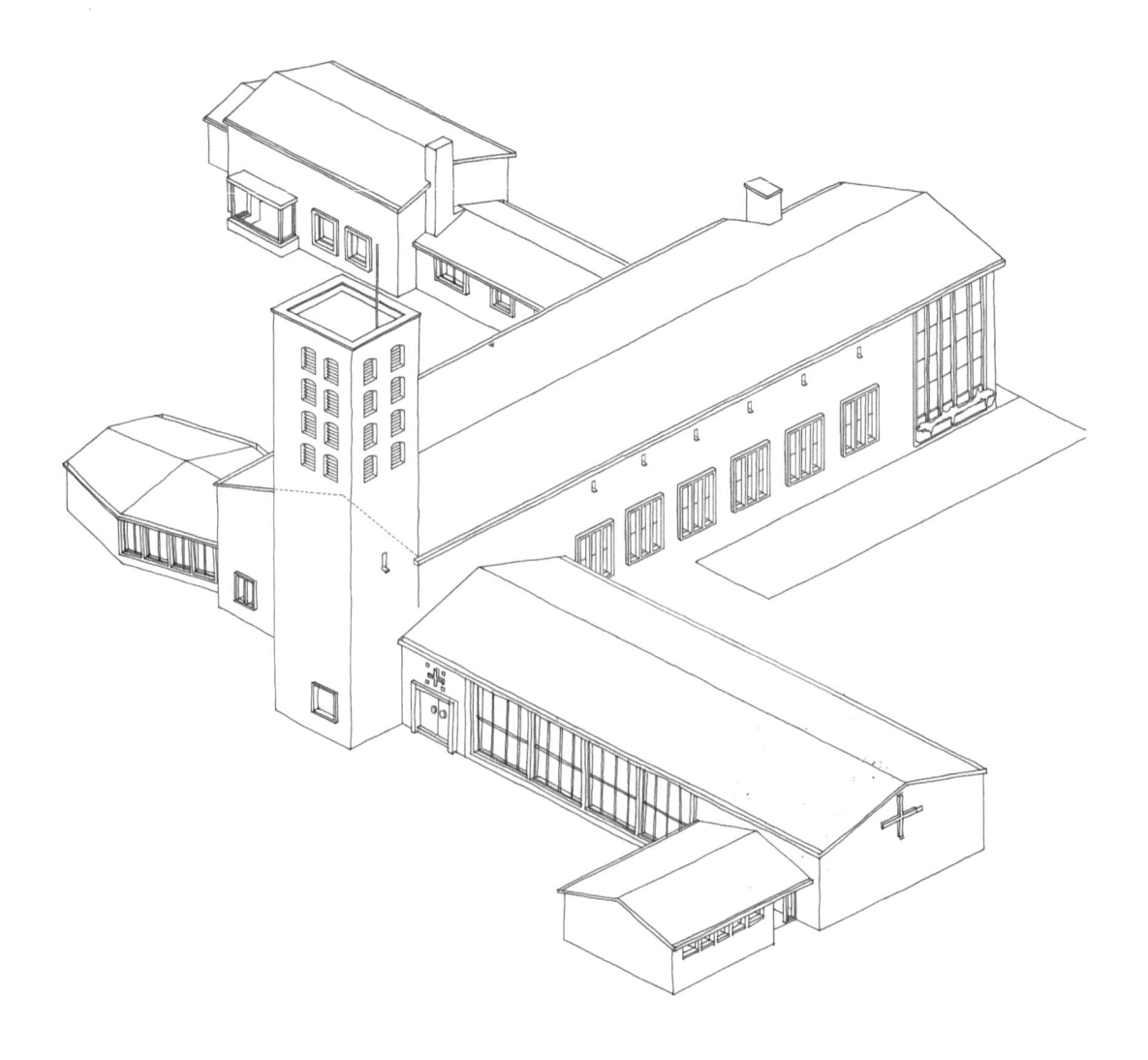

5.45 (BELOW)
Emmanuel Church isometric study of plan form showing spatial sequence and choreography

In terms of its spatial progression, the entrance axis (from both east and west) sits parallel with the nave, along its south side. It intersects with the cross axis of the hall which connects hall, vestibule and north-west chapel in enfilade across the western end of the nave. The north-eastern range is less formal but equally precisely aligned with toilets and vestries served by a corridor along their east side which is orientated to align with the stepped level change into the sanctuary. This also allows these spaces to face the enclosed gardens to the north.

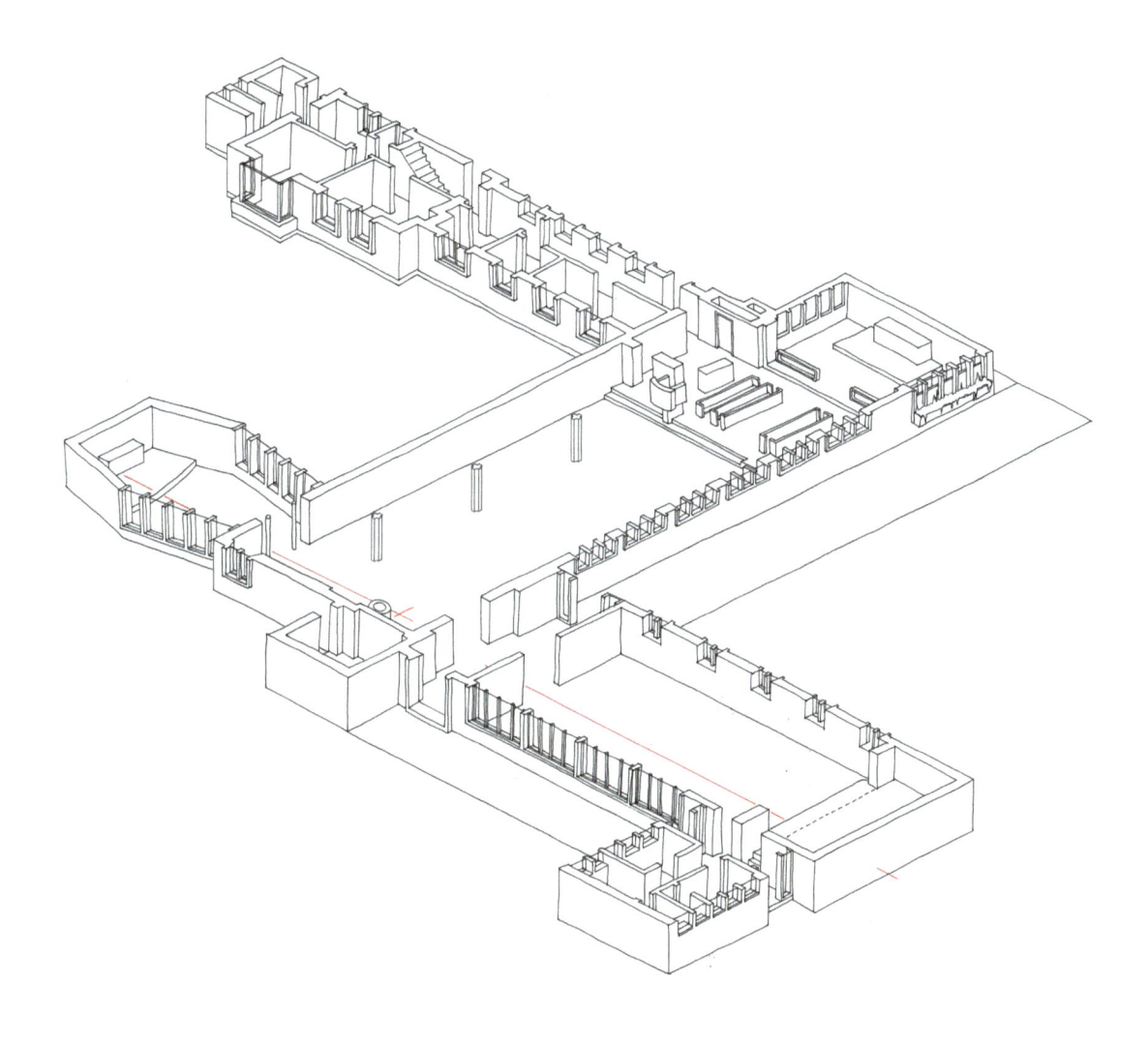

5.46 (BOTTOM RIGHT)
Emmanuel Church cross-axis of hall connecting nave and north-west chapel in enfilade

5.47 (RIGHT)
Emmanuel Church detail of timber quatrefoil columns and lintel with brass stars at entrance to north-west chapel

Twentyman designed the font, pulpit, altar rails, the organ console, and the choir stalls with the familiar ribbed pattern, also apparent on the main entrance doors along with the customary Twentyman-designed door handles. Although the altar is brought forward, the division between chancel and nave is quite marked with raised choir stalls on either side. Twentyman's concern for thematic detail is evident.

The cross pattée of the Bishop of Lichfield's Coat-of-Arms is repeated in the form of several smaller crosses in the east porch doorway decoration beneath it. Splayed Greek crosses, similar in design to the cross pattée, appear on the west porch door, east wall, both interior and exterior, and the entrance to the organ loft. The font pillar matches the cruciform nave pillars, and the wood-panelled east wall with alternating ribbed and shield sections matches the south interior door (5.42).

According to Pevsner, the church is 'much prettier than their pre-war work'.[18] It is certainly of very different design, and the increasing confidence with managing asymmetric volumes speaks of how far Twentyman had come since the formal compositions of the interwar churches.

A CHANGE IN STYLE THE 1950s

5.48
ST CHAD, RUBERY
THE SOUTH FACADE

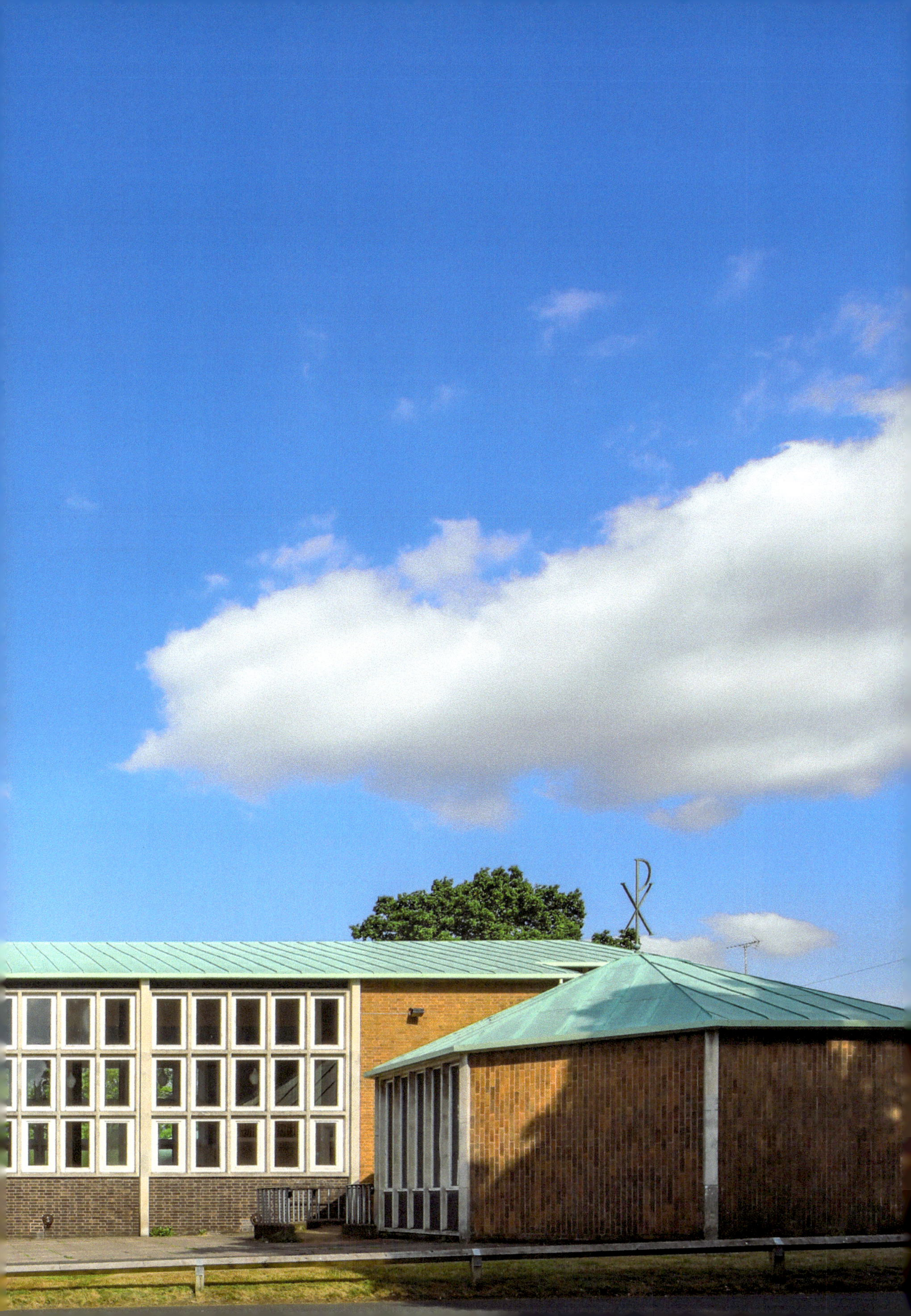

ST CHAD

RUBERY 1956-60

St Chad was built to replace a smaller wooden church of 1895, and to cater for the housing expansion that was occurring in the Rubery area after the war. Birmingham slums were being demolished and there was an influx of families into the area with new housing including high-rise flats. Many parishioners worked at the massive Longbridge Car Plant nearby, and the sanctuary light in the new church unusually was a rear motor light bulb symbolising the importance of the factory work.[19] The building costs were £40000. Most of the costs were covered by the diocesan Golden Jubilee Appeal, initiated by the then Bishop of Birmingham, Leonard Wilson (1897-1970). The parish had to find around £11000 which included the cost of the organ, resulting in several fundraising activities, including a 'buy-a-brick' scheme. Princess Margaret opened the church in 1960 (5.49).

5.49
Princess Margaret opening St Chad in 1960

5.50
ST CHAD, RUBERY
INTERIOR LOKING EAST

5.51
ST CHAD TOWER
FROM SOUTH-WEST

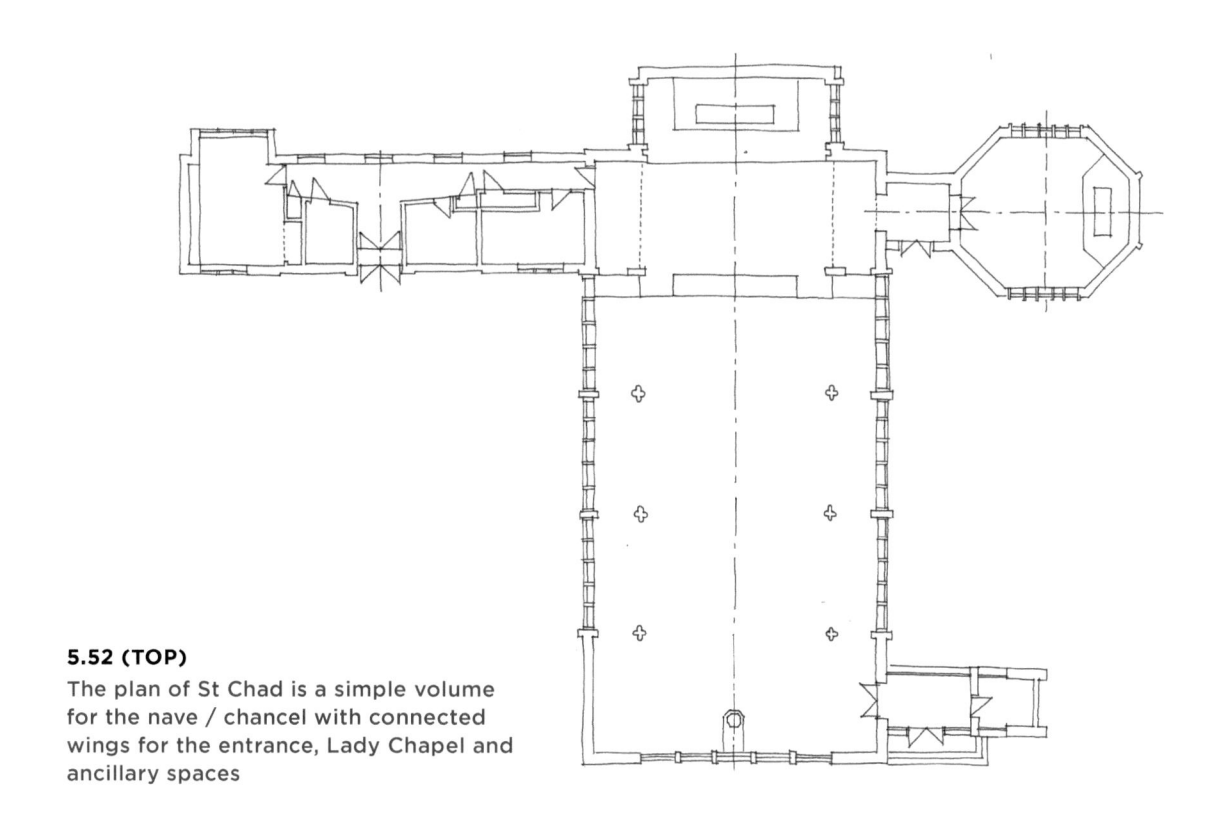

5.52 (TOP)
The plan of St Chad is a simple volume for the nave / chancel with connected wings for the entrance, Lady Chapel and ancillary spaces

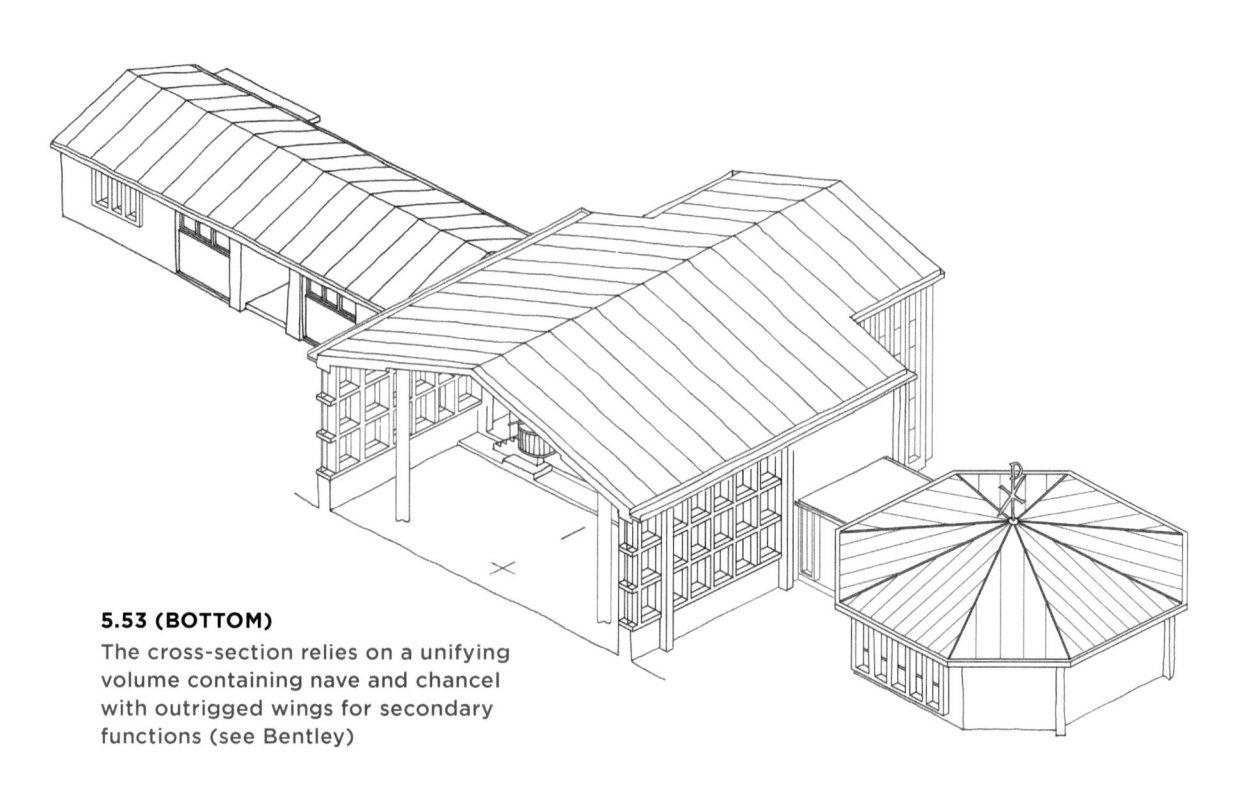

5.53 (BOTTOM)
The cross-section relies on a unifying volume containing nave and chancel with outrigged wings for secondary functions (see Bentley)

A CHANGE IN STYLE THE 1950s

5.54 (BELOW)
St Chad west frontage showing the plinths for the Geoffrey Clarke sculptures

5.55 (RIGHT)
St Chad west facade detail

A CHANGE IN STYLE THE 1950s

The church is built of a reinforced concrete portal frame, clad with brick and panels of black slate. In a note to parishioners about the building,[20] Twentyman mentions modern features found in his other churches built at this time, the special materials to assist acoustics (often unfortunately asbestos), and the electric underfloor heating. This was a solution common to all of Twentyman's churches which although an effective and sustainable strategy, has proved unreliable in the very long-term as the installations have outlived their design life.

The plan and massing are deceptively simple. A single volume, designed with seating for 400, contains nave, bays, and chancel, crossed with two perpendicular axial connections linking to the tower at the west end to form the entrance and creating links to a south chapel and a service wing to the south-east and north-east respectively. It has a standing seam pitched copper roof to the main volume echoed on the hexagonal Lady Chapel attached to the south-east.

The 70ft. open tower to the south-west has become less solid comprising two linked planes of brickwork encasing the flanks of a concrete frame, perhaps referencing the skeletal frames of Basil Spence's Coventry churches. The functional aesthetic is a clear progression from Darlaston.

5.56 (BOTTOM)
St Chad an early drawing of the west elevation showing figurative sculptures on the plinths originally intended for the Geoffrey Clarke sculptures

5.57
ST CHAD CHANCEL AND
EAST WALL RELIEF

5.58 (BELOW)
All Saints the pulpit carved in English oak by Don Potter

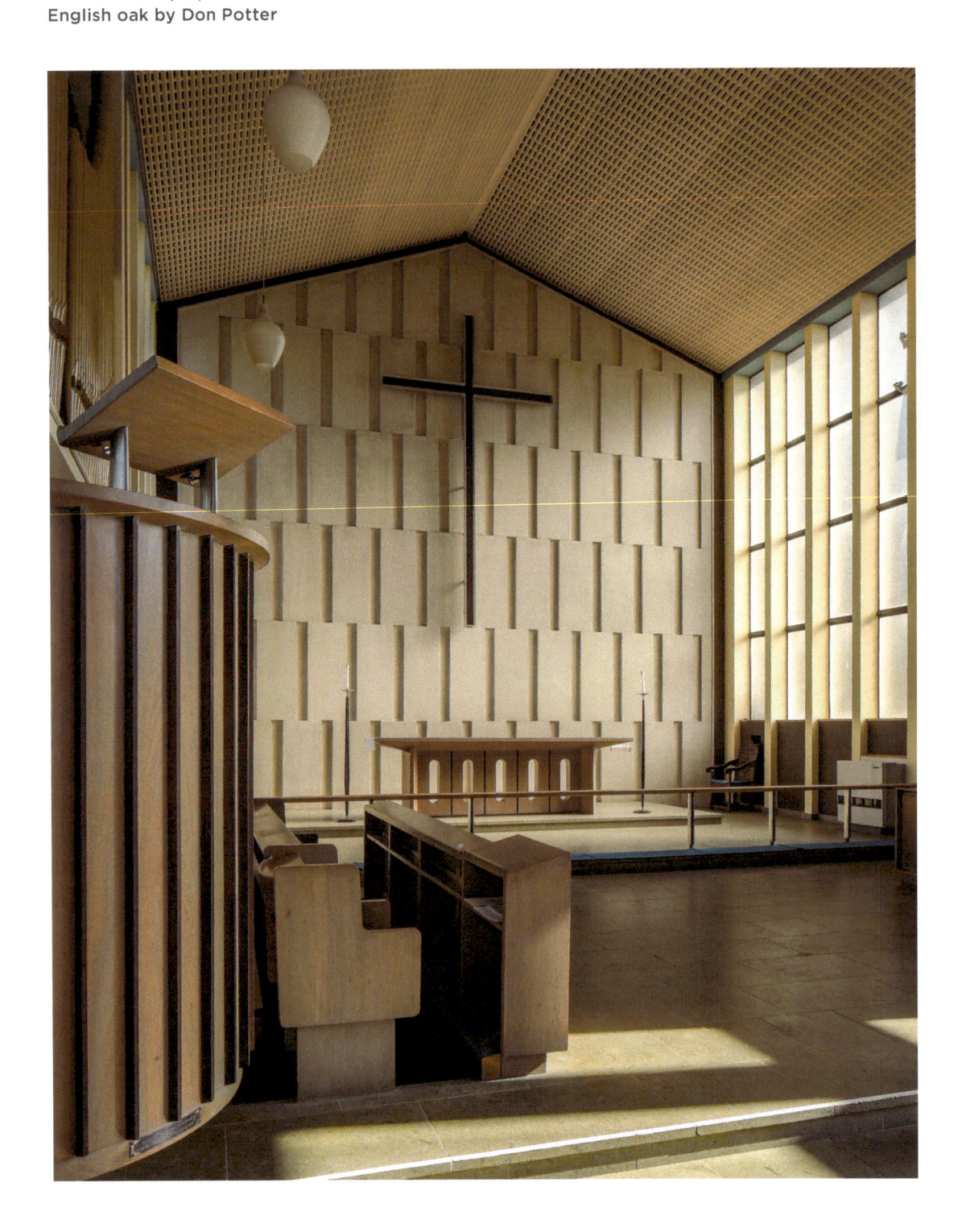

5.59 (BELOW)
All Saints the nave looking east

The exterior is similarly simple and functional, the west front designed to accommodate the Geoffrey Clarke sculptures.[21] A Twentyman drawing (2.10) exhibited at a Royal Academy Architecture Exhibition in 1957[22] shows the original idea was for figurative reliefs (also shown in 5.56). A hint of how these would have appeared had they not been rejected, and how different the facade would have been, can still be seen at the base of the tower where Clarke's Coat-of-Arms for the Bishop of Birmingham was allowed to remain (5.60), ironically also a symbolic work, but in this case accepted through familiarity with, if not entirely comprehension of, heraldic conventions.

There is a run of identical 15ft. tall mullioned windows along both the 50ft. north and south sides of the church together with full-length windows either side of the sanctuary filling the space with light. The deep mullions achieve the subtle lighting effect found in all Twentyman's postwar churches, and highlight the east wall of recessed, tiered, precast concrete slabs with a simple superimposed cross, matched by a similar cross on the exterior. The three bays of slim pillars utilise the same type of rounded cruciform quatrefoil style as at Emmanuel Church, Bentley, although at St Chad, they are painted a different colour, walnut.

A CHANGE IN STYLE THE 1950s

At Rubery however, the wide symmetrical nave has the effect of compressing the volume to create a more subtle, less linear and formal space than Emmanuel, despite the latter's subtly asymmetric form.

Colour is handled with the painterly finesse of the earlier churches. The sloping ceilings of the aisles are in a soft, powder blue (see Lady Chapel at Darlaston). This contrasts with the pale ivory of the central portion of the ceiling which is given texture by the slotted acoustic treatment, and aligns with the concrete panel of the east wall.

The effect is to emphasise the scale and directionality of the space. Against this backdrop, the Granwood flooring of the nave and stone of the chancel continue the muted theme, setting off the oak and walnut of the joinery to maximum effect. Although subtle, the overall result is highly effective, creating a peaceful and sophisticated interior, far removed from the busy road outside the west door.

The pale coloured boarding of the ceiling, the deeply mullioned windows, and the side-lit natural concrete of the east wall all create an illusion of spaciousness and an ever-shifting subtlety of illumination, very Scandinavian in character, referencing Alvar Aalto (1898-1976),[23] and hinting at the future work of Juha Leiviska (born 1936).[24] Kenneth Robinson, at the time Chief Assistant Editor of *The Architects' Journal*, in a piece explaining the multiplicity of architectural styles, highlights St Chad as 'light, elegant, and inviting – a building of its time'.[25]

St Chad marks the last of the series of 1950's designs, which have by this stage become a recognisable style. The move away from this in the 1960's, and experimentation with larger centralised forms in a more austere language, exemplifies the constant evolution of Twentyman's work. He tries out new ideas while always retaining a clarity of thought in their implementation.

5.60 (LEFT)
St Chad Arms of the Bishop of Birmingham the only remaining sculpture by Geoffrey Clarke on the west facade

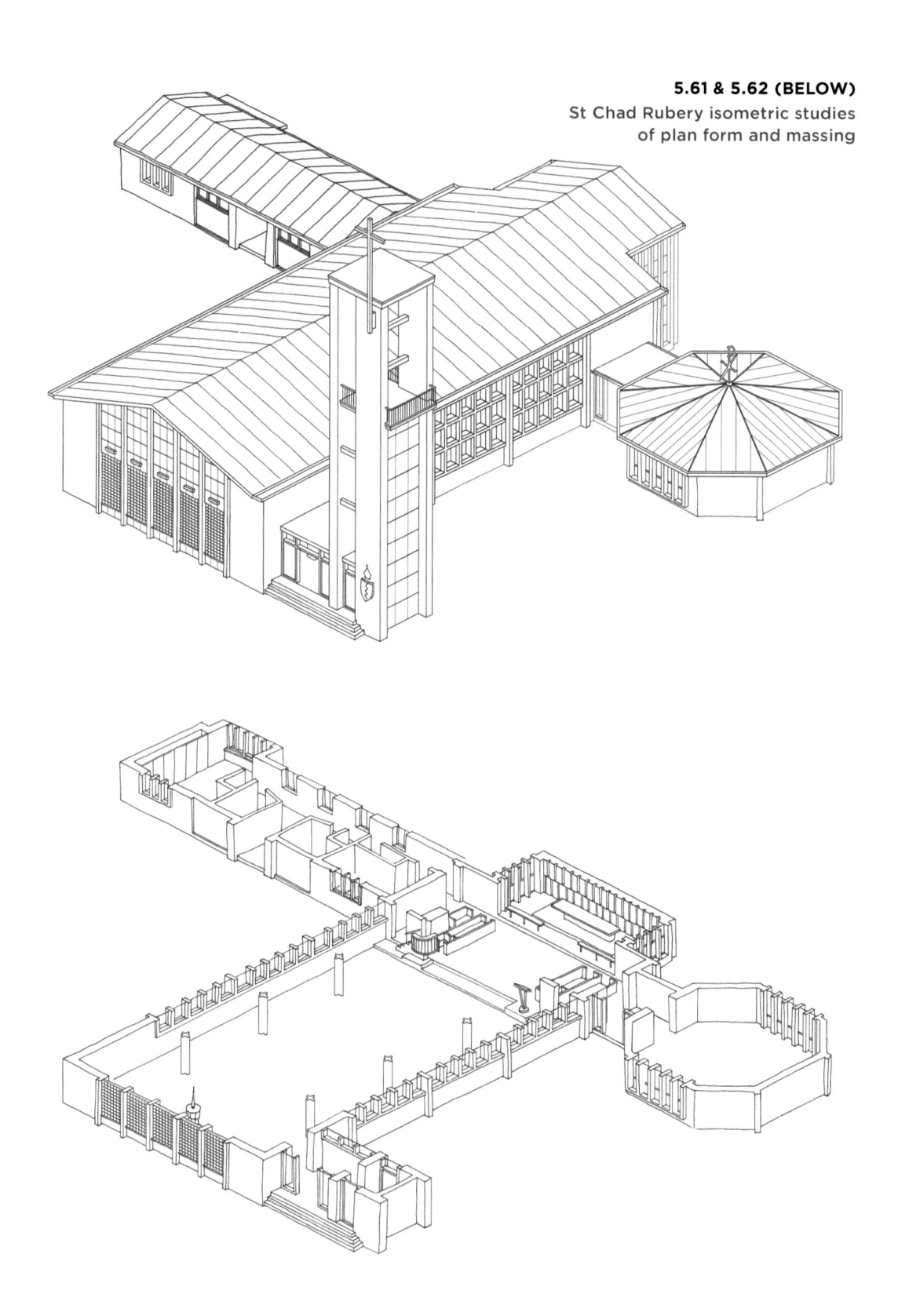

5.61 & 5.62 (BELOW)
St Chad Rubery isometric studies of plan form and massing

A CHANGE IN STYLE THE 1950s

5.63
ST CHAD CHANCEL

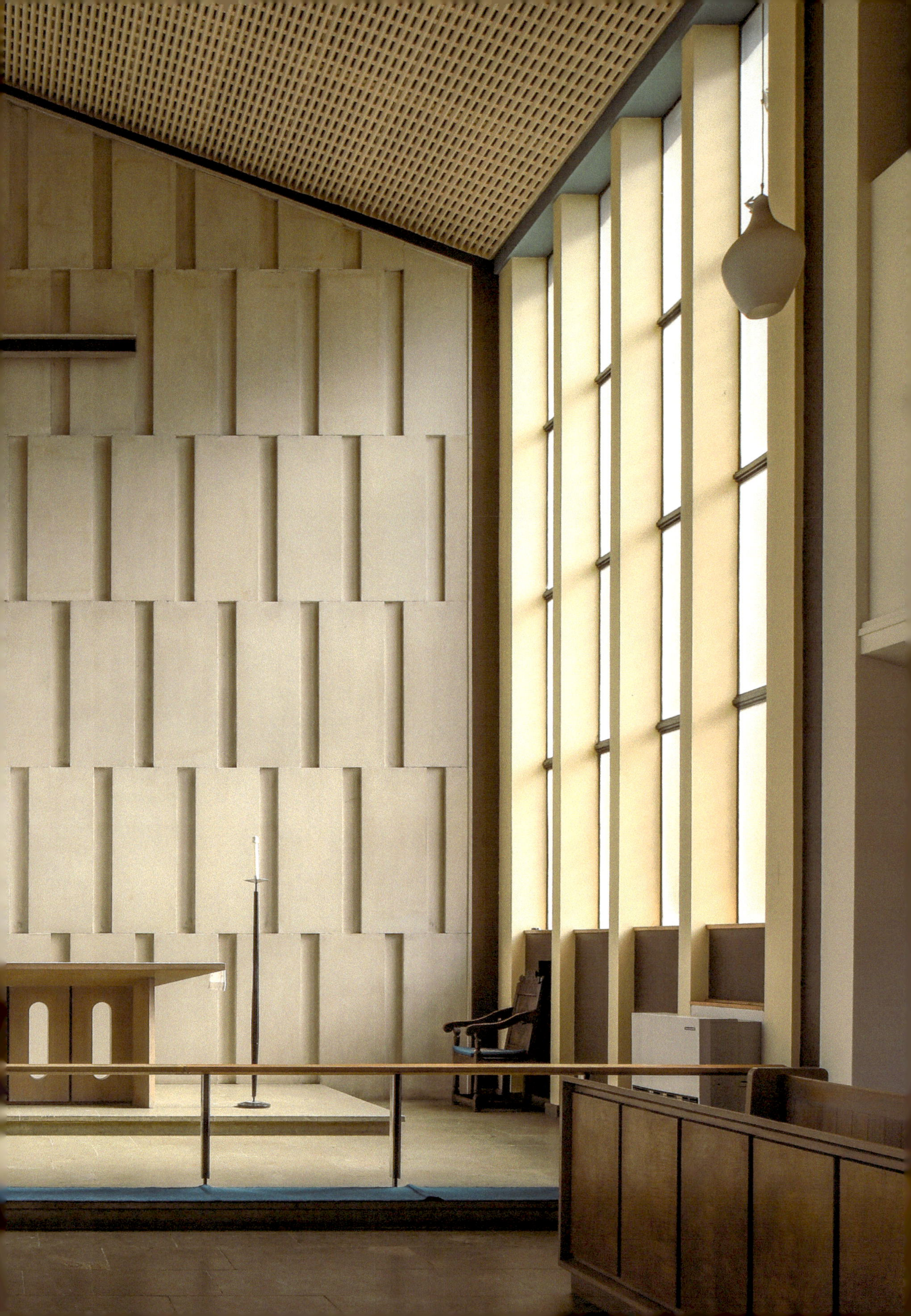

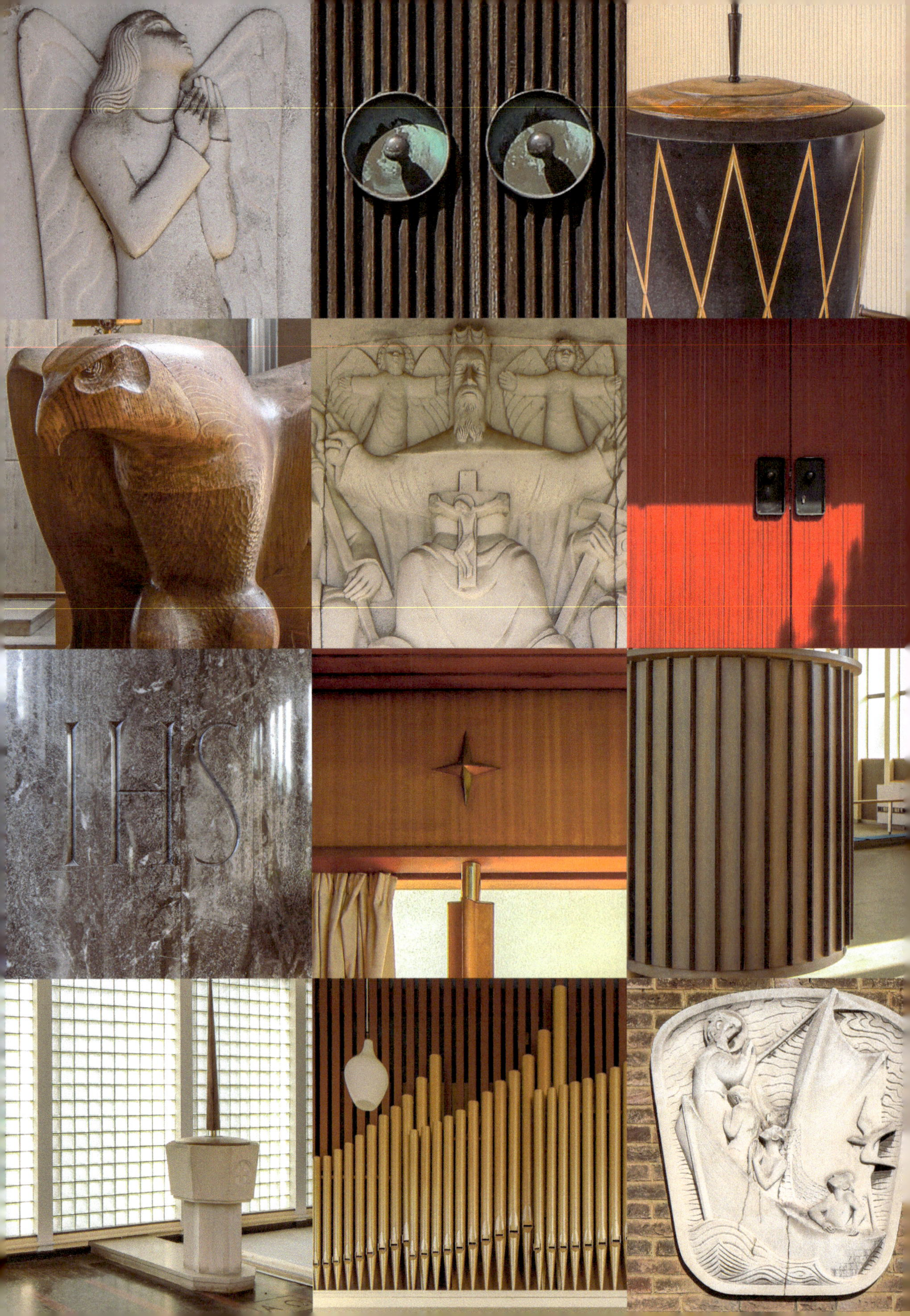
IHS

Notes

1. From a conversation with E. Lavender's daughter reported by Father Tony Hutchinson of Saint Martin.

2. J. Hares, 'Letter to RIBA Librarian', 25 November 1994, in *Alfred Richard Twentyman*, desk file, RIBA Library Archives.

3. P. Hammond, *Towards a Church Architecture* (London, The Architectural Press, 1962), p.10.

4. H. Myles Wright, (ed.), *Small Houses* (London: The Architectural Press, 1937), pp.78-79.

5. See Chapter 3.

6. 'All Saints Church, Darlaston', *Architect and Building News*, vol. 203, no. 7, 12 February 1953, pp.193-98.

7. W. Stock, *European Church Architecture 1900-1950* (Munich: Prestel Publishing, 2006), pp.110-16.

8. Stock, *European Church Architecture*, pp.124-28.

9. Stock, *European Church Architecture*, pp.142-47.

10. Personal communication from Aidan Ridyard, co-author of this book, whose father was Vicar of All Saints at the time.

11. *100 Years at St Nicholas, Radford* (Local Church Archives, n.d.), p.6.

12. C. Pickford, and N. Pevsner, *Warwickshire* (New Haven: Yale University Press, 2016), p.295.

13. 'St Nicholas, Radford', *The Architects' Journal*, 20 March (1958), p.423.

14. 'Iglesia, en Coventry', *Informes de la Construcctión*, 9, 87, (Enero 1957), pp.29-36.

15. Rubery Owen and Company Ltd.(Online). http://www.historywebsite.co.uk/articles/Darlaston/RO.htm.

16. Emmanuel local church archives.

17. 'Emmanuel Bentley', *The Architects' Journal*, 7 November (1957), 709-713.

18. N. Pevsner, *Staffordshire* (Harmondsworth: Penguin, 1975), p.297.

19. Archives of the vicar at the time, Revd. Canon F. Gordon Lacey (1926-2005), courtesy of his daughter, Rachel Owen, who also recalls a parish trip to see the tower bells being cast.

20. Revd. Lacey archives.

21. See Chapter 2.

22. 'Royal Academy Exhibition', *The Architects' Journal*, 9 May (1957), p.688.

23. G. Kidder-Smith, *The New Churches of Europe* (London: Architectural Press, 1964). pp.46-53.

24. R. Weston, *Key Buildings of the 20th Century* (London: Norton, 2010), pp.198-99.

25. K. Robinson, 'What is Architecture, Daddy?', *The Architects' Journal*, May 9, (1957), pp.688-89.

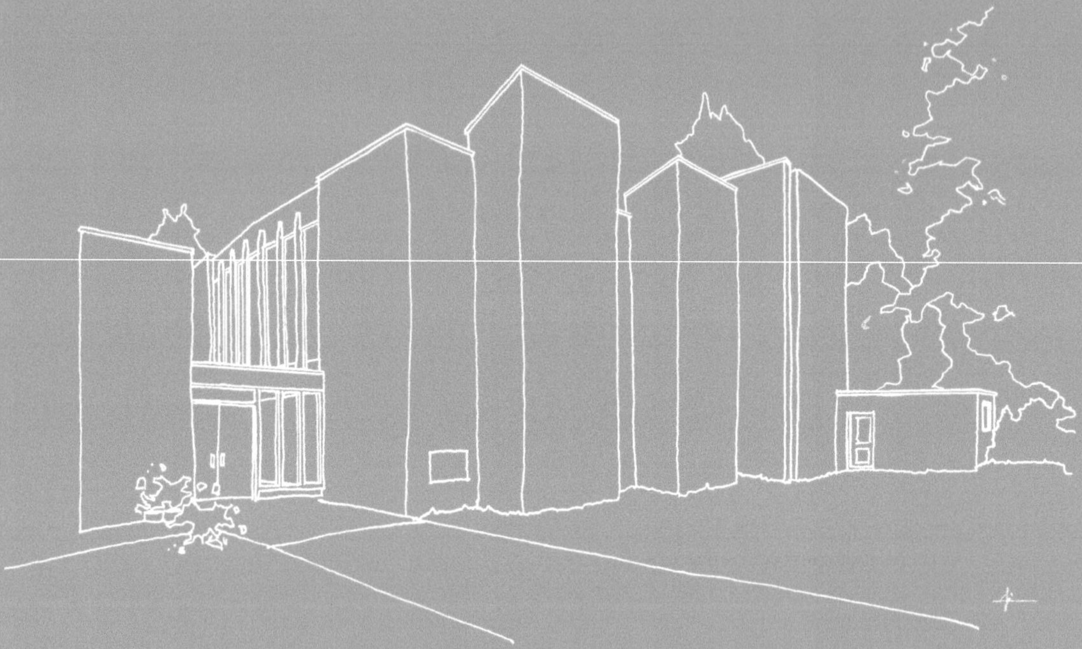

CHAPTER SIX

6

NEW DIRECTIONS THE 1960s

6.1 (RIGHT)
First Unitarian Church, Rochester NY plan Louis Kahn 1959-65

6.2 (BELOW)
Richards Medical Research Laboratories, Philadelphia Louis Kahn 1957-60

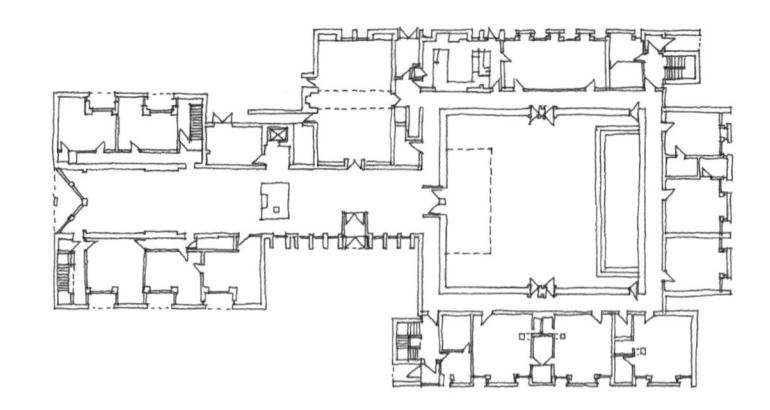

NEW DIRECTIONS

CHURCHES OF THE 1960s

Excluding Redditch Crematorium Chapel (1973), the last two churches that Twentyman designed, both around 1965, St Andrew, Whitmore Reans, Wolverhampton, and St Andrew, Grange, Runcorn, the latter his only church building outside the West Midlands, represent a final shift in Twentyman's ideas, and perhaps also in the attitudes of his clients.

Both churches show a more convincing architectural application of the New Liturgy, and a greater experimentation in the use of shape and space. That said, they are plainer and more austere as buildings within their site contexts, turning their attention inwards towards large central volumes and dramatic interiors. They still connect to their surroundings with spreading wings linking the churches with adjacent functions, but these are arguably less refined in their execution than in earlier works. The accomplishments of these last two churches are very much to be viewed by those congregating from within.

6.3 (ABOVE)
First Unitarian Church, Rochester
NY Louis Kahn 1959-65

ST ANDREW
WHITMORE REANS 1965

The Twentyman church replaced an earlier Victorian church destroyed by fire in 1964. The uncompromising monumental brick aspect of the exterior recalls the massive scale of Twentyman's St Gabriel and St Martin, but the 'blocky and convincing'[1] design is different. It could loosely be called 'Brutalist', though it is built of brick, not concrete, and the grouping of rectangular blocks and blank walls reveals a debt to Louis Kahn's Salk Institute (1959-65). The basic shape of the main body is square with a wider rectangular sanctuary at the east end (6.6), so that the congregation can gather around three sides of the more centrally-placed altar (6.8). The organ loft projecting from the south wall of the sanctuary (6.10 & 6.11) remains empty as funds were not forthcoming to cover the costs of a new organ.

An unusual feature is the solitary bell at low level on a beam attached to the exterior wall of the sanctuary. A bypass was planned beside the church, though never built, and Twentyman may have been concerned about noise, possibly a reason for the lack of conventional windows, natural light being directed from above and via two large windows above the sanctuary and entrance.[2]

Two brick bays extend on the north and south sides above the roofline, with concealed skylights providing downward light into the church, a device used by Louis Kahn in his First Unitarian Church in Rochester NY of 1962 (6.1 & 6.3). Externally these form a series of blind towers surrounding and defending the main volume, also recalling the brick towers of Louis Khan's Richards Medical Research Laboratories of 1957-60 (6.2).

6.4
ST ANDREW WHITMORE REANS
FROM THE GARDENS TO THE SOUTH

6.5
ST ANDREW WHITMORE REANS
SOUTH FACADE

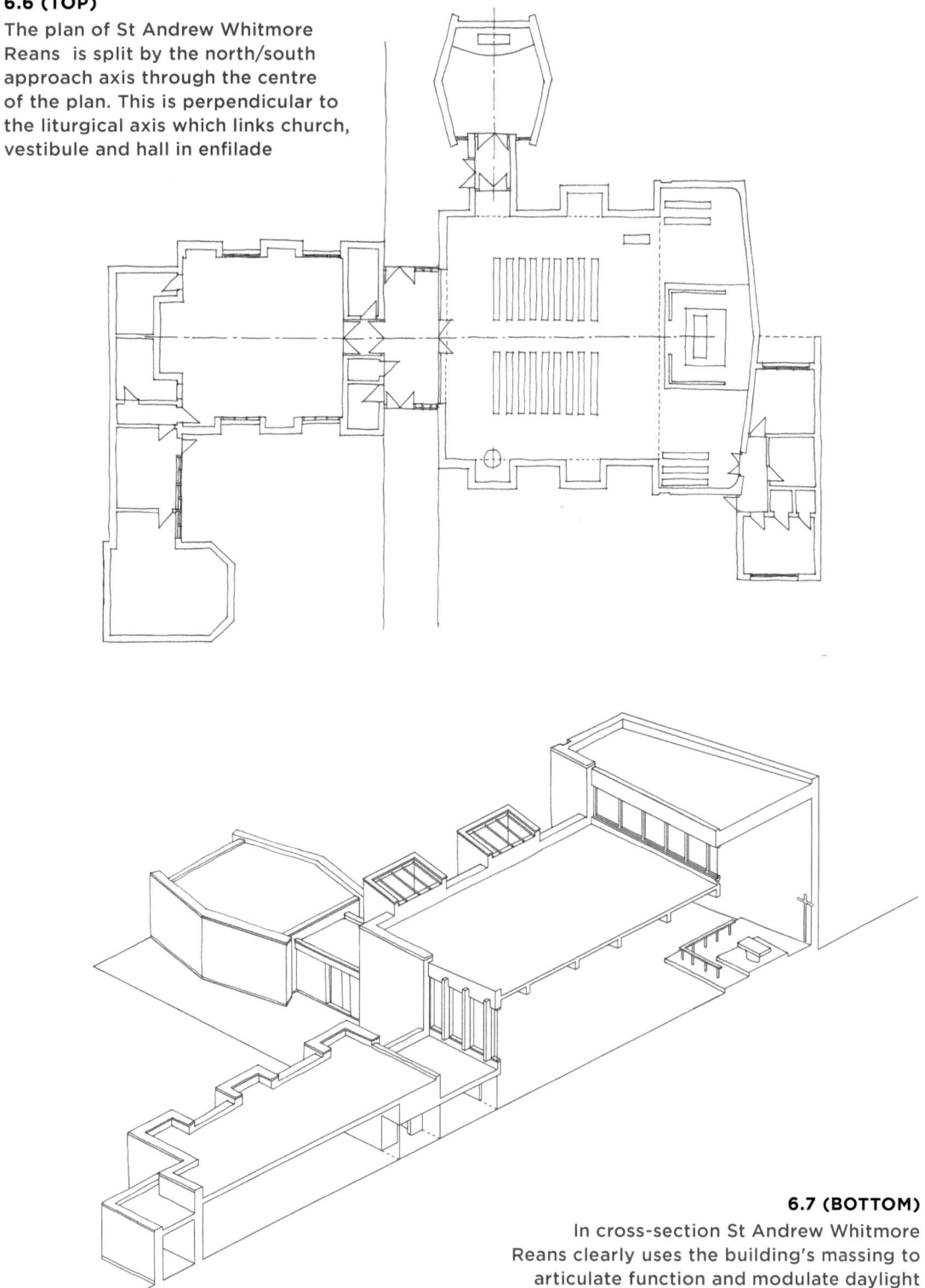

6.6 (TOP)
The plan of St Andrew Whitmore Reans is split by the north/south approach axis through the centre of the plan. This is perpendicular to the liturgical axis which links church, vestibule and hall in enfilade

6.7 (BOTTOM)
In cross-section St Andrew Whitmore Reans clearly uses the building's massing to articulate function and modulate daylight

6.8 (BELOW)
St Andrew Whitmore Reans the nave looking east suspended heaters are a later addition

6.9 (RIGHT)
St Andrew Whitmore Reans the altar a simple stone slab supported on curved mosaic columns

A row of square windows is provided at clerestory level bridging nave and sanctuary, a feature used in other later Twentyman churches, for example, Redditch Crematorium Chapel and St Andrew, Grange. Elsewhere these are clear glass, but the unusual feature here is the dramatic abstract Piper and Reyntiens stained-glass west window above the entrance, representing St Andrew's life as a fisherman on the Sea of Galilee (6.15). Twentyman rarely designed a glazed west or east window, and this was the only time he used stained glass, perhaps because of his concern for 'constructional purity',[3] or his preference for the light-enabling properties of clear glazing. The higher cost of stained glass in comparison with clear glass may have also played a part, but Whitmore Reans is very much of its time, and is part of the movement towards swathes of coloured glass influenced by the new Coventry (consecrated in 1962) and Liverpool Metropolitan (1962-67) Cathedrals. The cost of the Piper window was high in proportion to the rest of the building. Piper's fee alone was £1,000 (6.11).

Compositionally the organisational planning of the building is highly functional and shows the clear influence of Kahn. The entrance axis, as at Bentley, allows an approach from north or south into a vestibule the full width of the church. Here sliding screens can open up the east side of the space allowing it to become a part of the

NEW DIRECTIONS THE 1960s

6.10 (BELOW)
St Andrew Whitmore Reans
south side of the nave

6.11 (RIGHT)
Twentyman's letter (signed by George Sidebottom) enclosing Piper's invoice

main church increasing its capacity significantly. On the right-hand west side of the entrance is a set of buildings more conventionally constructed with several windows, which contain community rooms, a hall, lounge, kitchen, and games room.

The most telling achievement of St Andrew is the way Twentyman handles natural daylight, with his usual aplomb, but in a completely new style. It shows an evolution of architectural language while maintaining a consistency in compositional priorities.

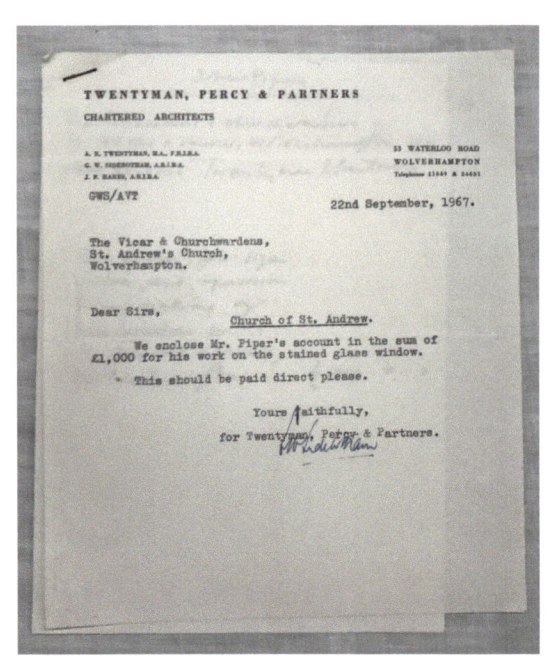

6.12 (BELOW)
St Andrew Whitmore Reans
chancel with clerestory above

6.13 (ABOVE)
St Andrew Whitmore Reans isometric studies of plan form and massing

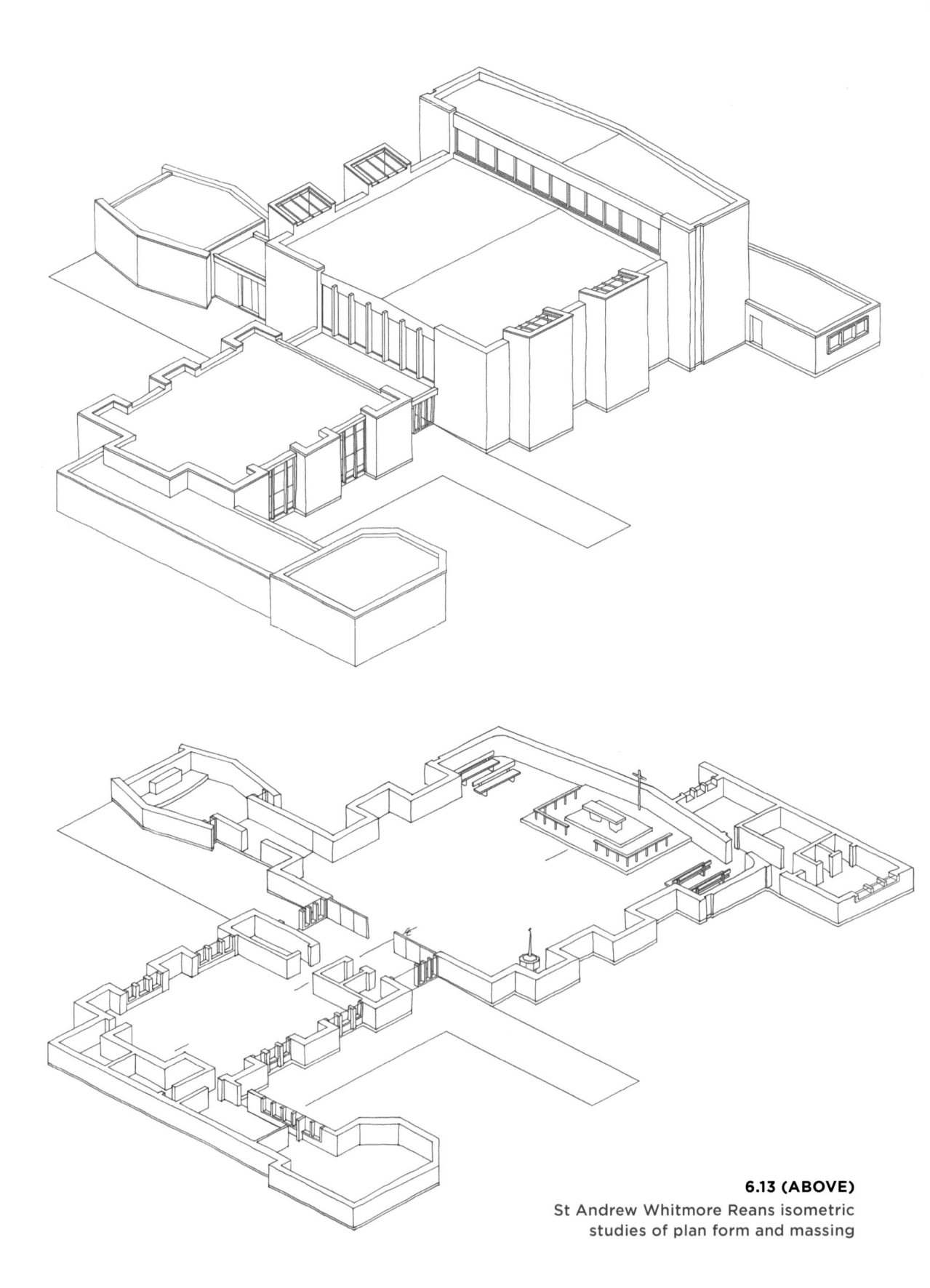

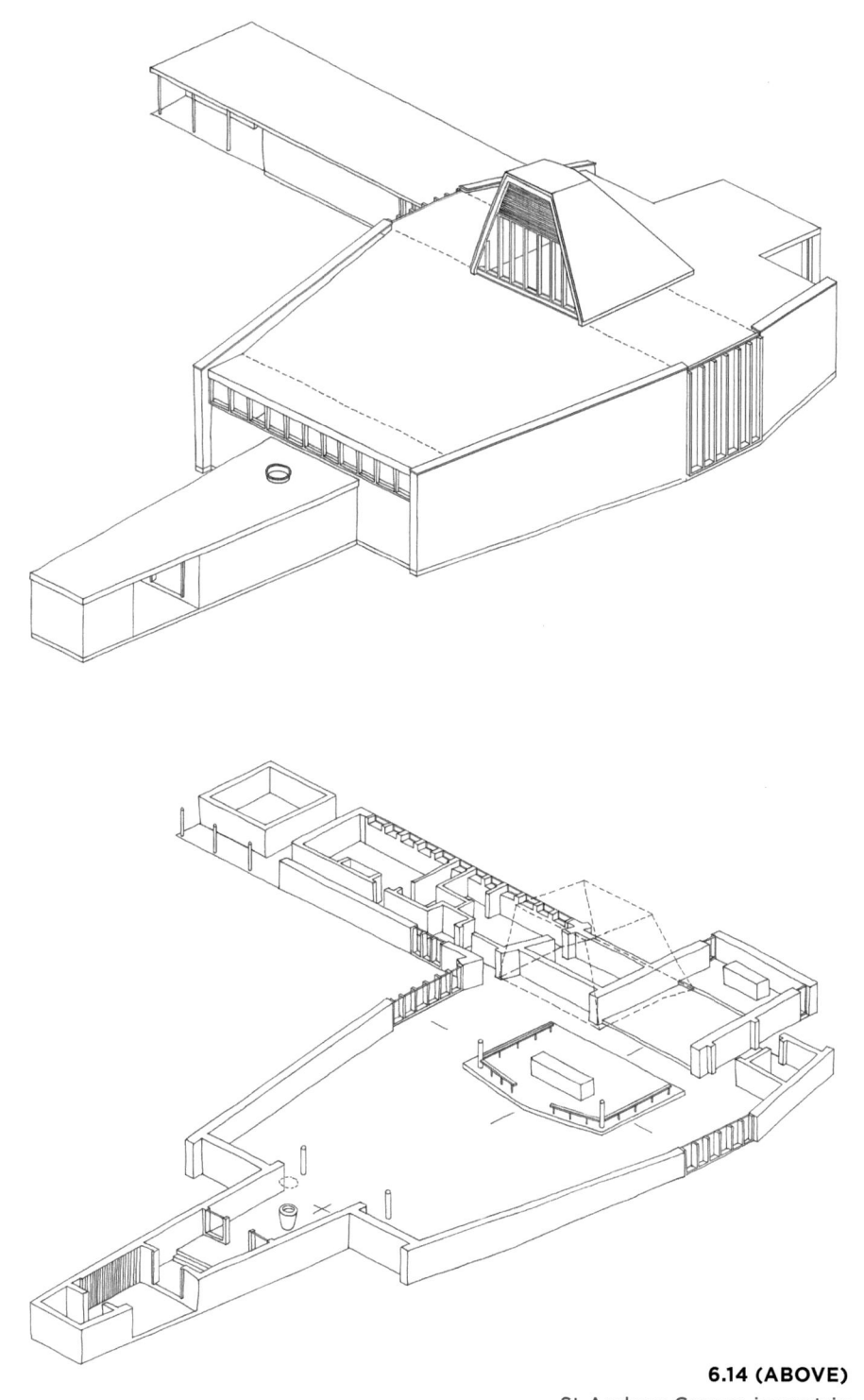

6.14 (ABOVE)
St Andrew Grange isometric
studies of planform and massing

6.15
ST ANDREW WHITMORE REANS
WEST WINDOW BY JOHN PIPER AND
PATRICK REYNTIENS

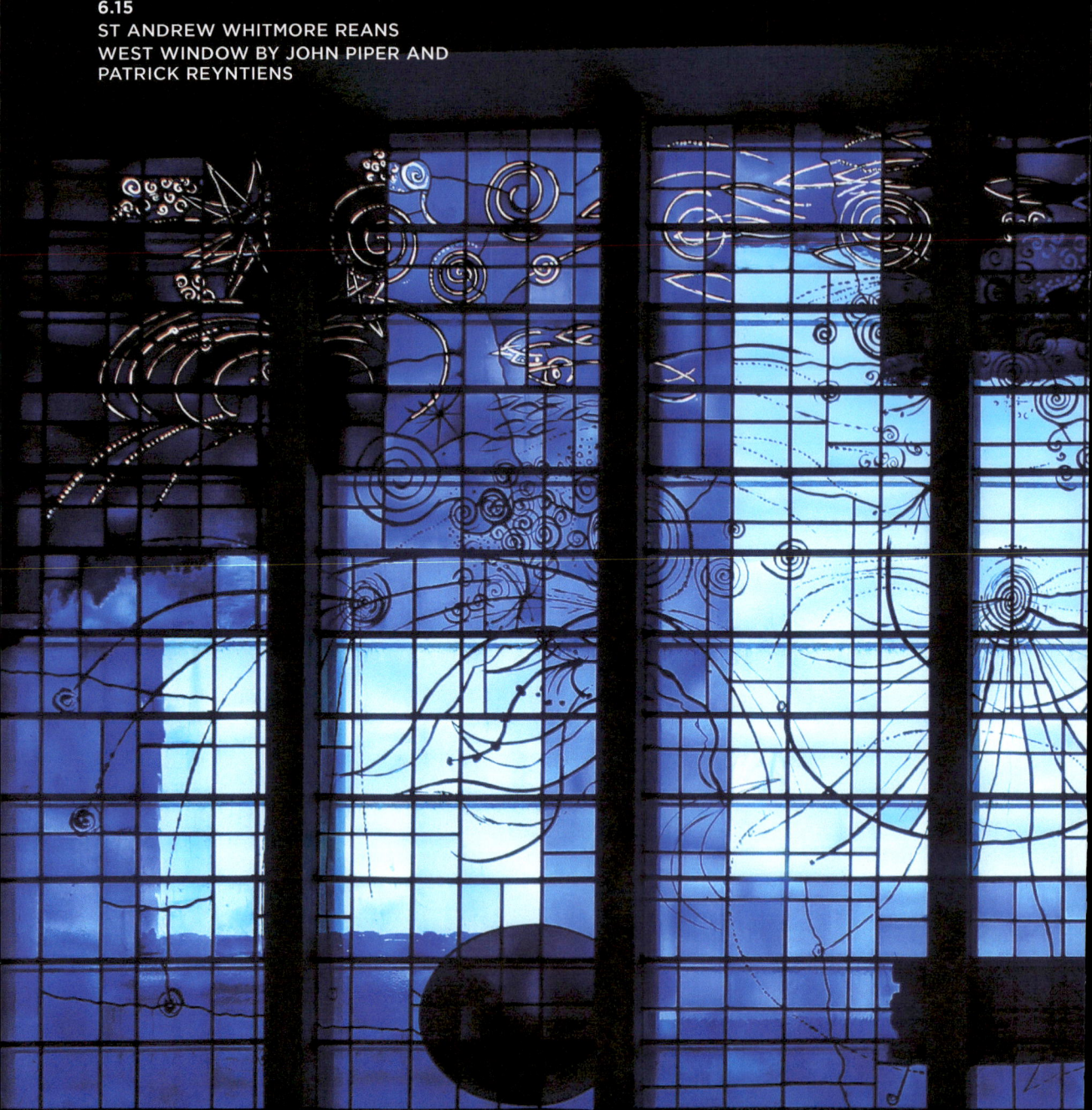

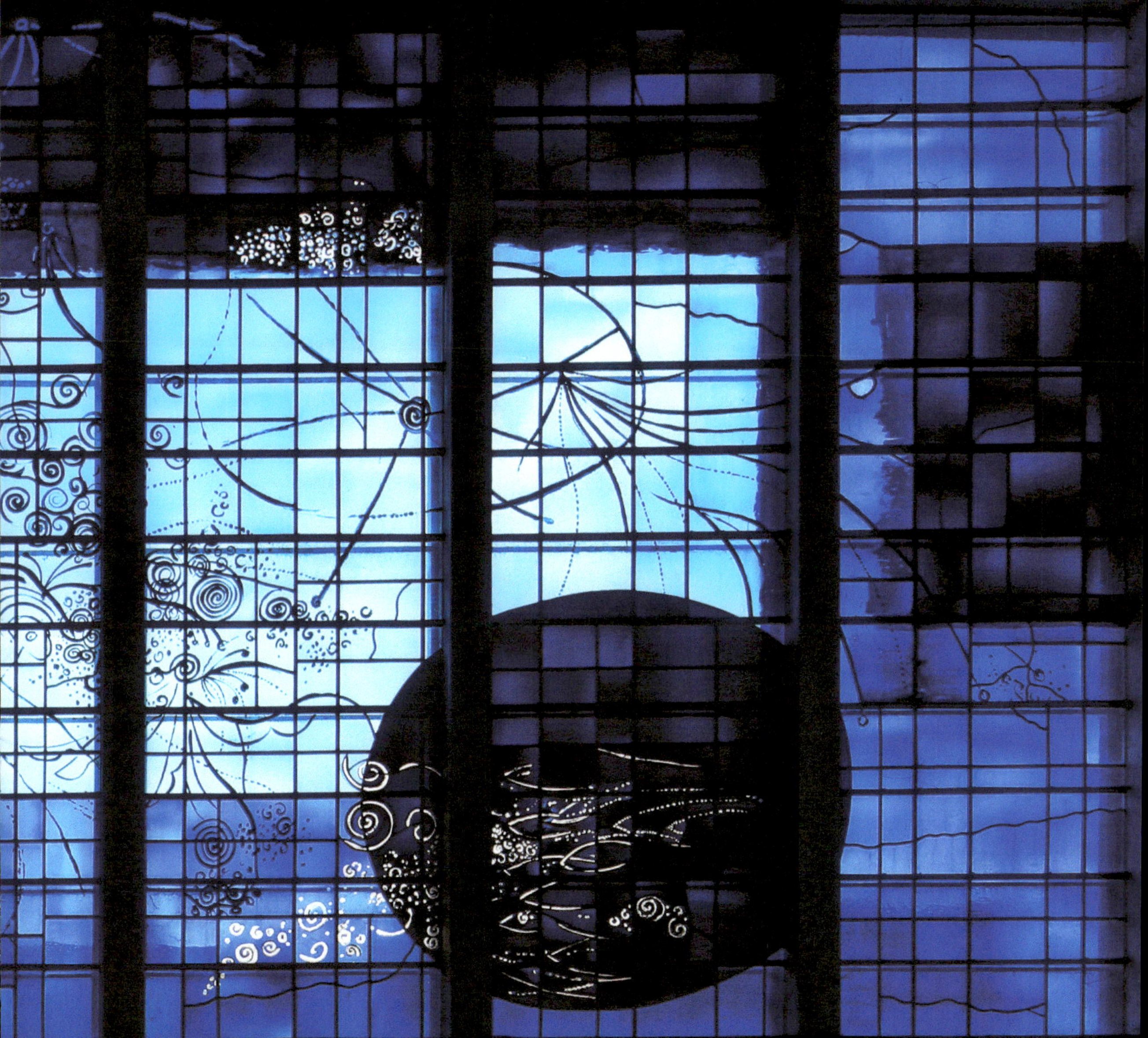

ST ANDREW

GRANGE, RUNCORN 1965

The development of St Andrew, Runcorn demonstrates the approach adopted in this book in practice, showing the importance of the religious, social, and political context in the life history of a church's architecture. Like Redditch, Runcorn was one of Britain's second generation New Towns (1961-64), built around the established historic urban centre next to the River Mersey.

A comparison between an Ordnance Survey (OS) map of the 1950s and that of the 1960s, (6.21 & 6.22), highlights the rapid development of the Town Hall Estate, later the Grange Estate, which prompted the need for a church to serve the new community, as part of the New Town. Assisted by weekly collections of sixpence a week for five years, a hall, doubling as a church, was dedicated in 1959 by Gerald Ellison, Bishop of Chester from 1955-73[4] who promised 'a separate church and parsonage when the life of the area had been built up to justify it and the means were available.'[5]

The eventual outcome was the new Twentyman church and vicarage opened in 1965, shown together with the separate hall, demolished in 2015, in the 1980s OS Map (6.23). In plan (6.18) the west wing of the building is unusually long, and narrow. It acts as the entrance to the church, orientating visitors onto the main liturgical axis and widening towards the main eight-sided brick structure 'to approximately resemble the shape of a fish',[6] St Andrew being a fisherman.

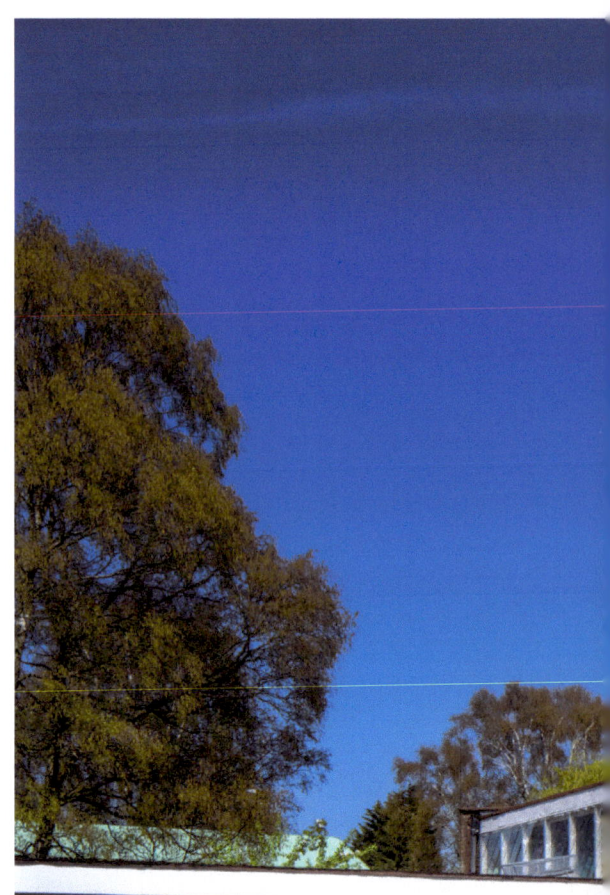

6.16
ST ANDREW GRANGE
FROM SOUTH-WEST

6.17
ST ANGREW GRANGE CHANCEL
& LANTERN FROM THE EAST

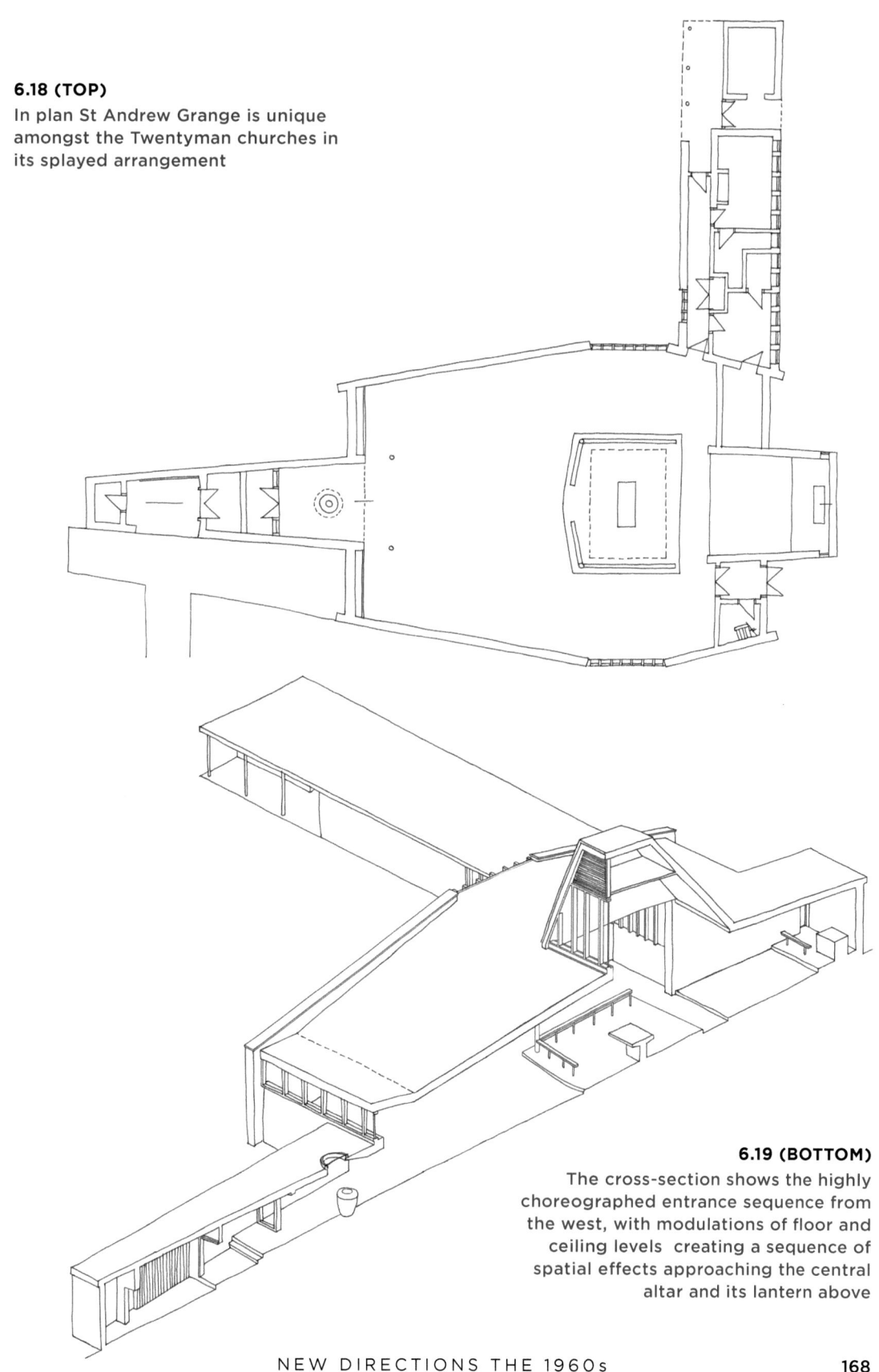

6.18 (TOP)
In plan St Andrew Grange is unique amongst the Twentyman churches in its splayed arrangement

6.19 (BOTTOM)
The cross-section shows the highly choreographed entrance sequence from the west, with modulations of floor and ceiling levels creating a sequence of spatial effects approaching the central altar and its lantern above

6.20 (BELOW)
St Andrew Grange from south-east with three lancet windows to the belfry above the door

Perhaps Twentyman knew of Byrne's 1949 fish-shaped church in Kansas City, which Hammond believed 'a fundamentally mistaken approach to church planning...the concern with structure rather than function'.[7]

St Andrew's wide shape enables seating on three sides of the altar as at St Andrew, Whitmore Reans, and, if required, a fourth side accessed from the Lady Chapel open behind the altar (see the cross-section 6.19). Light is provided from above, centred over the altar by glazing in the vertical west side of a copper-clad lantern, the fin-like structure on the church roof. This structure continues the fish motif, an innovative alternative to a small traditional tower or spire, but sufficient to signal the church's presence to the houses and businesses around it (6.20).

The church at Grange also has a small belfry, but it has been squeezed in above the east door and is only articulated behind three minimal, louvered slits between door head and parapet. Light comes from full-length windows on the north and south walls, and narrow full-length windows either side of the Lady Chapel which provide further natural light, but the dominating features, as at Whitmore Reans, are the west facing clerestory, above the entrance, and that in the central lantern.

The interior wood-boarded ceiling is gently angled as the roof slopes up and down from west to east. An unusually plain font is of Portland stone and there are original Twentyman celebrant chairs.

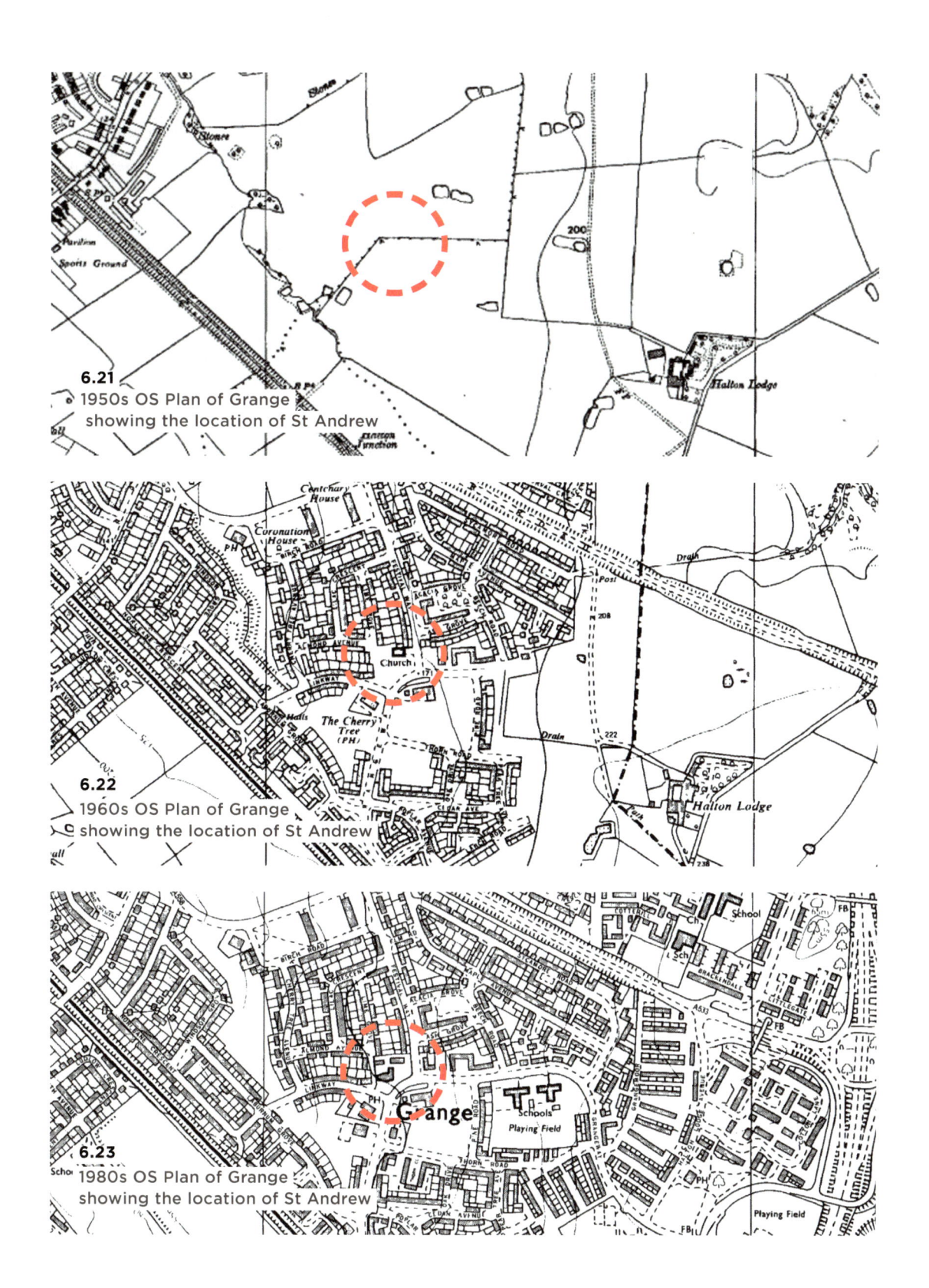

6.21
1950s OS Plan of Grange showing the location of St Andrew

6.22
1960s OS Plan of Grange showing the location of St Andrew

6.23
1980s OS Plan of Grange showing the location of St Andrew

NEW DIRECTIONS THE 1960s

6.24
ST ANDREW GRANGE
ORGAN LOFT SCREEN

A long projection at right angles to the chancel containing toilets and vestry leads northwards to the separate vicarage, recalling the implied cloisters of earlier work, yet less refined as it has to adjoin the more complex irregular octagon geometry of the main church. More successful is the western projection forming storage spaces and a covered porch using the same octagonally-generated splays as the main church. This relies on a classic Twentyman device of directional change, as the porch has a blank back wall, forcing the turn to the east, where the effect is a heightened sense of perspective, with dramatically splayed vanishing points adding drama to the western approach into the interior. No sources of direct light are visible, but the effect is transcendent, light drawing the eye in sequence from font to sanctuary to Lady Chapel beyond, as an allegory of the Christian journey itself (6.29).

6.25
ST ANDREW GRANGE
ALTAR & LANTERN

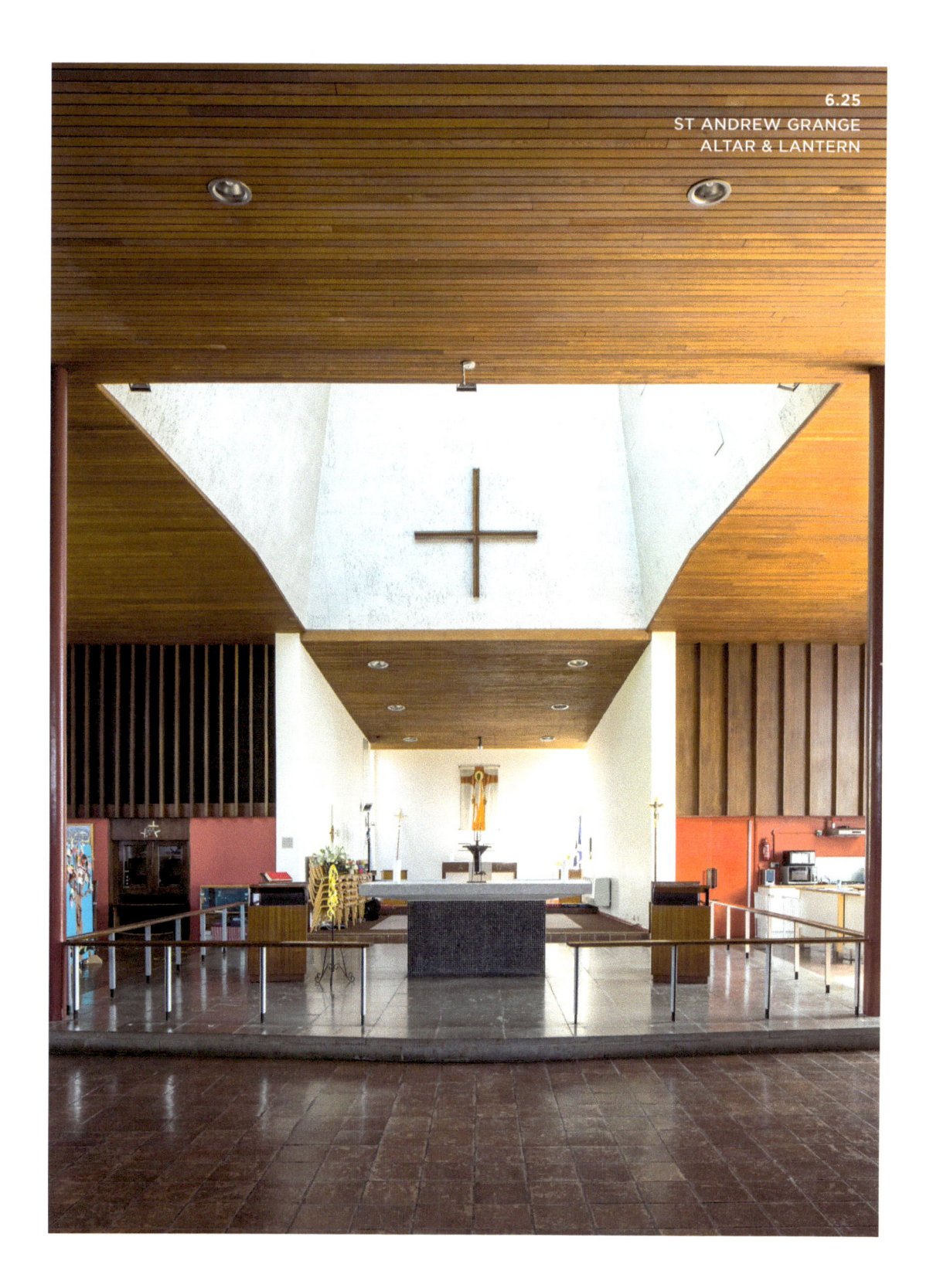

6.26 (BELOW)
The nave looking east

6.27 (BOTTOM)
The concrete central altar finished in mosaic

6.28 (BELOW)
The nave looking west with lantern & clerestory windows across the full width of the space

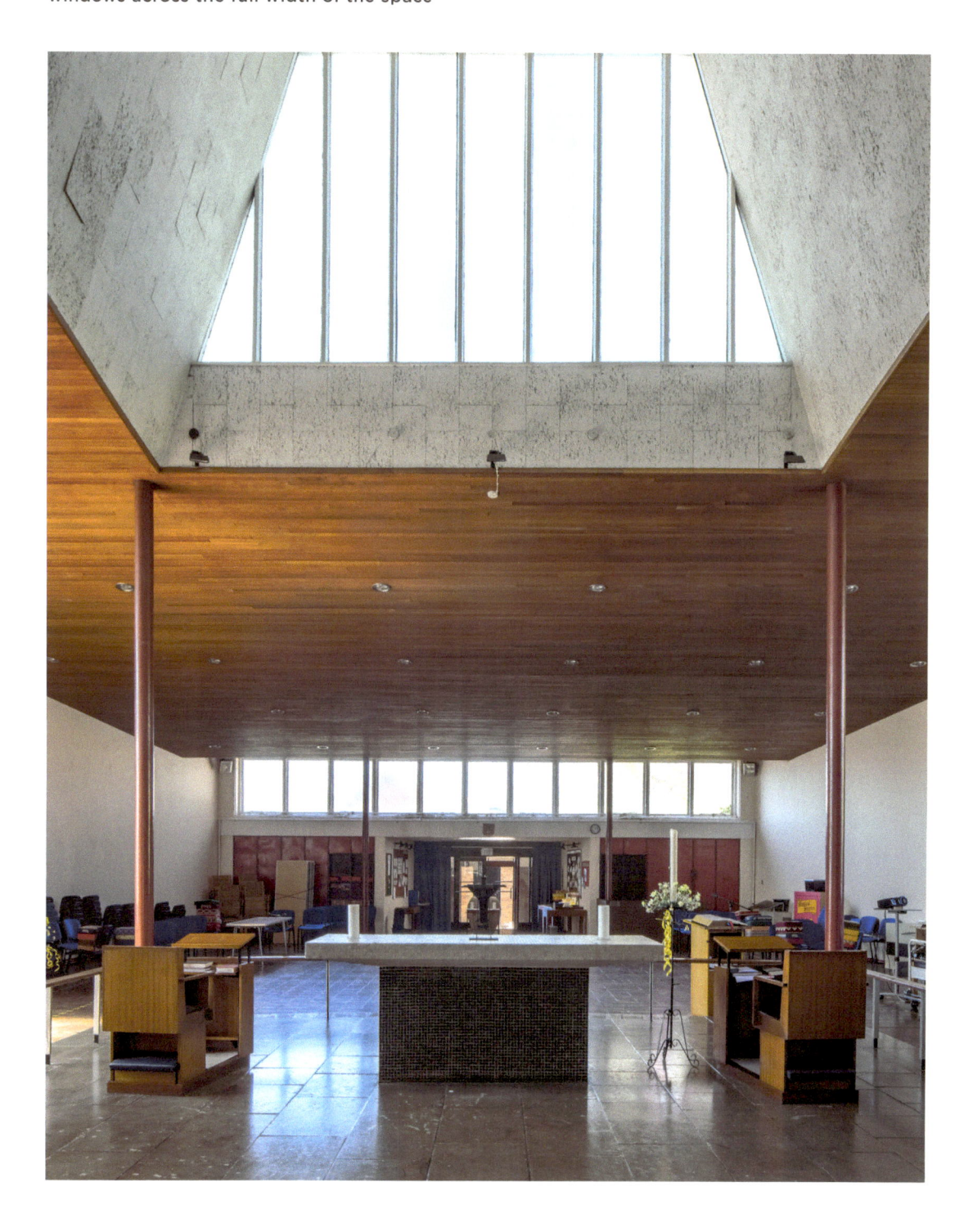

6.29
ST ANDREW GRANGE ENTRANCE
SEQUENCE FROM THE WEST

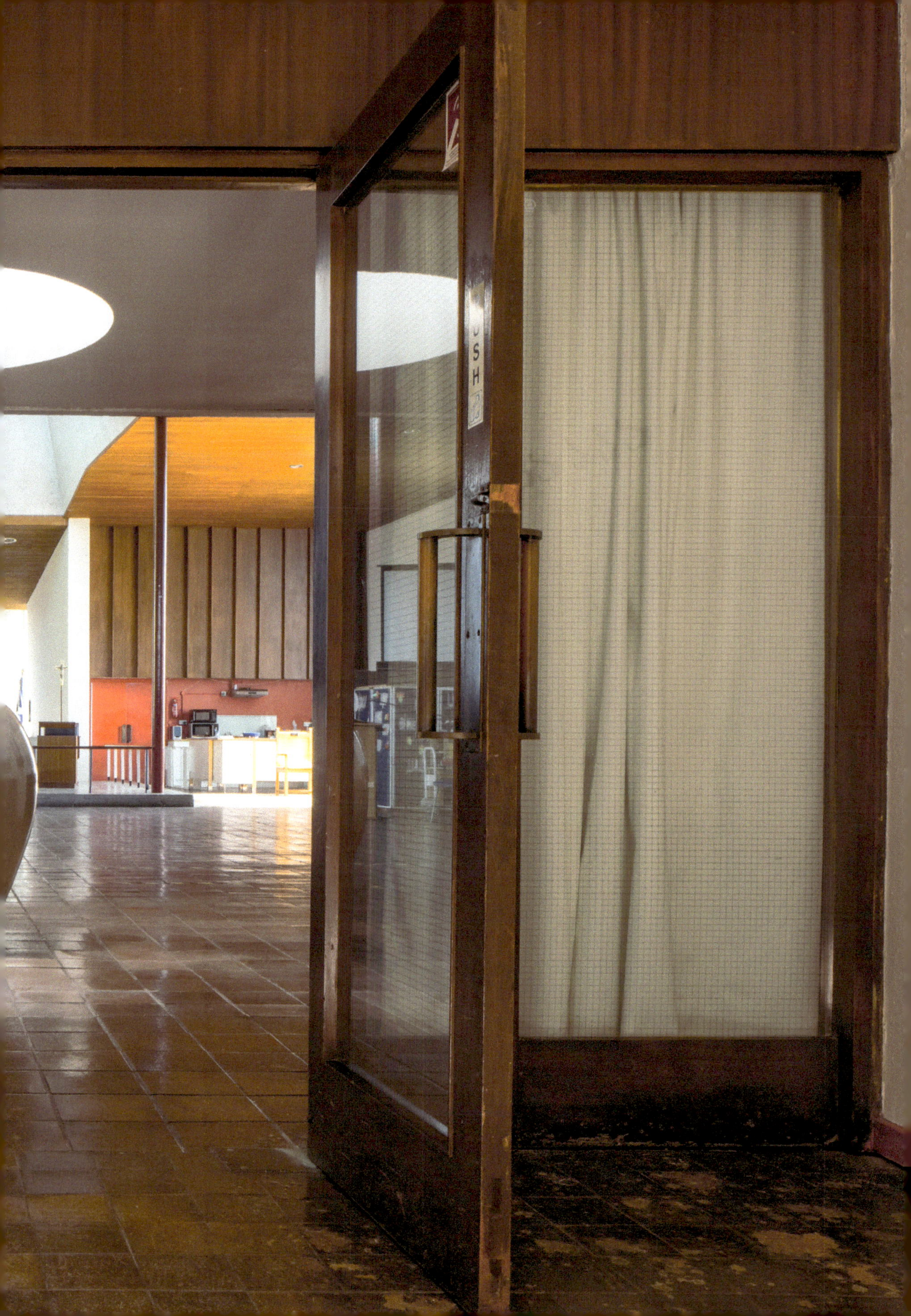

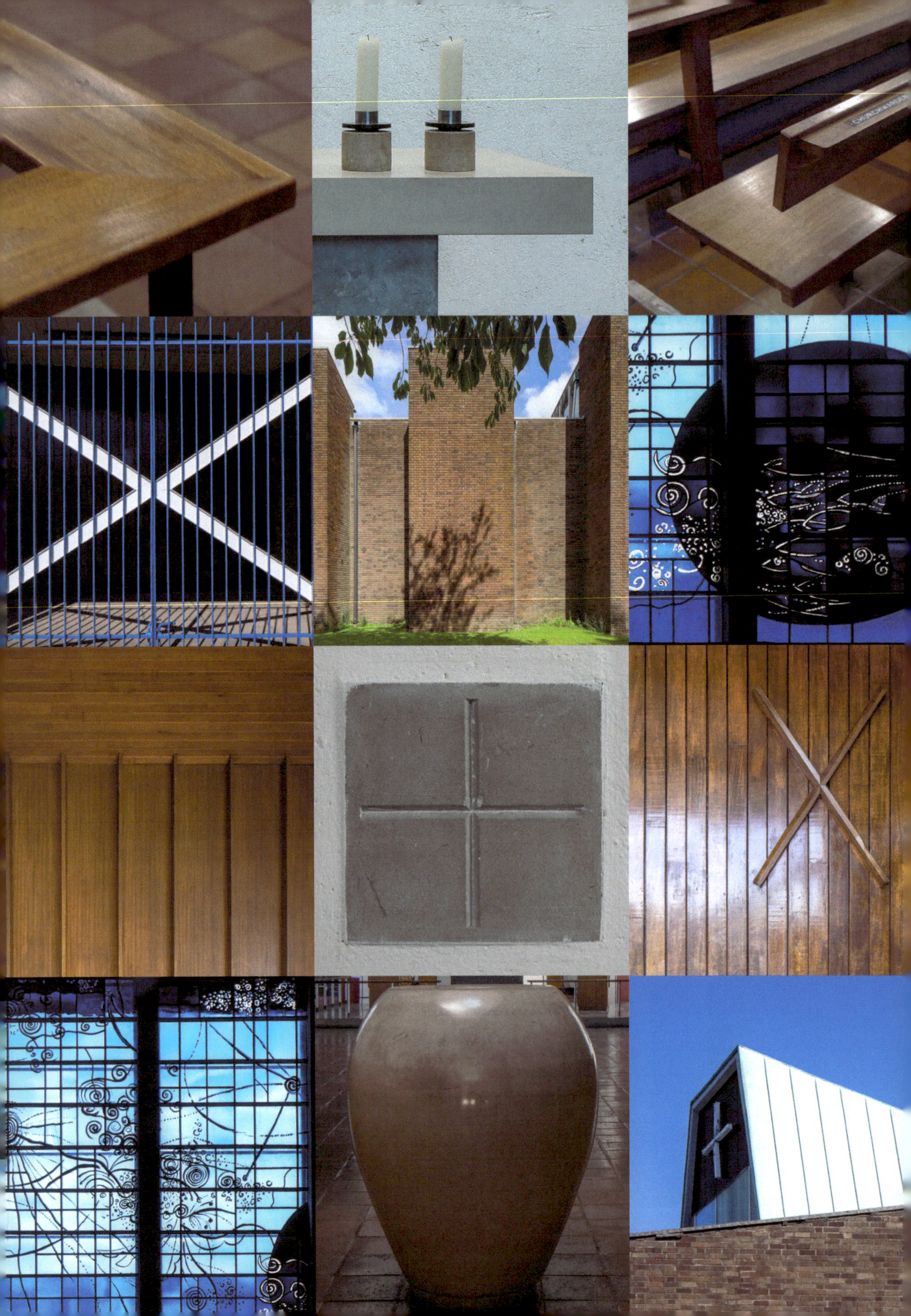

Notes

1   N. Pevsner, *Staffordshire*, (Harmondsworth: Penguin), p.324.

2   A. Chipping, St Andrew's Church, Whitmore Reans. (Online). http://www.historywebsite.co.uk/interesting/standrews/standrew01.htm.

3   Myfanwy Piper, Correspondence. Wolverhampton Record Office, ref. D/TWM/4.

4   *St Andrew* – Souvenir Programme for 21st Anniversary Celebrations, 1965-86. Cheshire Record Office Archives, ref. P169/3714/4/3.

5   *The Guardian*, December 3, 1959. Cheshire Record Office Archives, ref. P169/3714/4/4/3.

6   *St Andrew* – Souvenir Programme, p.6.

7   P. Hammond, *Liturgy and Architecture* (London: Barrie and Rockcliff, 1963), p.82.

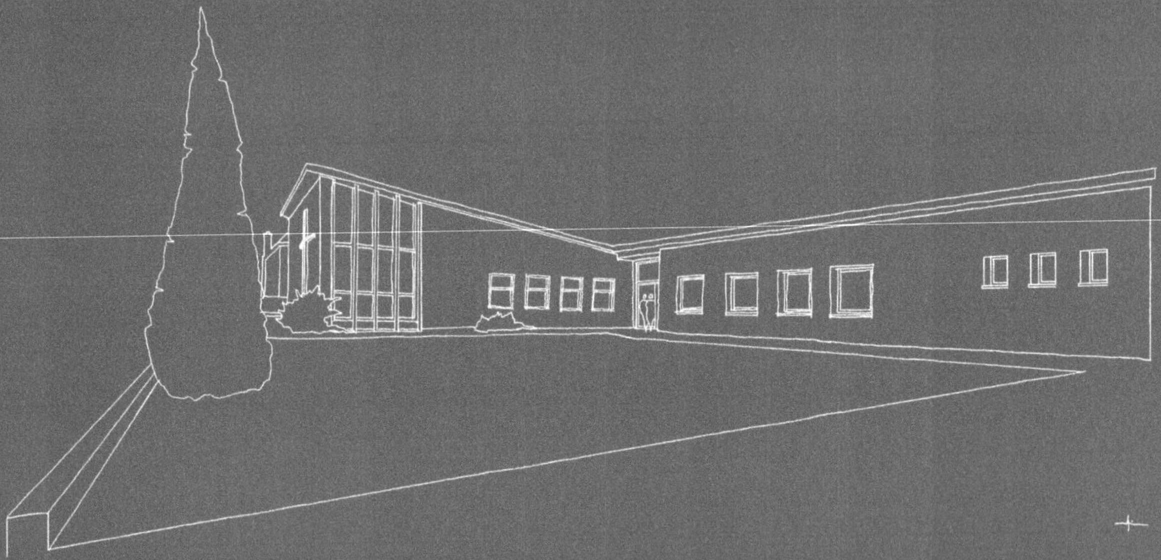

CHAPTER SEVEN

7

THE 'UNKNOWN' TWENTYMAN CHURCHES

7.1 (RIGHT)
St Gregory the Great, Wednesfield in 2021 with the original Twentyman church visible in the background

THE TWO 'UNKNOWN' TWENTYMAN CHURCHES

WEDNESFIELD & LANESFIELD

Our research has identified what appear to be two unrecorded Twentyman churches in addition to the generally accepted list of nine. Both are clearly designed in the Twentyman style of the period and include the detailing and materials seen in Twentyman's other churches, in their construction and fittings.

In a letter to the RIBA Librarian of 25 November 1994, John Hares, a retired practice partner, lists Twentyman's commissions, including 'a small combined church and hall subsequently extended by others' in Blackhalve Lane, Wednesfield.[1] A visit to the address confirms that this building still exists (7.1) and is clearly attributable to Twentyman in its architectural language. It is now used solely as a community hall attached to the more recent St Gregory the Great Church, subsequently built on the adjacent plot, although not designed by Twentyman.

7.2 (ABOVE)
St Gregory the Great, Wednesfield the vestigial chancel of the original Twentyman block can be seen in the step in the eaves line

The classic Twentyman full-height side windows to the chancel are also evident although they are now bricked up

7.3 (ABOVE)
St Gregory the Great, Wednesfield the north elevation (street frontage) of the original Twentyman block now the Church Hall. The compositional parallels with Rubery are clear, as is the use of materials from the slender concrete mullions to the slate tiled spandrel panels

ST GREGORY THE GREAT

WEDNESFIELD 1954

The 1940s Ordnance Survey (OS) map shows no buildings on the present site, but a 1950s OS map (7.5) shows the Twentyman building clearly designated as St Gregory the Great, built around 1954.[2] The 1970s OS map (7.6) shows the new St Gregory the Great attached to the former church, now designated on the map as a hall, which complements information from parishioners who gave 1966 as the date of the new church.

At the east end inside the present hall is a raised area indicating the former position of the chancel, and a further step for the altar position, evidence of its past use as a church. The old altar is in the present St. Gregory's Lady Chapel and has the Alpha/Omega symbols found in other Twentyman churches, for example, St Martin and The Good Shepherd, and two choir stalls remain in the new church recognisable as Twentyman designs. These features are shown clearly in a photograph showing the 1954 interior (7.7), which also reveals its similarity with The Good Shepherd (1955). Both are dual-purpose churches, designed so that the chancel, framed by a proscenium-style arch, can be separated from the nave area, creating a space for alternative functions.

The hall (the former Twentyman church) is small and of simple rectangular design with a pitched copper roof. There are replacement windows on the north and south sides, but the west wall has a typical Twentyman feature, a large window, with seven long rectangular lights inserted into typical, slim precast concrete pillars, below which are concrete and slate spandrel panels (7.3 & 7.8). The composition as well as its relationship to the adjacent street frontage is very similar to that of St Chad Rubery, albeit at a reduced scale.

7.4 (LEFT)
St Gregory the Great, Wednesfield the original Twentyman altar has been relocated into the Lady Chapel of the new church building

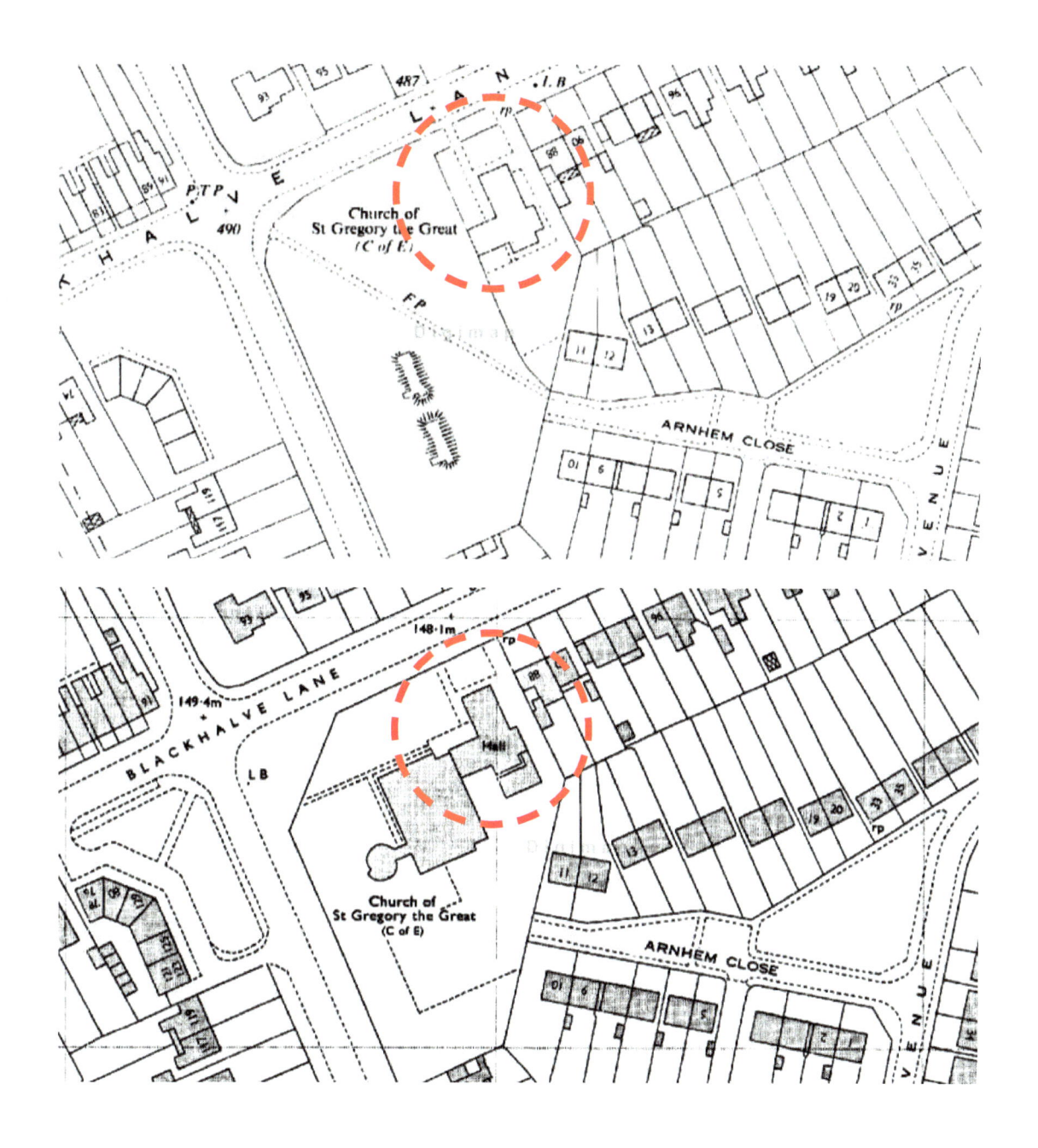

7.5 (TOP)
1950s OS Plan of Wednesfield showing the original Twentyman church building

7.6 (BOTTOM)
1970s OS Plan of Wednesfield showing the addition of the later church building to the west

7.7 (BELOW)
St Gregory the Great Wednesfield
interior in the 1950's

7.8 (BELOW)
St Gregory the Great Wednesfield
now functioning as the church hall

LANESFIELD METHODIST CHURCH

WOLVERHAMPTON 1960

John Hares' letter also lists Lanesfield Methodist church in Laburnum Lane, Lanesfield, designed by Twentyman and Percy in 1960, and confirmed by existing plans.[3] A church was needed to replace a chapel in nearby Spring Road and to service the new housing estates.[4]

The church has a different design from other Twentyman churches, cost being a consideration, estimated at the time as £15,000. It is a simple rectangular brick church with a sloping mono-pitch roof, the higher end accommodating an organ brought from the old chapel and creating a lofty sanctuary. The space is flooded with natural light from a large floor-to-ceiling window on the north-east corner, characteristically concealing the light source from the congregation behind a projecting pier (7.12).

7.9 (BELOW)
C.G. Percy (centre) at the laying of the foundation stone in 1960

7.10
LANESFIELD METHODIST CHURCH

**7.11
LANESFIELD METHODIST CHURCH
CHANCEL AND ORGAN**

Another typical Twentyman motif is the large cross set on the plain masonry of the east end wall; this time (unusually) in black painted metal which has a slightly tapering profile (7.10).

The interior ceiling is cedar wood, and mahogany furnishings are also designed by Twentyman. The plans show a multi-purpose building. A curtain, now removed, between the piers in the nave, could convert the church to a 200-seat hall if required. The composition is similar to that at Castlecroft, creating a primary, flexible space which changes orientation when functioning as a church or as a hall, with a raised platform at the west end to act as a stage. This space is supplemented by a side wing containing school and committee rooms with associated ancillary spaces.

An impressive pulpit and tester, placed centrally on the east wall of the chancel, was designed but apparently not constructed (Compare photos of interior 7.11 and drawing of pulpit 7.17).

7.13 (OPPOSITE BELOW)
The mono-pitch volume of the nave showing the full height chancel windows

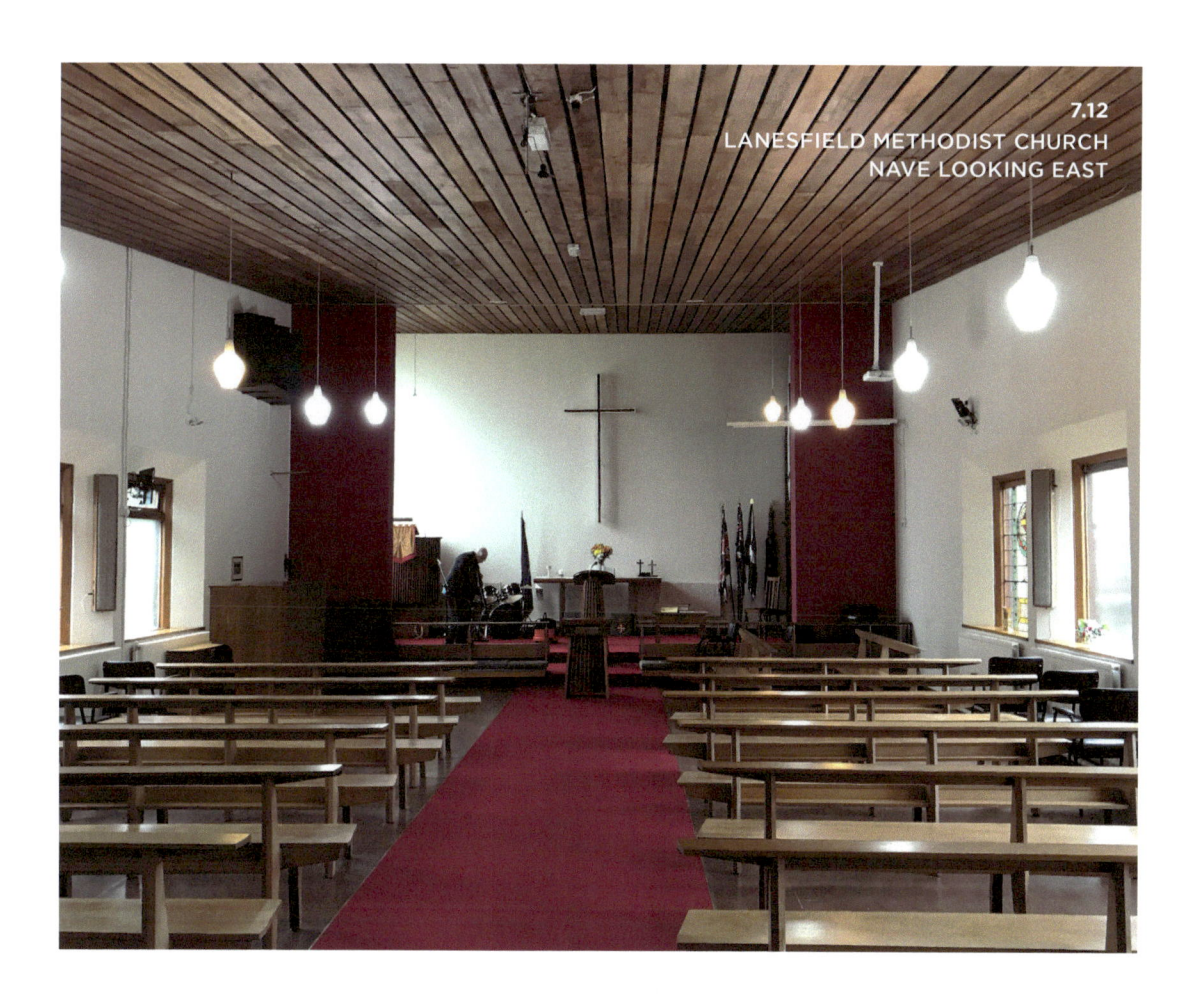

7.12
LANESFIELD METHODIST CHURCH
NAVE LOOKING EAST

THE 'UNKNOWN' TWENTYMAN CHURCHES

7.14 (BELOW)
The bespoke seating in the nave in African mahogany

7.15 (BOTTOM)
The chancel rail in African mahogany and polished stainless steel

The local church archives mention 'Mr C. G. Percy – the architect', a partner in Twentyman, Percy, and Partners, and he is shown assisting during the ceremony for the laying of the foundation stone (7.9).

It is likely that Twentyman oversaw the design of the church, since it is in the list Hares prepared as a tribute to Twentyman, with the day-to-day administration of the contract and liaison with the client delegated to Percy, a role mentioned explicitly in an obituary for Percy.[5]

7.16 (BELOW)
THE NORTH-EAST WINDOW UNDER CONSTRUCTION MULLIONS ARE IN TIMBER AS OPPOSED TO THE PRE-CAST CONCRETE OF THE EARLIER CHURCHES, A DETAIL ALSO FOUND AT ST ANDREW GRANGE

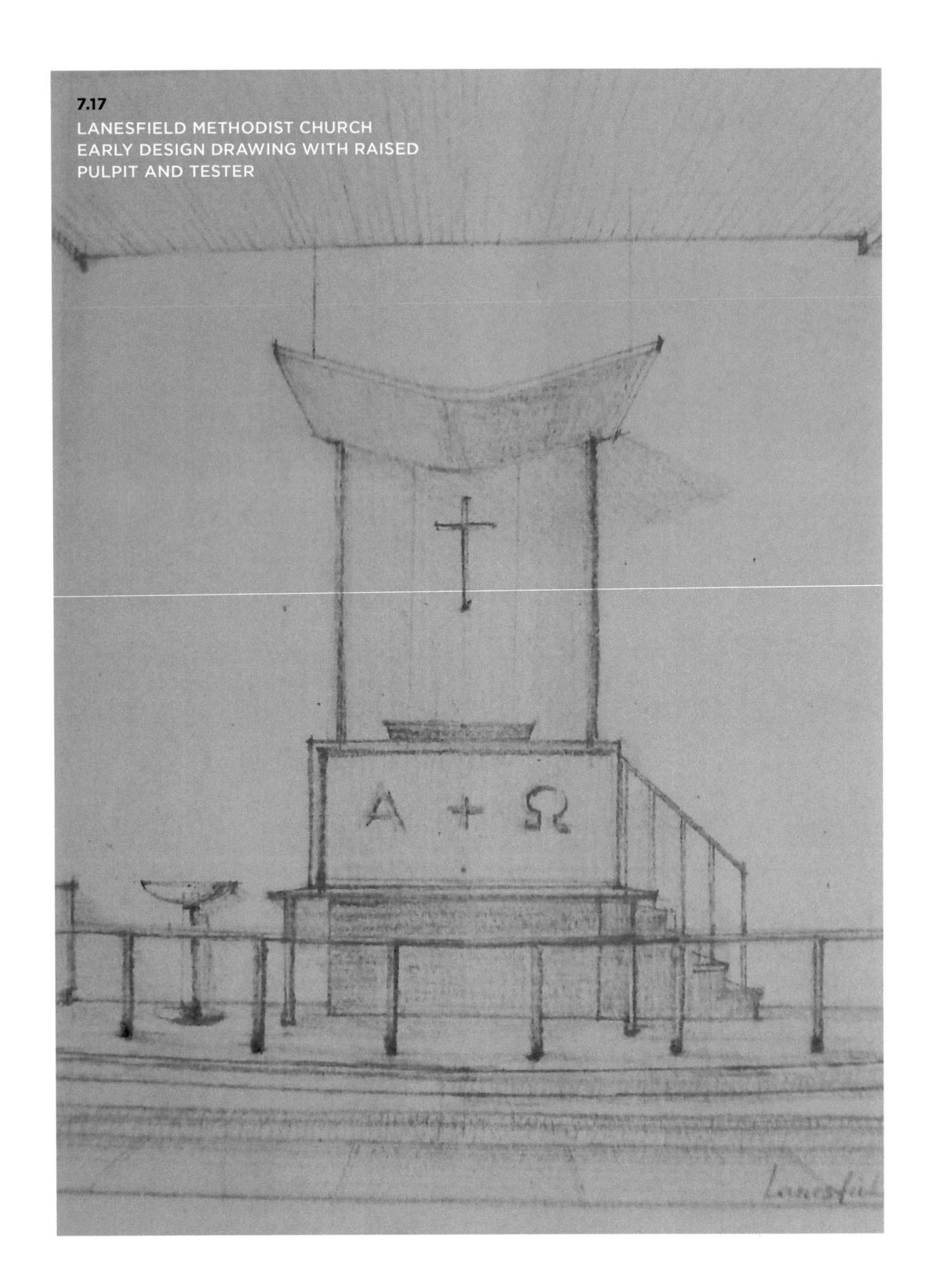

7.17
LANESFIELD METHODIST CHURCH
EARLY DESIGN DRAWING WITH RAISED
PULPIT AND TESTER

Notes

1   *Alfred Richard Twentyman*. Desk file, RIBA Library.

2   A panel in the present church records 1954 as the date of the first incumbent of the earlier church.

3   *Plans of Lanesfield Methodist Church by Twentyman and Percy*, 1960. Wolverhampton Record Office Archives, ref. M/LF.

4   Lanesfield Local Church Archives.

5   A. Miller, *Charles Geoffrey Percy (1914-63), An Obituary* (n.d.). Desk file on request, RIBA Library.

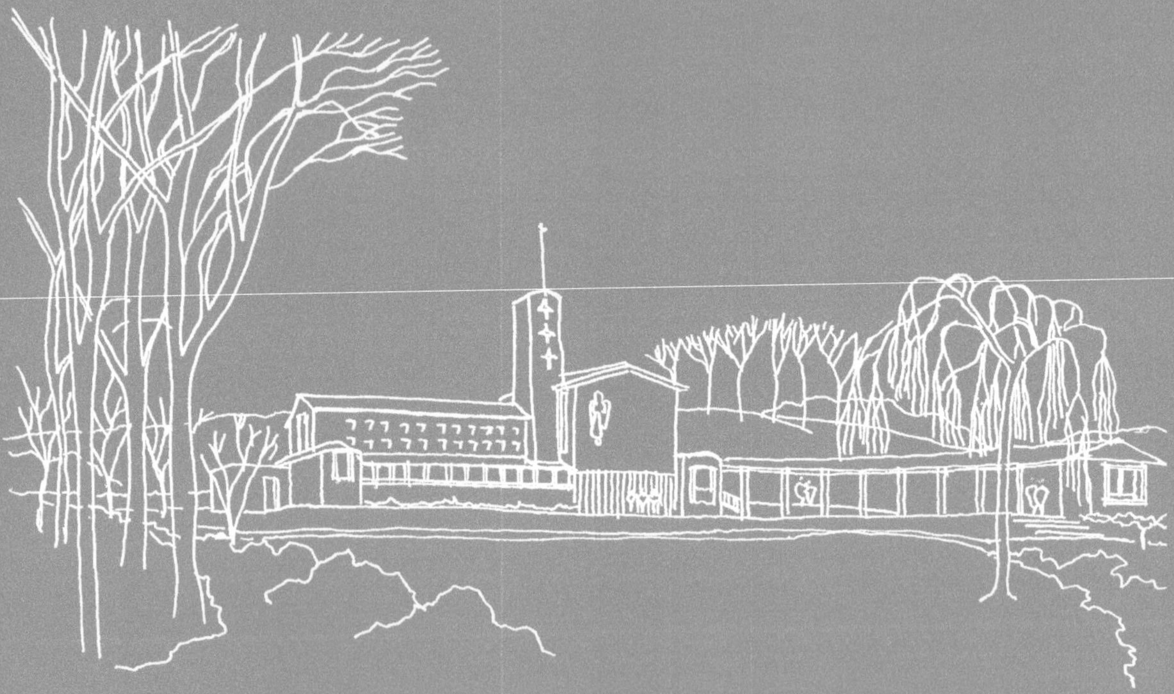

CHAPTER EIGHT

8

THE CREMATORIUM CHAPELS

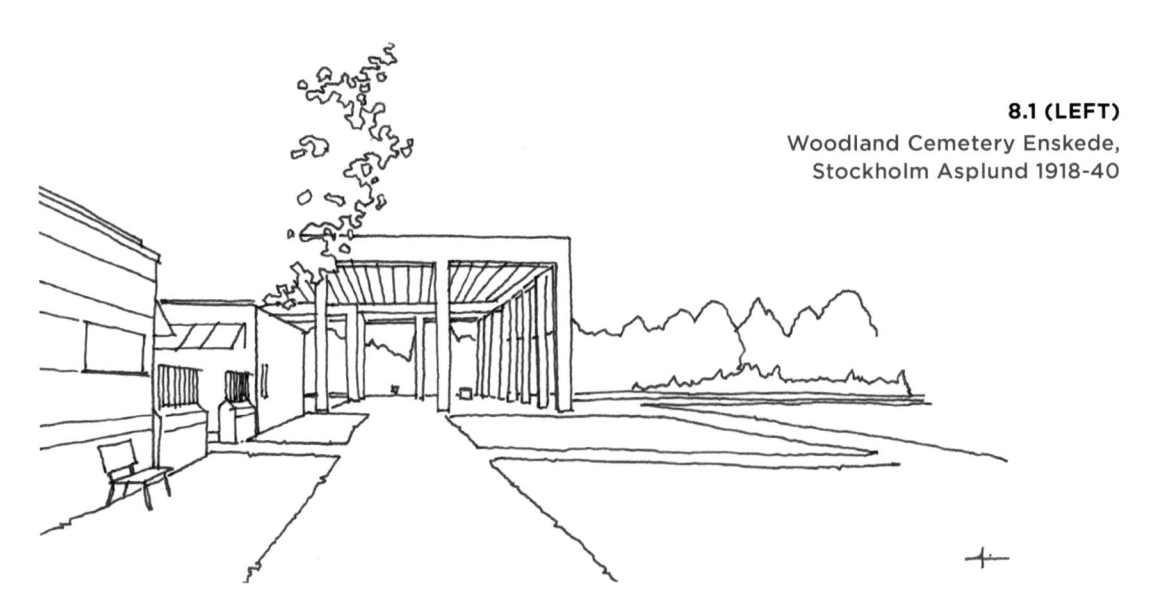

8.1 (LEFT)
Woodland Cemetery Enskede, Stockholm Asplund 1918-40

THE CREMATORIUM CHAPELS

WOLVERHAMPTON & REDDITCH

Both the churches and the crematoria projects illustrate how Twentyman was clearly influenced by the Swedish architects Gunnar Asplund (1885-1940) and Sigurd Lewerentz (1885-1975). Their work from 1918-1940 on the larger scale 100-hectare Enskede Woodland Cemetery on the outskirts of Stockholm had defined the new typology for the next generation of architects around Europe.[1] We have already mentioned Twentyman's 1955 paper on the design of crematoria. In the article he explicitly makes reference to Asplund's work.

Asplund and Lewerentz' design captured a mixture of Nordic classicism and modern functionalism, and reflected a less church-oriented, non-denominational, but still transcendental view of death.

It was part of a public health move away from city burials for hygienic reasons, but also an aesthetic twentieth-century shift in Sweden towards an elevated role for landscape, and a wider acceptance of its equivalence with architecture.[2]

Enskede was the first overtly modern cemetery in Western Europe to exemplify in its features the rejection of a traditional cemetery design of straight avenues lined with gravestones and tombs, instead integrating landscape, memorial, and architecture as a *Gesamtkunstwerk*. The gravestones at Enskede, for example, were of a small standard size and dispersed among wooded areas, blurring the defined typologies into a single whole. The original site was partially forested, with disused gravel pits, and Asplund and Lewerentz used both the natural and their own artificially-created landscapes as an integrated component of architecture.

8.2 (RIGHT)
Bushbury Crematorium signed watercolour by Richard Twentyman 1954

8.3 (ABOVE)
Bushbury Crematorium north terrace & cloister (balustrade added later)

BUSHBURY CREMATORIUM

WOLVERHAMPTON 1954

Bushbury Cemetery, two miles north of Wolverhampton centre, has a 16-hectare hilltop site with a lawn layout style opened in 1949 to serve the growing population of the town. The Crematorium was designed by Twentyman in 1954, with an additional 1970 chapel not by Twentyman himself but by his younger partner, George Sidebottom.

Cremation had long been promoted as an alternative to burial. Prior to cremation being made legal in 1885, William Robinson (1838-1935), a respected horticulturist and later advocate of the 1902 Golders Green Crematorium, had advocated its use not only on hygienic but also aesthetic grounds, highlighting, somewhat idealistically, the importance of landscape:

> **...everything we can desire for the artist is not only possible but easily attained. Soft, green, undisturbed lawns; stately and beautiful trees in many forms; ground undisturbed,...a background of surrounding groves; no hideous vistas of crowded stone...** [3]

Cremation gradually became more accepted, and Bushbury Crematorium's development reflected more positive attitudes toward cremation in Britain, though to many it was still an unfamiliar event. The number of cremations in England grew in the 1950s rising to 15% of total funerals. As populations expanded, cremations continued to increase in the 1960s and 1970s, encouraged by more relaxed religious attitudes, including the 1963 lifting of the ban on Roman Catholic cremation by Pope John Paul II.

8.4
BUSHBURY CREMATORIUM
MAIN ENTRANCE

8.5 & 8.6 (BELOW & BOTTOM)
German Military Cemetry Cannock
Chase plan and view from west

8.7 & 8.8 (RIGHT)
Bushbury Crematorium front entrance
and rear terrace (pictured in 1954)

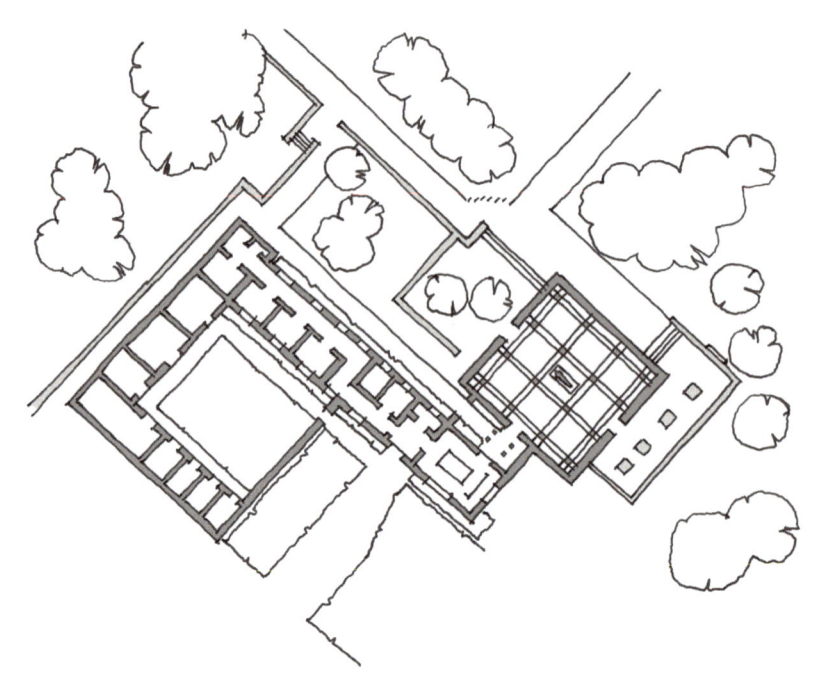

The new building's significance at the time was highlighted in three architectural journal articles. In one of those articles,[4] a painting by Twentyman (8.2) shows the balanced nature of the building design: the north elevation of the crematorium with the lower ancillary block to the east, the tower and chapel in the centre, and the sweeping curved cloisters contouring the existing hill to the west.

Twentyman adopted Asplund's approach on a reduced scale at both his Bushbury (1954) and Redditch (1973) crematoria. The Woodland Cemetery must surely have also influenced design of the nearby German Military Cemetery (listed Grade I) on Cannock Chase, Staffordshire, built in 1964 and dedicated in 1967. The architects were Harold Doffman and Peter Leach of Stafford, and landscaping was undertaken by Diez Brandi, a German architect, together with local landscape architect consultants, Lovejoy and Partners. The Cannock Chase Cemetery's striking feature is the way it visually extends northwards with no apparent boundary between it and the surrounding heathland interspersed with trees, reminiscent of a northern German landscape.

THE CREMATORIUM CHAPELS

8.9
BUSHBURY CREMATORIUM
FORMAL ENTRANCE & *PORTE COCHÈRE*

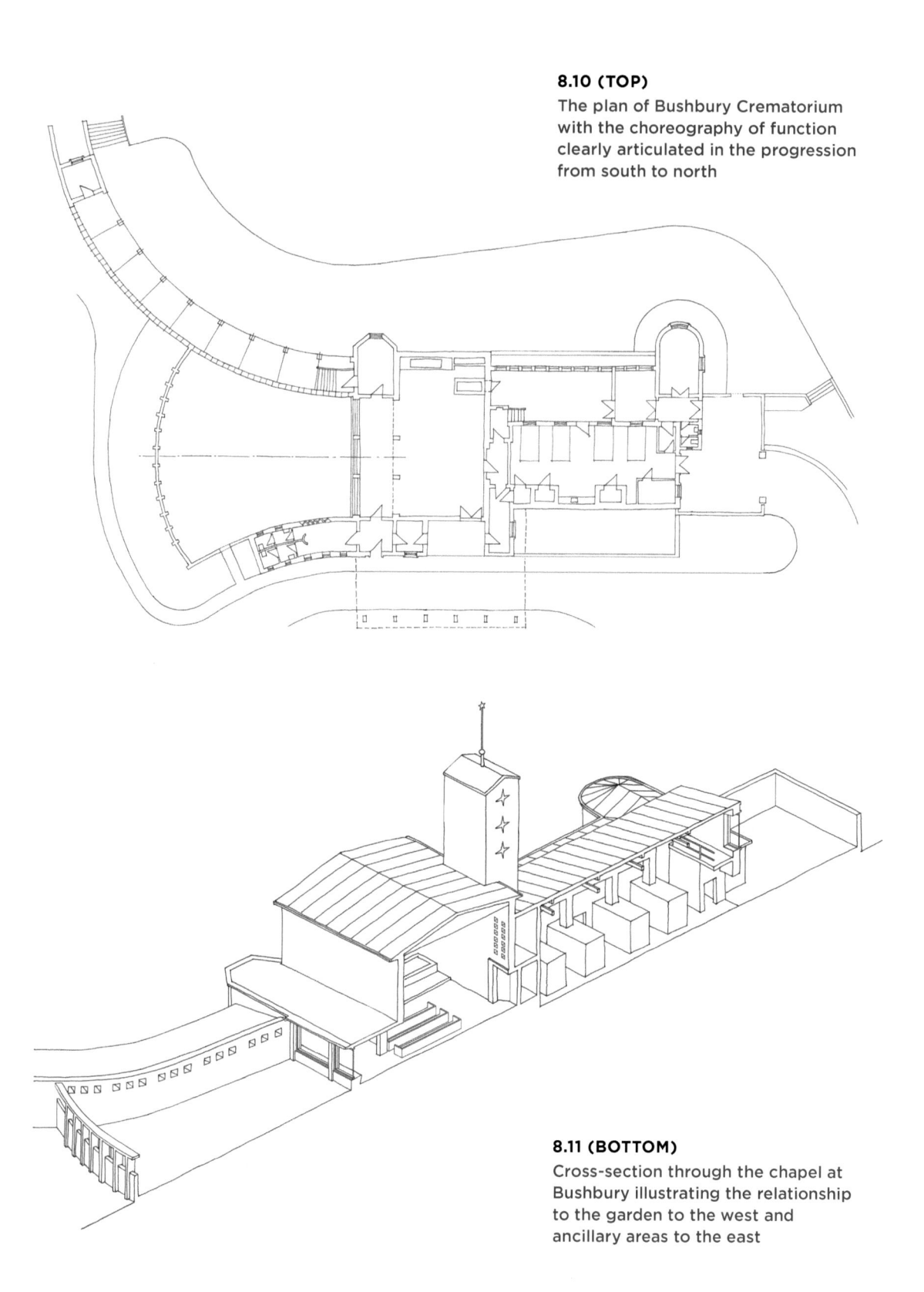

8.10 (TOP)
The plan of Bushbury Crematorium with the choreography of function clearly articulated in the progression from south to north

8.11 (BOTTOM)
Cross-section through the chapel at Bushbury illustrating the relationship to the garden to the west and ancillary areas to the east

THE CREMATORIUM CHAPELS

8.12 (BELOW)
Bushbury Crematorium north-facing cloister and terrace

The Enskede Woodland Cemetery has three chapels, one by Lewerentz, the Chapel of Resurrection (1925), and two by Asplund, the Woodland Chapel (1920), and the Crematorium and Chapel of the Holy Cross with the smaller attached Chapels of Hope and of Faith (1940). It is to the Chapel of Faith that Twentyman refers in his 1955 article as 'a splendid example of a friendly and intimate yet dignified interior'.[5] A photograph of the Chapel of Faith in the article shows the plain white walls, a supporting pillar but no aisles, and high-placed rectangular side windows casting light on the catafalque, aspects which recall Twentyman's church design around the same period at All Saints, Darlaston (1952), Emmanuel, Bentley (1955), and St Chad, Rubery (1956). Twentyman includes a second photograph from the Crematorium Chapel of Resurrection, Hope, and Memory (1944) in Borås, Sweden, by Harald Ericson (1890-1972), and comments on the 'dramatic, but noble, effect obtained by the extreme simplicity, and clever lighting'. He explicitly associates his work with that of Asplund and Ericson by adding a third photograph of an interior view of his own Bushbury Crematorium Chapel showing the simplicity of design he, too, favoured (8.15).

8.13
BUSHBURY CREMATORIUM
VESTIBULE

THE CREMATORIUM CHAPELS

8.14 (BELOW)
Bushbury Crematorium chapel in 2020

His Bushbury photograph also shows the three Portland stone doves on the wall to the right of the altar sculpted by Don Potter, recalling the reliefs by Ivar Johnsson on the altar wall of Asplund's Chapel of Faith, and similar reliefs in the Borås chapel.

In his article, Twentyman suggests general design guidelines for crematoria which he had earlier applied to Bushbury Crematorium. The site should give 'a distant view over open country' and preferably be 'well-wooded'.[6] He mentions that cremation is a relatively new procedure, so the design should have the effect of providing reassurance to mourners. He is critical for that reason of an unnamed foreign example with 'a windowless chapel with a black floor, lit only from one hole in the roof', a description that could, ironically, also fit Asplund's Woodland Chapel. Twentyman does not deny its architectural quality, but raises the question of its negative effect on mourners. The architect, he says, 'has to walk a tightrope between comfortable vulgarity…and excessive nobility'.[7]

The buildings at Bushbury are grouped together as a single composition on an elevated site. The ground slopes away to the north-west with the crematorium and chapel affording a gently undulating view of the wooded countryside and a park to the north/north-west, an aspect still remarkably countrified despite inevitable housing expansion since 1954. The terrace which mourners approach after the ceremony is in shade, yet overlooking a sunlit landscape.

8.15
BUSHBURY CREMATORIUM CHAPEL IN 1954

Twentyman, in his article, is concerned with the efficient and smooth movement of mourners, and the crematorium building is accordingly carefully designed to facilitate a ritualised sequence of events to minimise their stress, while effortlessly choreographing their movement from space to space. The building is designed to welcome and then gently separate coffin and mourners along two diverging circulation patterns.

The cortège arrives in funeral cars which, after depositing the mourners under a *porte cochère*, circle around to park opposite the exit from the cloisters (8.7). The coffin is carried from the hearse to the chapel catafalque to the right of the altar. At the end of the ceremony, it is removed from the chapel to the side before being lowered to the transfer room and cremator.

THE CREMATORIUM CHAPELS

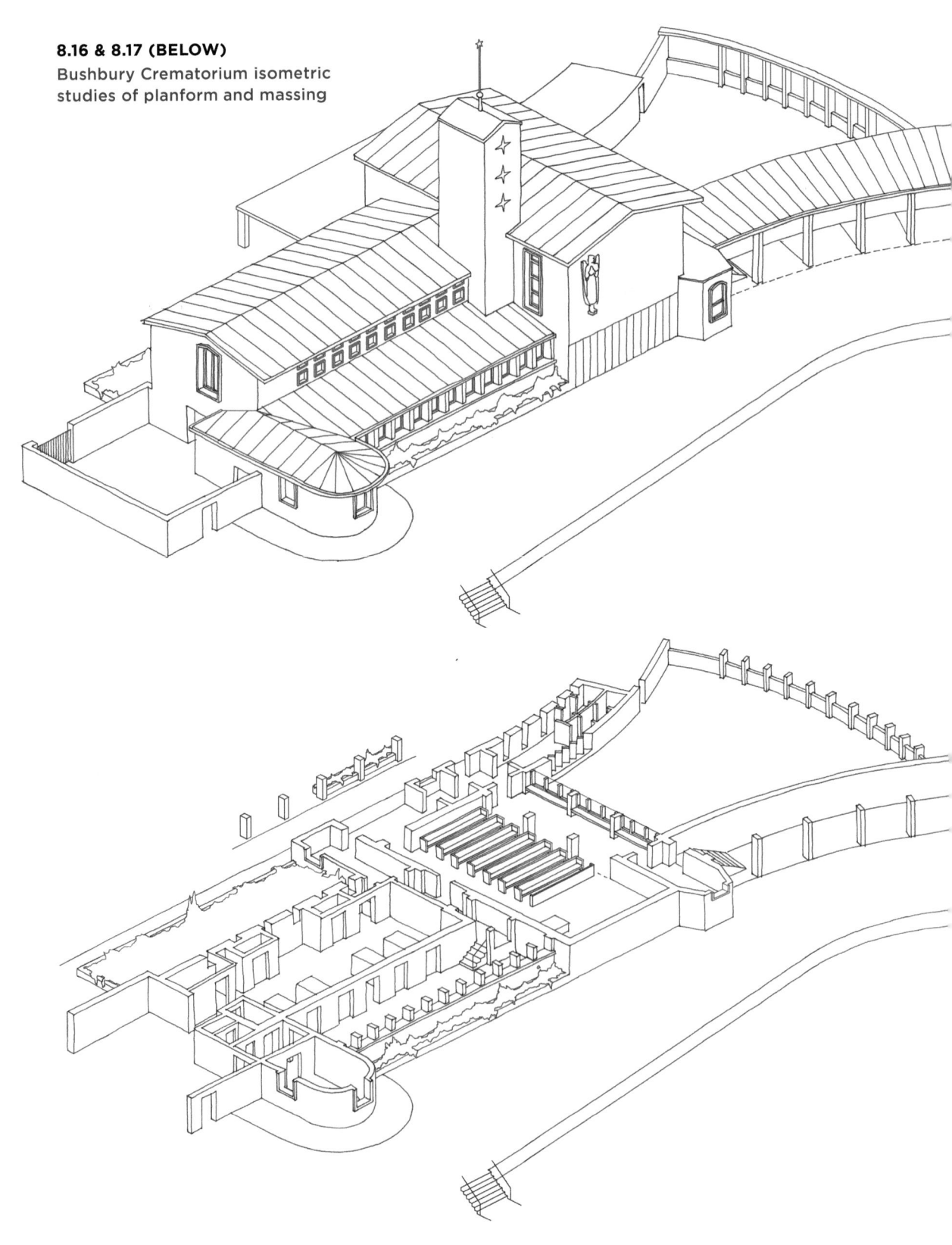

8.16 & 8.17 (BELOW)
Bushbury Crematorium isometric studies of planform and massing

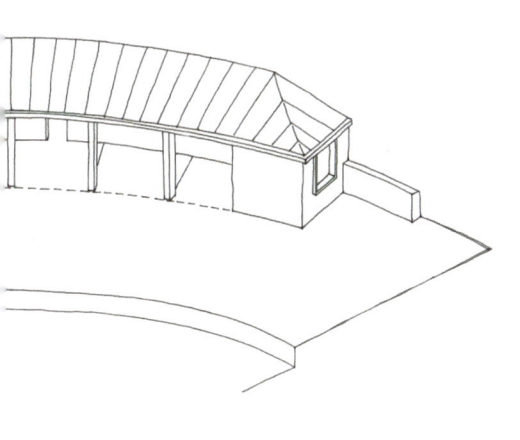

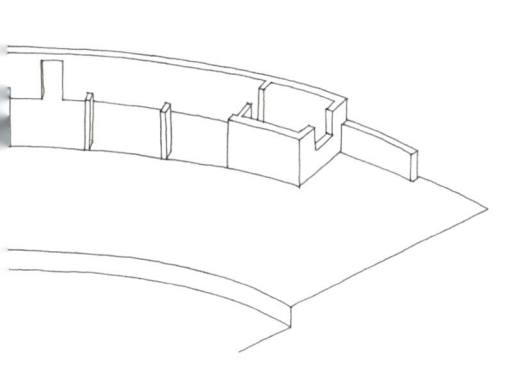

8.18 (RIGHT)
Angel in Portland stone on the east wall of the chapel, by Don Potter

THE CREMATORIUM CHAPELS

8.19 (ABOVE)
View from the chapel into the concealed garden area imediately to the west

The mourners enter the chapel by the same main door on the south side of the chapel as the coffin, but they leave by a second on the north side to the covered cloisters overlooking countryside and a Garden of Remembrance with space for wreaths, then exit to the waiting cars. The floor plan shows this circulation, effective also in providing physical separation from preceding and subsequent funeral groups.

External walls are of cream-coloured brick in Flemish bond with some rectangular stone slabs. Window surrounds are of stone or slate, and the roofs and downpipes were originally finished in copper with standing seams patinated green. Twentyman mentions the chimney should not be disguised 'as a Gothic church with smoke pouring from the belfry windows',[8] but designed sensitively so that it is not factory-like. Bushbury's chimney is a four-sided tower with three vertically placed four-pointed metal cruciform stars attached on its north and south sides, and a five-pointed metal star crowning a slender mast-like spire. The four-pointed star motif is repeated along the length of the metal balustrades on the north side of the cloisters (8.3), and occurs elsewhere in his churches of this period, notably at Darlaston and Bentley.

The 'simple but not austere' interior of the chapel has familiar Twentyman decorative features (8.15), including mahogany doors with six pairs of raised rectangular panels matching the panels on the altar front and the lectern; rounded bench ends; and exposed concrete roof beams. The altar is a focal point and behind it is an oak cross on fluted mahogany boarding, with the catafalque placed on the right-hand side.

8.20
**BUSHBURY CREMATORIUM
ORGAN *NICHE* IN CHAPEL**

THE CREMATORIUM CHAPELS

8.21 (LEFT)
Bushbury Crematorium gardeners' store with carved Phoenix by Don Potter

8.22 (RIGHT)
Twentyman's commended submission for the new Kirkcaldy Crematorium competition published in *The Architect and Building News* June 1954, page 729

North aisle windows look out onto an enclosed garden providing privacy for those in the chapel, recalling Asplund's similar method of separating his three chapels so that, if required, services could take place concurrently.

Similar chapel garden windows were designed by Sanger and Rothwell (S&R) in their 1954 winning competition entry for Kirkcaldy Crematorium. They had already used such windows in a 1953 crematorium chapel conversion in Oldham.[9] Twentyman also submitted a design for Kirkcaldy (8.22), receiving a commendation, but his design, unlike that for Bushbury Crematorium, did not include windows replacing the north wall. Grainger, referring to S&R's window design, believes that such a feature, reducing the division between internal and external worlds, 'would define British post-war crematoria'. Both Twentyman and S&R, therefore, realised the potential of such windows to create 'a space that invited engagement with nature and the living world'. The direction of influence, if any, between Twentyman and S&R, has not been established, nor is it clear whether S&R were aware of Asplund's earlier work at Enskede.

Commended — LAVENDER, TWENTYMAN & PERCY

CREMATORIUM. DUNNIKIER PARK. KIRKCALDY

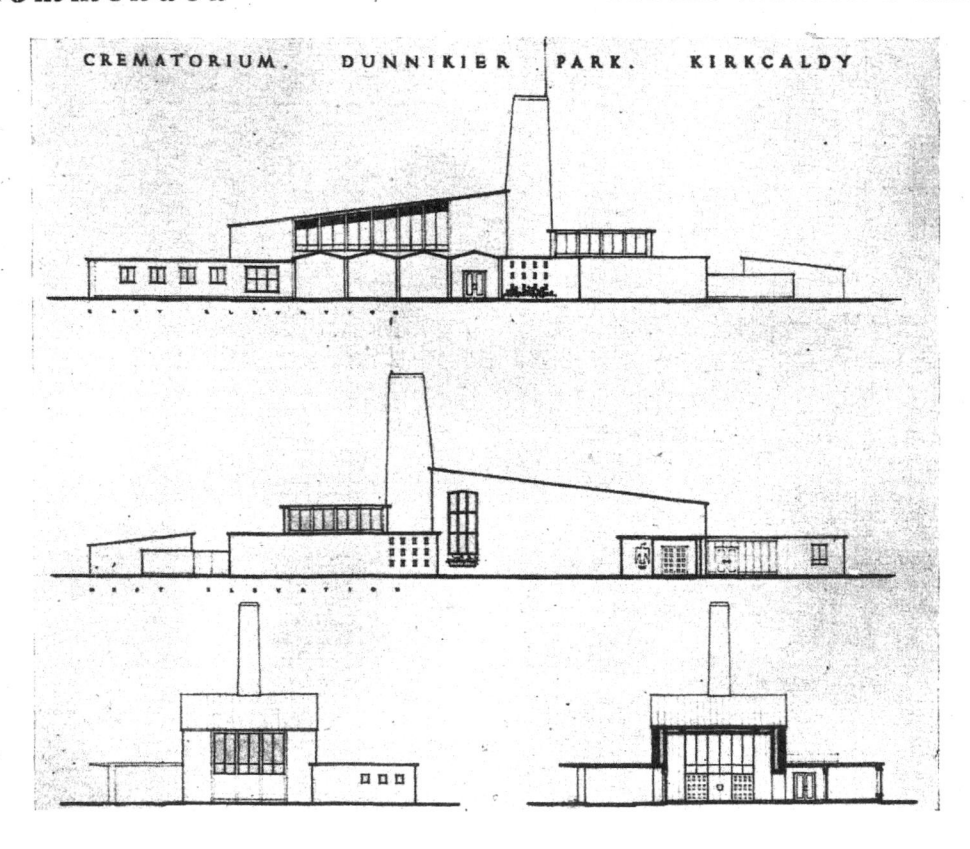

KEY
1. COVERED SPACE
2. ENTRANCE HALL
3. GENERAL WAITING
4. OFFICE
5. VESTRY
6. CHAPEL
7. LOGGIA
8. COMMITTAL CHAMBER
9. CREMATION ROOM
10. STAFF ROOM

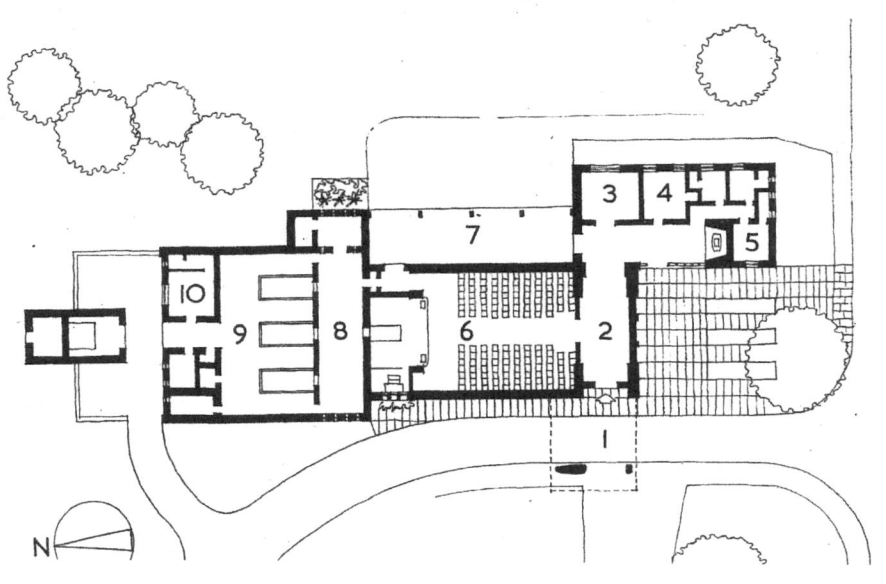

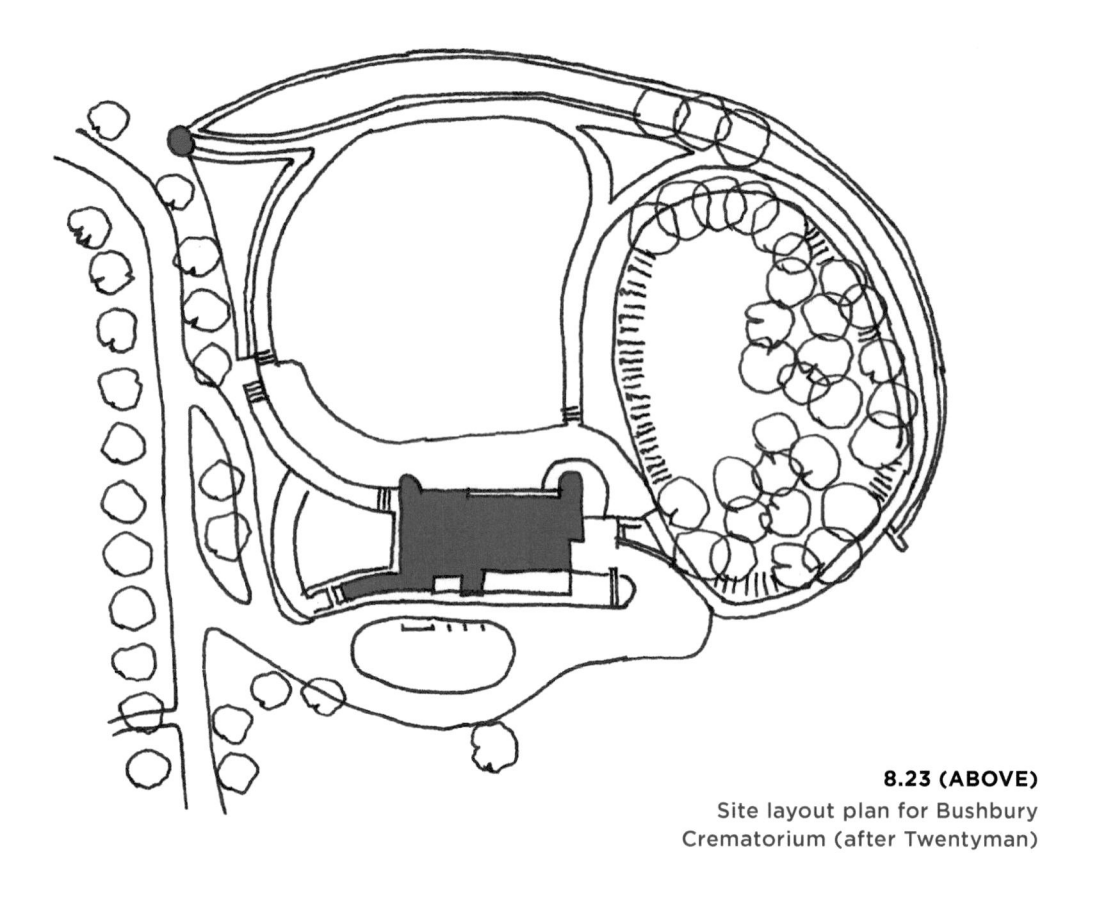

8.23 (ABOVE)
Site layout plan for Bushbury Crematorium (after Twentyman)

Returning to Bushbury, a window with a Book of Remembrance overlooks the view north over the gardens and the landscape beyond. Twentyman made provision for an organ rather than the 'deplorable method of relaying gramophone records'[10] in an alcove on the south chapel wall with, above it, a set of small rectangular openings four across by six down to improve acoustics.

Don Potter was given three Portland stone sculpture commissions at Bushbury: three Doves on the chapel's east wall, a 12-foot high Angel on its external north wall overlooking the terrace, and a Phoenix attached to an unusual circular brick toolshed for the gardeners, now relatively hidden in the grounds to the north-west of the main building. The Angel recalls the monumental sculpture of St Martin, at Twentyman's St Martin Church, Parkfields, also by Potter, and similarly placed on a blank expanse of brick wall for maximum effect.

8.24
BUSHBURY CREMATORIUM
CLOISTER EXIT

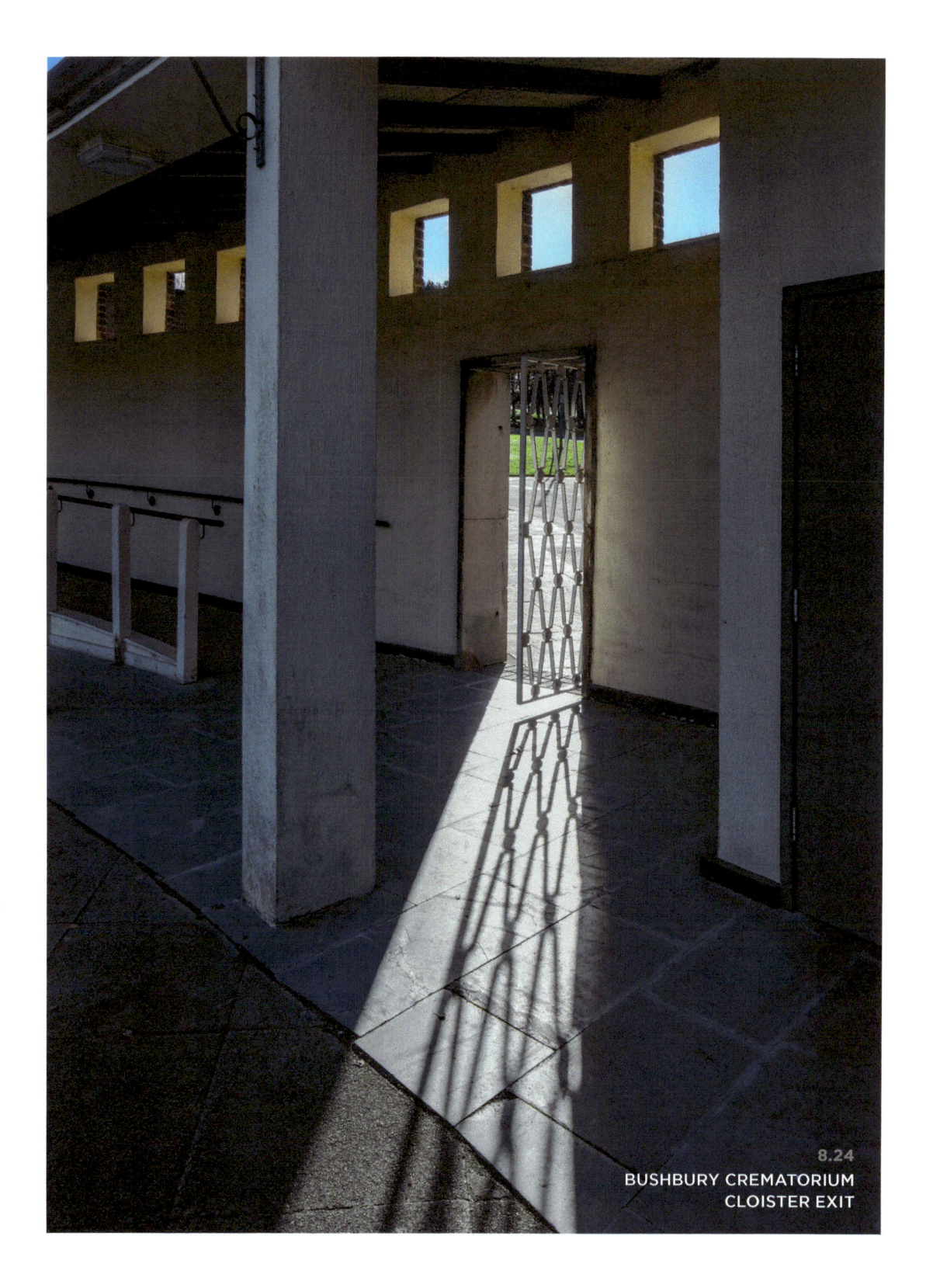

8.25
BUSHBURY CREMATORIUM
SOUTH FACADE

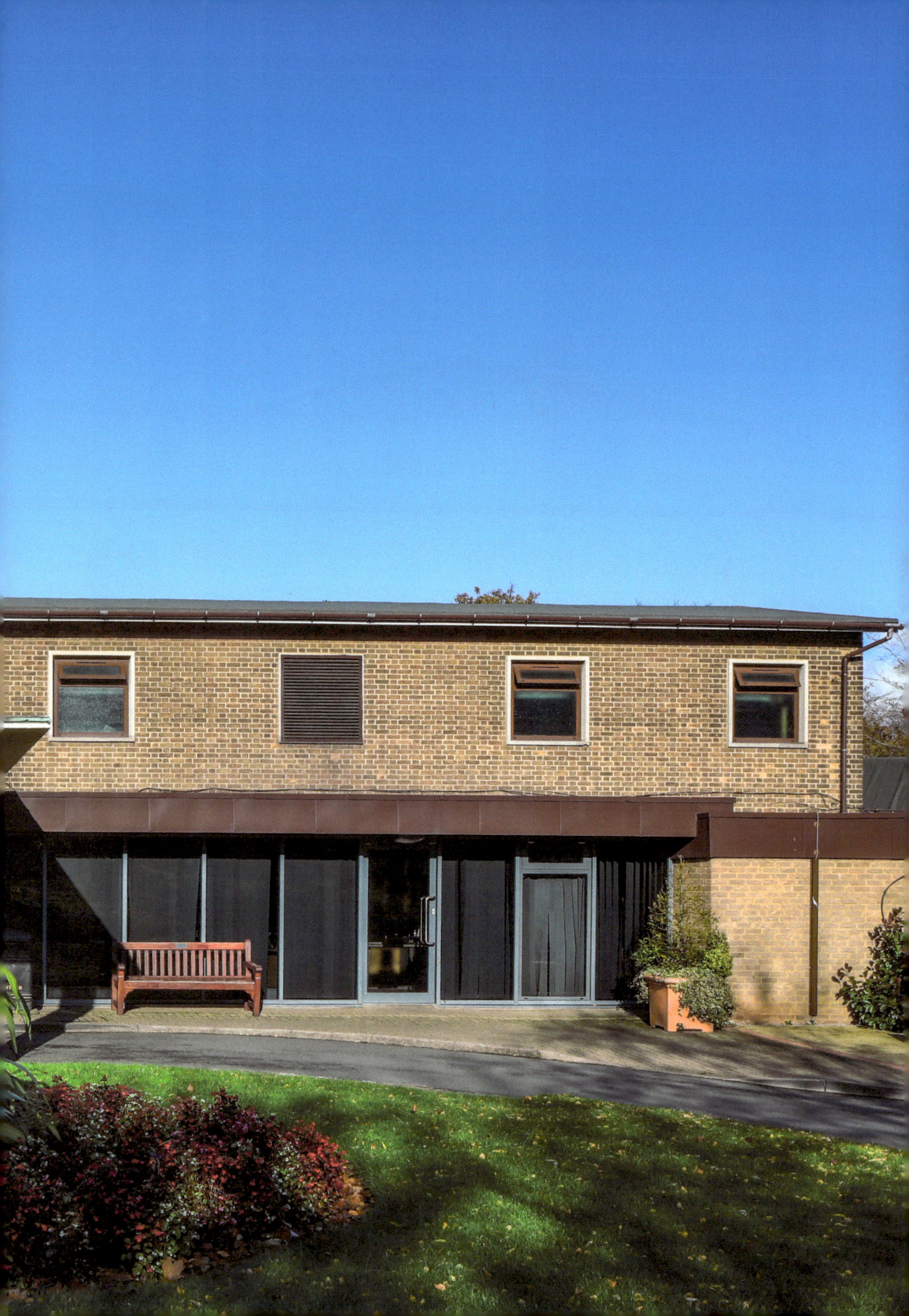

REDDITCH CREMATORIUM
WORCESTERSHIRE 1971-73

Redditch Crematorium, which includes Twentyman's last chapel before retirement in 1977, shares many of the features found at Bushbury, and in particular its simple choreography of coffin and mourners entering together and gently parting ways. It similarly reflects Twentyman's established attitude to the design of crematoria and Brooks and Pevsner describe it as a 'model example'[11] of the architectural typology of the period.

It was planned as early as 1955, but its construction became more urgent following Redditch's designation as a Second Phase New Town in 1964, at the same time as Runcorn, where Twentyman built St Andrew, Grange in 1965. Redditch New Town was to cater for population expansion and overspill from Birmingham. In 1984 the population of 80,000 represented a threefold increase from its 1964 figure. Such population increases inevitably created greater demand for cemetery and crematorium provision.

As at Bushbury, the crematorium is on the edge of the town, on an elevated site overlooking countryside towards the River Arrow. A central axis orders the whole plan, aligned on the dominant mass of the chapel. Asymmetric wings balance the composition with the low brick and stone ancillary building housing administration and cremation functions, clustered together with the tower to the west and the Memorial Corridor, an evolution of the curving cloister at Bushbury, and Room of Remembrance to the southeast.

8.26
REDDITCH CREMATORIUM

THE CREMATORIUM CHAPELS

8.27
REDDITCH CREMATORIUM
EAST FRONT

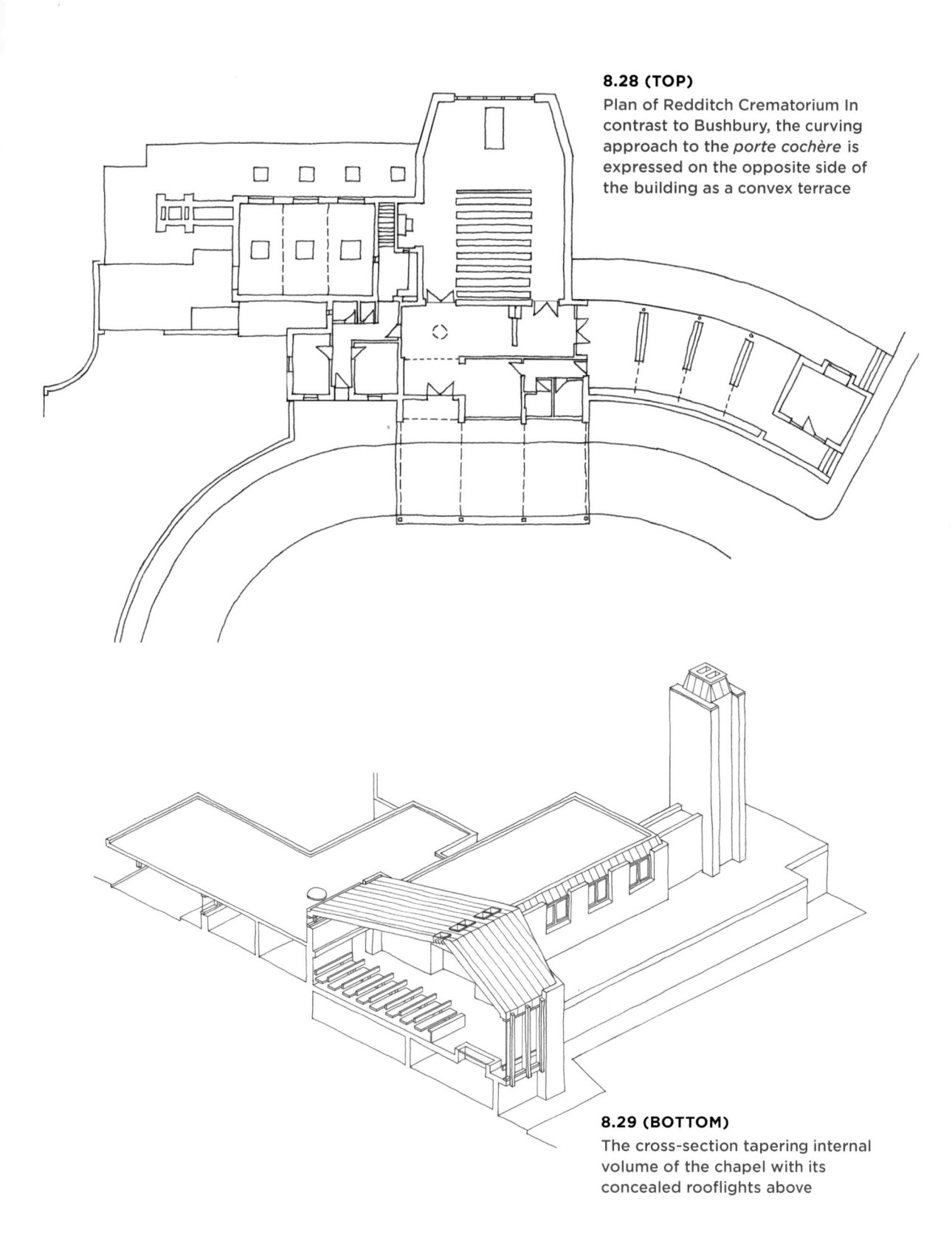

8.28 (TOP)
Plan of Redditch Crematorium In contrast to Bushbury, the curving approach to the *porte cochère* is expressed on the opposite side of the building as a convex terrace

8.29 (BOTTOM)
The cross-section tapering internal volume of the chapel with its concealed rooflights above

THE CREMATORIUM CHAPELS

8.30 (ABOVE)
Redditch Crematorium east frontage

8.31 (TOP RIGHT)
Redditch Crematorium sloping site to east of chapel pictured in 1973

8.32 (BOTTOM RIGHT)
Site layout plan for Redditch Crematorium (after Twentyman)

These wings form an implied cross axis which intersects the main central one just outside the chapel, reinforcing the choreography of use. The coffin and the mourners enter the architectural focal point of the taller chapel along the main north-east to south-west axis together, before separating into the north-west and south-east wings respectively.

The whole complex is built on top of a low hill, yet blocks the views until the chapel itself is entered, when the panoramic window shows the ground sloping away to the north-east. The chapel has an asymmetric pitched roof, similar to St Andrew, Grange in geometry, originally with copper standing seams. This material remains only on the splayed cladding of the perimeter of the main roof, although it is echoed in the form of the small detached chapel, which is now an office, to the south-east. The chimney, north-west of the chapel, is designed as a rectangular tower with vertical diaphragm walls connected by recessed brick cross walls, creating recessed panels, similar in construction to the bell tower at St Chad, Rubery (1956-60), and is surmounted by a low copper cupola.

With his customary attention to detail, Twentyman specified in his drawings the colour red for the tarmac on the approach roads,

THE CREMATORIUM CHAPELS

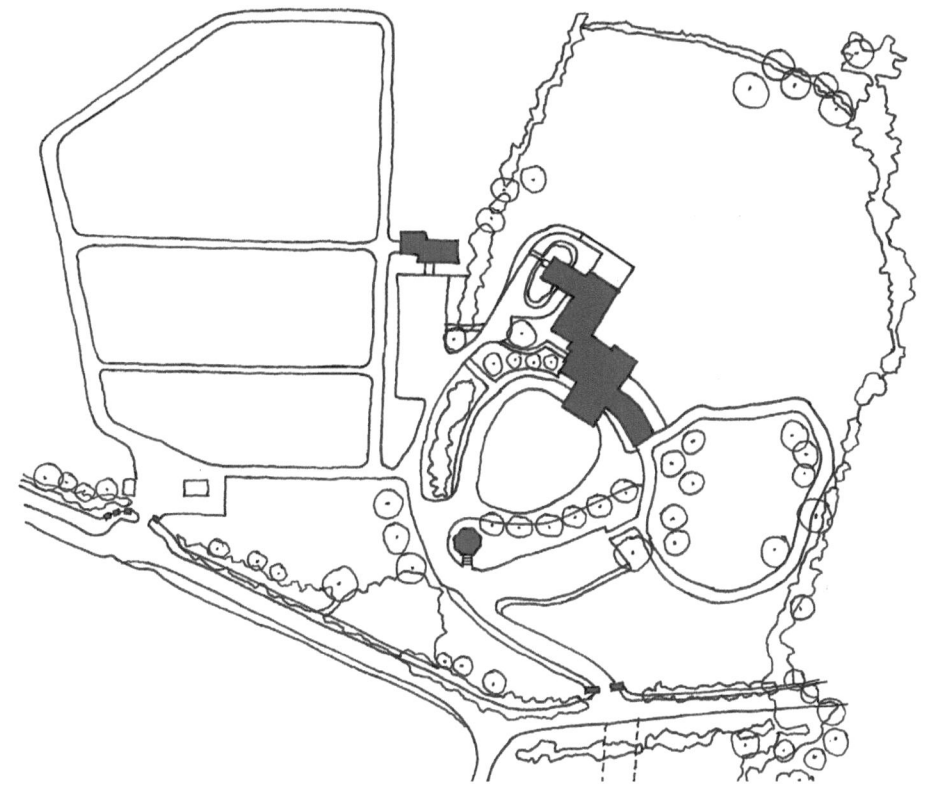

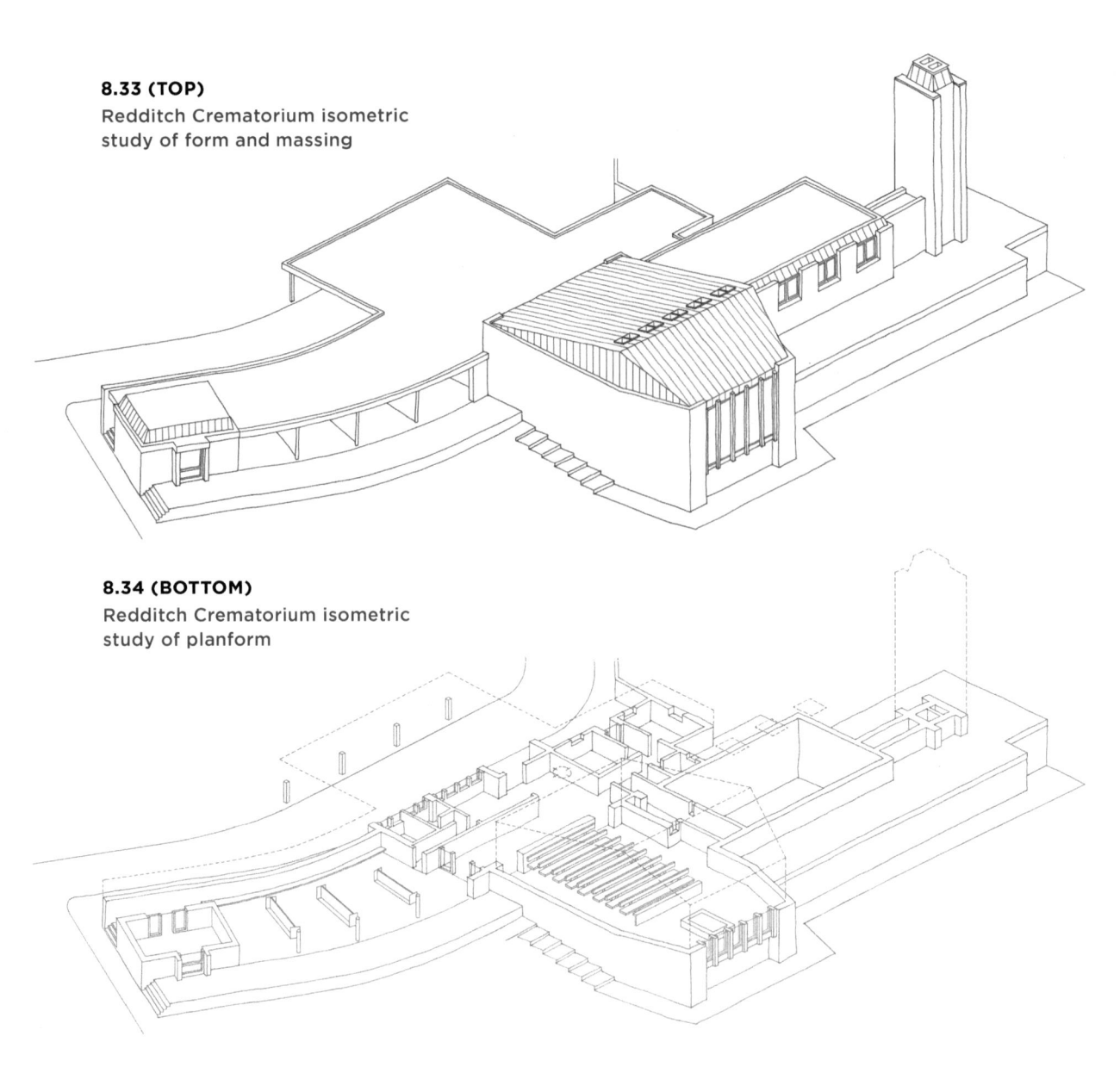

8.33 (TOP)
Redditch Crematorium isometric study of form and massing

8.34 (BOTTOM)
Redditch Crematorium isometric study of planform

a topic he also mentioned in his 1955 article in connection with Bushbury. He believed a black finish 'was ugly and depressing'. The alternatives were 'a coloured concrete...or a tarmacadam road with a surface of fairly large uncoated chippings of a suitable colour',[12] a stipulation providing a fascinating insight into his wider views on the impact of colour in design.

As he had done successfully at Bushbury almost twenty years previously, Twentyman provided for the movement of mourners from the moment they entered the site as much as within the buildings. The drive sweeps up the hill to a flat-roofed *porte cochère* with a direct entrance to the lobby, signalled with a circular rooflight (8.38), a device Twentyman also employed at the Church of the Good Shepherd, Castlecroft

8.35 (ABOVE)
Redditch Crematorium approach to the chapel from the west pictured in 1973

(1955) and St Andrew, Runcorn (1965) to mark the intersection of axes. Coffin and mourners then move through doors into the north aisle of the chapel. At the end of the service, the catafalque lowers the coffin to the transfer room on the floor below, while mourners return through west doors at the end of the south side of the chapel. This led to an external covered terrace area connecting with the surrounding landscape. Now glazed, the curving Memorial Hall and Room of Remembrance form another shaded cloister looking north-east over the gently undulating North Worcestershire countryside (8.30 8.31 & 8.37).

The chapel, with a capacity of eighty seated and eighty standing, has white rough-cast side walls narrowing slightly to accentuate the ceremonial 'east end' with a centrally placed free-standing catafalque behind which is a simple cross (8.39).

THE CREMATORIUM CHAPELS

8.36 (TOP LEFT)
Redditch Crematorium eastern entrance to terrace and loggia past the Chapel of Remembrance pictured in 1973

8.37 (MIDDLE LEFT)
Redditch Crematorium the terrace and loggia looking out over the landscape to the north-east pictured in 1973

8.38 (BOTTOM LEFT)
Redditch Crematorium internal circulation lobby linking the chapel and the west-facing *porte cochère* pictured in 1973

8.39 (BELOW)
Redditch Crematorium
the chapel looking east

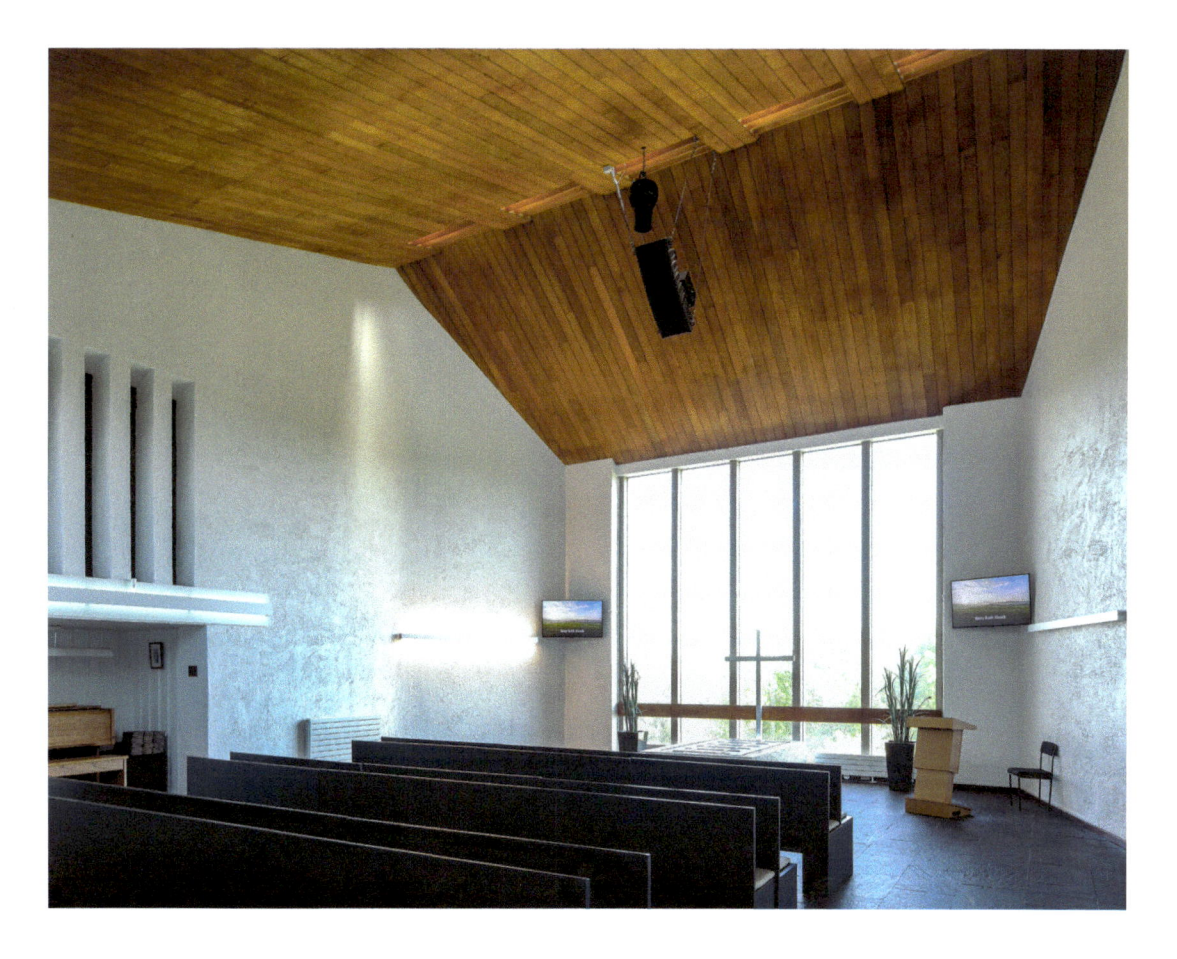

Twentyman, rather than designing his usual unglazed east wall articulated by materiality and architectural detail, was clearly influenced by the uniqueness of the Redditch site, overlooking the Arrow Valley and the site of the ruined Cistercian Bordesley Abbey. He successfully captured this outlook over the surrounding countryside by providing an almost fully glazed east window of five, tall, mullioned lights reaching just short of the eaves (8.27). The slight rotation of the plan towards the north, heightens the effect, as at this orientation, the landscape is in full sun for most of the day. Further light is provided by three sets of triple banked rectangular windows in the west clerestory, catching the afternoon sun. The angled roof is of slatted Columbia Pine providing an attractive warm glow in contrast with the otherwise plain white walls (8.39 & 8.40), while hiding five roof lights, creating Twentyman's signature illuminance from a concealed source of natural light.

8.40
REDDITCH CREMATORIUM
THE CHAPEL

Betty Ruth Alcock

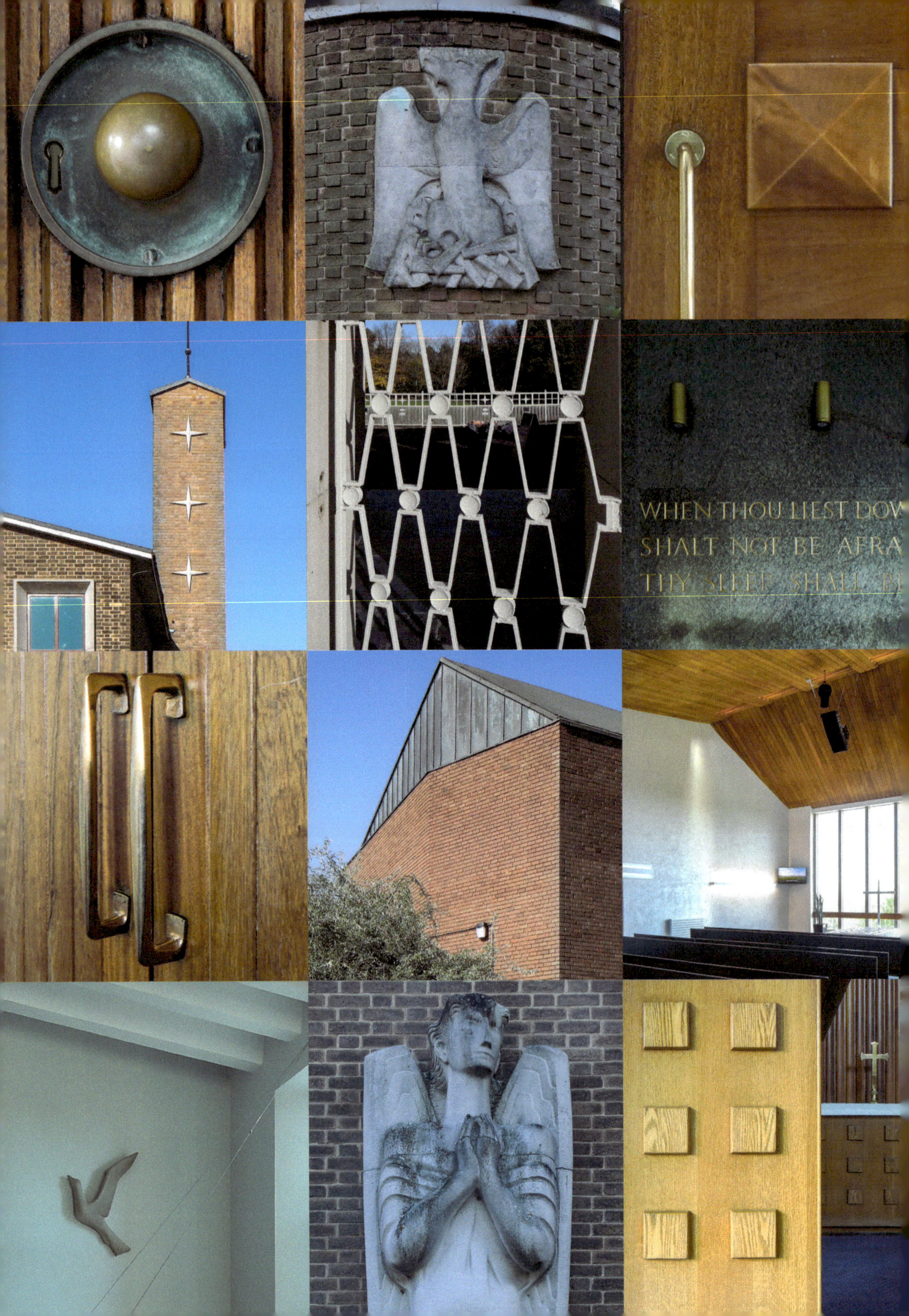
WHEN THOU LIEST DOV
SHALT NOT BE AFRA
THY SLEEP SHALL B

Notes

1 M. Woollen, *Erik Gunnar Asplund* (London: Routledge, 2019).

2 C. Constant, *The Woodland Cemetery*, (Stockholm: Byggförlaget, 2008), p.78.

3 W. Robinson, *God's Acre Beautiful* (London: The Garden Office, 1882), pp.13-14.

4 'Proposed Crematorium for Wolverhampton' *The Architect and Building News*, vol. 201, no. 4343, March 13, (1952), pp.311-13.

5 A. R. Twentyman, 'The Design and Layout of Crematoria', *Royal Sanitary Institute Journal*, 75, 7, July, (1955), p.502.

6 Twentyman, 'Design of Crematoria', p.500.

7 Twentyman, 'Design of Crematoria', p.504.

8 Twentyman, 'Design of Crematoria', p.504.

9 H. Grainger, *Designs on Death* (Edinburgh: John Donald, 2020), pp.159-165

10 Twentyman, 'Design of Crematoria', p.501.

11 A. Brooks and N. Pevsner, *Worcestershire* (New Haven: Yale University Press, 2007), p.90.

12 Twentyman, 'Design of Crematoria', p.506.

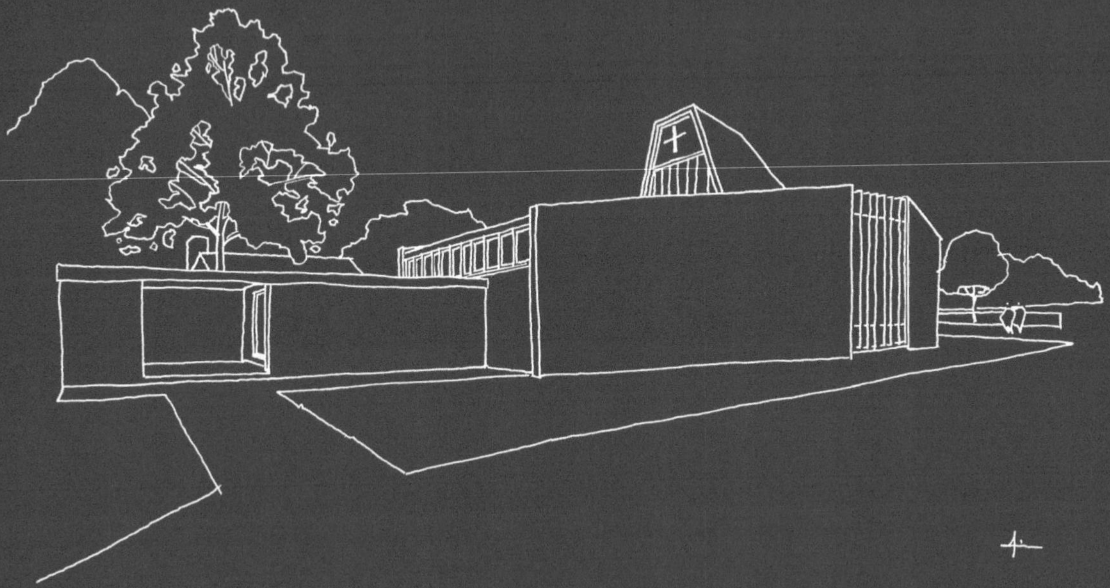

CHAPTER NINE

9
CONCLUSIONS & REFLECTIONS

CONCLUSION

Twentyman's professional life spanned fifty years of the twentieth century from the 1920s to the 1970s, a period which moved away from historicism to modernism in all cultural activities including architecture, the former vividly illustrated by the Victorian drawing of Joseph Lavender's bicycle factory (9.2). It was a time characterised by industrial expansion, population movements, suburban housing developments, and, of relevance to this book, extensive church building, all of which impacted Twentyman's architectural output. He skilfully managed such social, political, and ecclesiastical developments, successfully balancing client needs and wants against inevitable budgetary constraints and materials supply shortages.

The motivation for this book was to bring Twentyman's work, especially his churches, to a wider audience, and review the evidence of Twentyman's skill and development as an architect and the influences on his work. During our researches, it became clear that Twentyman worked on a variety of secular projects as well as his churches.

His output in the 1930s, in addition to the churches of St Gabriel and St Martin, included a number of public houses and individual house commissions, the latter providing impressive exemplars of the modern movement of the time. In the post-war period from the 1950s to 1970s, the churches described in this volume constituted his major architectural contribution, and arguably represent his best work, but he also took on larger institutionally-based projects including commercial offices and schools, reflecting a more buoyant regional economy and expansion of postwar educational provision. This secular work has suffered from the same inattention as Twentyman's ecclesiastical architecture and similarly requires re-examination in due course.

Twentyman's church design narrative is not one of revolution but of evolving innovation.

9.1 (OPPOSITE)
AA Journal, October 1946 Richard Twentyman standing on far right

9.2 (BELOW)
Joseph Lavender, June 1896 design for cycle factory, Wolverhampton

The Architectural Association Journal, 34, 35, 36 Bedford Square, London, W.C.

Vol. LXII. 706.　　　　　　　　　　　　　　　　　　　　October 1946

DENMARK AND SWEDEN, 1946

The party on board the 'Kronprinz Frederik'
Photograph: F. McManus

From left to right (standing): E. L. Bird, F. J. Samuely, A. H. H. Jenkins, Mrs. Brandon Jones, J. Brandon Jones, Mrs. McManus, R. M. Maitland, E. B. O'Rorke, Mrs. Dawbarn, Mrs. O'Rorke, K. Peacock, E. Armstrong, Mrs. Armstrong, L. F. I. Wolters, E. Shires, I. R. M. McCallum, A. R. Twentyman. (Sitting): K. W. Douglas, Graham Dawbarn, H. J. W. Alexander, G. I. C. Highet, Miss E. Caldicott (second row), Mrs. Chitty, A. M. Chitty, K. W. Grieb

He changed from designing massive and defensive-looking structures in the 1930s to more modern approaches in the postwar period, with an emphasis on lightness of structure and spatial openness, and a constant concern to utilise the effects of natural light. In this respect, his influences were 1930s English architects and earlier European architects. His exposure to modern Scandinavian architecture during his Architectural Association training became a lifelong interest and is clearly evident in his architectural designs. Significantly, he participated in the AA's trip to Denmark and Sweden in 1946 (9.1).

He steered a course between advocates of an extreme functional design and those supporting a more transcendental experience, the latter assisted by his subtle use of modern sculpture and his own total design features, down to details of doors and furnishings. He realised practical needs were also important, for example the provision of uninterrupted sightlines to the altar. As a consequence, he gradually replaced aisles with pierced walkways, and eventually moved to an open nave design. He also strove to produce buildings that were long-lasting, required little maintenance, and were well-lit and warm, with good acoustics.

Two striking features of his churches, each facilitated through the development of reinforced concrete and glazing materials, are the internal vistas from west to east, culminating in an originally-designed east end wall, and his use of large windows to create space and exploit natural light. He used sophisticated design techniques to avoid glare and vary light intensity from low to high, from nave to sanctuary. His use of glazing in Bushbury crematorium chapel removed the barriers between a private interior and an exterior landscape and recalled the principles of Frank Lloyd Wright's 'organic' architecture: '...we have no longer an outside and an inside as two separate things. Now the outside may come inside, and the inside may, and does, go outside'.[1]

Twentyman's architecture evolved throughout his career. As society changed and ecclesiastical demands changed with it, Twentyman adapted and developed, and was able to design to his clients' satisfaction as well as produce substantial buildings worthy of analysis today. The result is a variety of churches from the utilitarian simplicity of a small, multipurpose church like the Church of the Good Shepherd, Castlecroft, to the imposing Emmanuel, Bentley. He was still innovating towards the end of his career with the uncompromising massing of St Andrew, Whitmore Reans, the novel splayed shape and lantern of St Andrew, Runcorn, and the panoramic east window at Redditch crematorium chapel. He believed 'the creation of an enduring building, having dignity and the right devotional atmosphere was an absorbing problem to the architect, and one giving great scope to the imagination'.[2] Those three elements, 'dignity', 'atmosphere', and 'imagination', provide a fitting summative evaluation of his work.

9.3
EMMANUEL CHURCH, BENTLEY

CONCLUSIONS & REFLECTIONS

9.4
ST NICHOLAS RADFORD
WATERCOLOUR OF NAVE
AUGUST 1951

AUGUST 1951

ST. NICHOLAS C

RCH, COVENTRY

LAVENDER, TWENTYMAN & PERCY F/ARIBA
CHARTERED ARCHITECTS
2, WATERLOO RD., WOLVERHAMPTON.

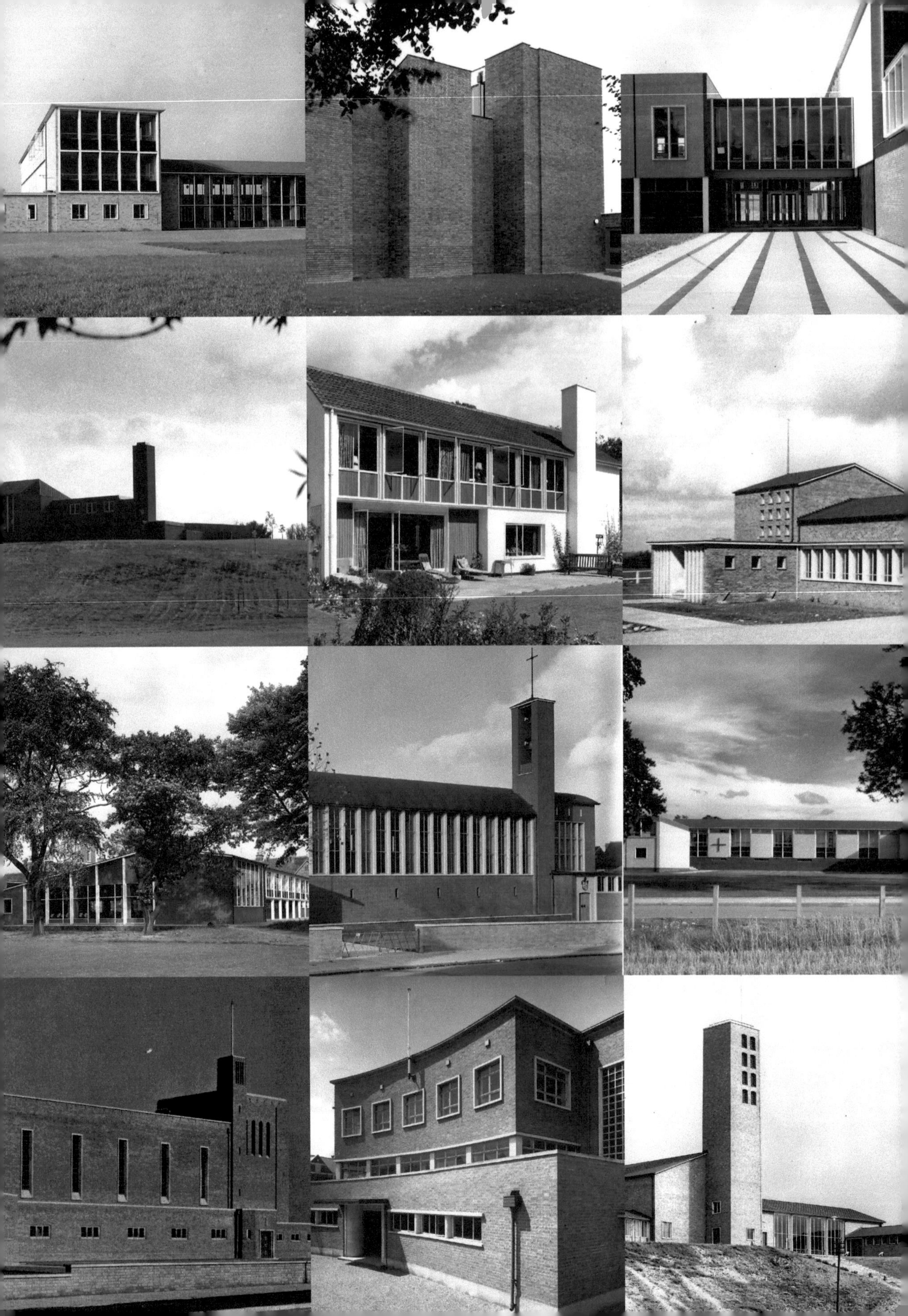

Notes

1   F. L. Wright, *An Autobiography* (New York: Horizon Press 1977), p.363.

2   'Church Designing Lecture', *Wolverhampton Express and Star*, (27 March 1939).

LIST OF TWENTYMAN CHURCHES & CREMATORIA

St Gabriel, Fullbrook, Walsall	1937-39*
St Martin, Parkfields, Wolverhampton	1937-39*
All Saints, Darlaston	1952*
Crematorium Chapel, Bushbury, Wolverhampton	1954
St Gregory the Great, Wednesfield, Wolverhampton	1954
Church of the Good Shepherd, Castlecroft, Wolverhampton	1955
St Nicholas, Radford, Coventry	1954-55
Emmanuel, Bentley, Walsall	1955-57*
St Chad, Rubery	1956-60
Lanesfield Methodist Church, Wolverhampton	1960-61
St Andrew, Whitmore Reans, Wolverhampton	1965
St Andrew, Grange, Runcorn	1965
Crematorium Chapel, Redditch	1973

*Listed Grade II

LOCATIONS OF TWENTYMAN CHURCHES & CREMATORIA

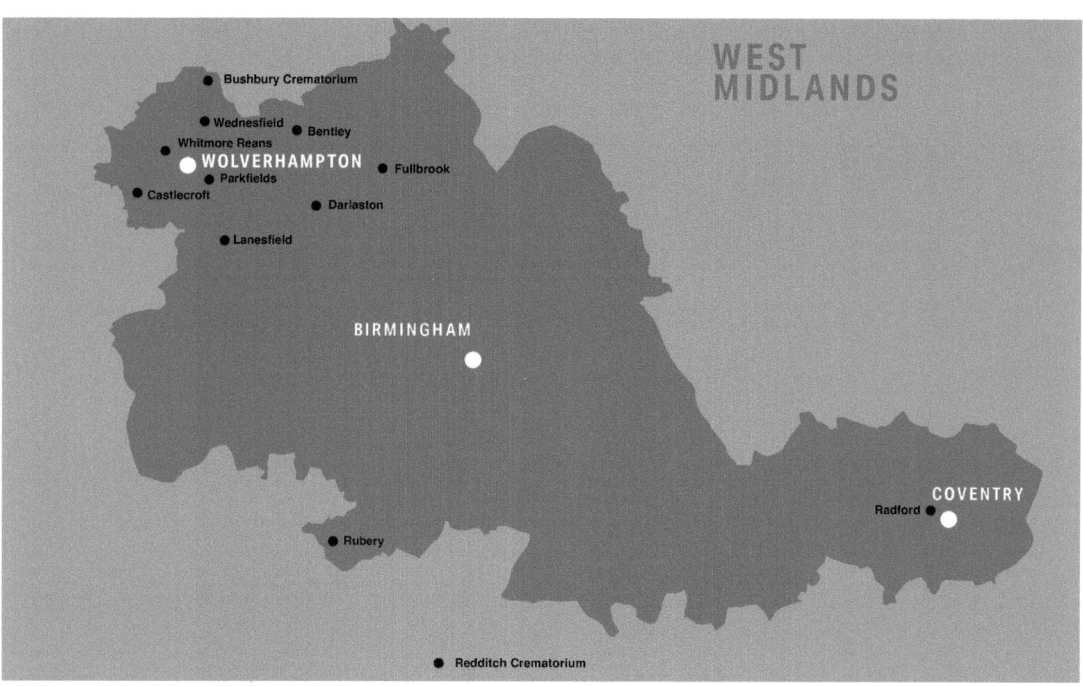

244

ILLUSTRATION CREDITS

The authors have made every effort to contact copyright holders , and apologise for any errors or omissions.

All line drawings are the work of Aidan Ridyard. All photographs, unless credited otherwise, were taken by John East, to whom we are extremely grateful for his help and support.

Aidan Ridyard
1.12
7.1 7.2 7.3 7.8 7.12 7.13 7.14 7.15
8.6
9.3

All Saints Church Archive (Darlaston)
3.1 3.3 3.4

Architectural Association Archives
1.9 1.10 1.11
9.2

Bob Morgan (Philippines)
5.2

Bushbury Crematorium Collection
8.2

Chris Kennedy
1.8
7.4

George Sidebotham Archive
0.5 0.6 0.8
1.14
3.5
7.7 7.11 7.16 7.17
8.8 8.15 8.19 8.31 8.35 8.36 8.37. 8.38
9.1

Historic England, 'Britain from Above'
4.22

Informes de la Construtión, CSIC (Spain)
2.5
5.25 5.26

Lanesfield Church Archive
7.9

Private family collection
1.2 1.7 1.13

Ray McGinley RIAI
4.25

Revd Claire Turner
2.10 2.11

Revd Gordon Lacey Archives
5.49

St Andrews Church Archive (Whitmore Reans)
6.11

St Nicholas Church Archive (Radford)
5.33
9.4

Staffordshire Archives
1.3 1.4 1.5

Wikimedia Commons
2.7
4.1
6.2 6.3

Wolverhampton Art Gallery
1.1 1.6
2.13 2.14

INDEX

Albi Cathedral 26-27

All Saints, Darlaston 26-27 38 45 83 85-98 107 205

Architectural Association 15-19 53 236

Asplund, Gunnar 55 197 207 213

Cachemaille-Day, Nugent 15 53

church art 33 38 77

church funding 45 47 85 71

Church of the Good Shepherd, Castlecroft, Wolverhampton 28 99-106 183 225 237

Clarke, Geoffrey 33-5 142

Coventry Cathedral 29 33 45

Crematoria 53 197 207 213

Crematorium Chapel, Bushbury, Wolverhampton 199-218 237

Crematorium Chapel, Redditch 157 219-230 237

Emmanuel Church, Bentley, Walsall 26 45 117-30 142 205 217

Enskede Cemetery, Sweden 197 205 213

form and function 26 28-29 35 53

functionalism v transcendence 28 77 91 139 142 157 197 236

Gesamtkunstwerk 33 197

Hammond, Peter 29-31 61 77 83 169

housing developments 45 71 133 207

Kahn, Louis 153 157

Lanesfield Methodist Church, Wolverhampton 181 187-93

Lavender, Ernest 3 19 67 83

liturgical reforms 29-31 77 95 151

Liverpool School of Architecture 25 55 77

materials 6 25 28 31 83-4 139 181 235

Maufe, Edward 15 26 53 61 77

Mies van der Rohe 28 73

Modernism 6 25-40 61 83 84

multipurpose churches 28 31 45 189

Piper, John 19 33 34 38 157

population expansion 85 219

Potter, Don 19-20 33 38 73 77 91 109 207 215

reconstruction and renewal 44-48

Rubery Owen 45 117

Scandinavian architecture 17 25 55 143 236

Schwarz, Rudolf 25 29 53 94 103

Spence, Basil 33 35 45 47 59 139

St Andrew, Grange, Runcorn 31 151 165-76 219 223 225 237

St Andrew, Whitmore Reans, Wolverhampton 19 31 38 151 153-61 237

St Chad, Rubery 26 28 33 45 133-46 183 205 223

St Gabriel, Walsall 30 45 53 55-63 71 73 75 83-4 153

St Gregory the Great, Wednesfield 181 183-6

St Martin, Wolverhampton 20 26 31 38 53 67-78 83 84 85 89 91 153 183 215

St Nicholas, Radford, Coventry 29 38 45 103 107-14

Twentyman brothers
    Bilbrook Manor 11 19
    Claverley 11
    education 15
    family firm 11 13 15
    interests 13-14
    war service 19

Twentyman, Anthony
    artistic contacts 15

Twentyman, Grace (née Evill) 11 19

Twentyman, Harold 11 13

Twentyman, Richard
    aisles and passageways 6 26 59 61 75 91 94 111 236
    art 33 38 77
    colour 53 75 142 143 225
    competitions 67 213
    crosses 31 59 61 75 89 103 109 129 142 189 211 226
    design 6 28 31 33 38 53 61 77 83 84 91 99 107 129 139 143 153 181 187 201 205 207
    development 6 31 235
    doors 61 91 103 129 211
    fittings and furnishings 28 33 38 61 189 236
    influences - see Asplund, Kahn, Maufe, Scandinavian architecture, Schwarz, Velarde
    light 6 47 75 78 91 103 121 142 153 159 187 205 236-7
    secular architecture 84 235
    space 75 77 83 91 143 151 183 208 213
    training – see Architectural Association
    views on architecture 31 53 225
    windows 26 47 53 91 94 213 237

Velarde, Francis 25 55 94

ACKNOWLEDGEMENTS

We are immensely grateful to the numerous people who gave up their time and shared their knowledge with us, and without whom this publication would not have been possible. They include the relatives and friends of the Twentyman brothers who gave us invaluable information and narratives that communicated so well the brothers' life history, interests, and personalities.

We thank also the supportive clergy, churchwardens, and parishioners of the Twentyman churches who showed interest in our research and provided access to personal and church archives, including Father Tony Hutchinson of St Martin, Parkfields, John Wallbridge of St Andrew, Whitmore Reans, Reverend Claire Turner of St Chad, Rubery, and the daughter of Reverend Gordon Lacey, the former Vicar of St Chad, Rubery. The photography records of Gordon Sidebotham, former practice partner of Richard Twentyman, were generously loaned by his daughter.

We applaud the dedicated staff consulted at the Henry Moore Institute, Birmingham University, Bodleian, RIBA, and Warwick University Libraries, and the Birmingham, Chester, Shropshire, Stafford, Walsall, and Wolverhampton Record Offices.

Edward Bottoms, the Architectural Association Archivist, Carol Thompson at Wolverhampton Art Gallery, and Alexa Buffey of the National Trust patiently answered queries and facilitated further contacts, as did Andy Foster, Malcolm Dick of West Midlands History, and Judy Davies and Sue Burns of Bilbrook and Claverley History Societies respectively.

David Owen, formerly Chairman of the Rubery Owen Company, provided a family connection to the building of Emmanuel Church, Bentley, encouraged us, agreed to write a Preface, and generously supported this publication. Roy Albutt, Roger Button, Juliet Dunmur, Georgina Maltby, and Caroline Walker advised us on the self-publishing process.

The outstanding photographs are by John East and the impressive design is by Julia Berrisford. Hilary Grainger of the University of the Arts, London very kindly agreed to lend her expertise to create a perceptive and significant Foreword. Claire O'Mahony and Julian Holder of the University of Oxford were crucial catalysts.

Finally, we thank our respective families, Judith Kennedy, Penny Lane-Ridyard and Sienna Ridyard for their unstinting patience and support.

CK and AR

ABOUT THE AUTHORS

Chris Kennedy

Following a career as a professor in Applied Linguistics at the University of Birmingham, Chris gained a Masters degree in the History of Design and a Postgraduate Certificate in Architectural History from Oxford University. His interests are in 20th-century architecture and design. After a chance visit to a Twentyman church, Chris became an admirer of Twentyman's architecture.

c.j.kennedy@bham.ac.uk

Aidan Ridyard

Managing Partner at Burrell Foley Fischer Ridyard Architects and a member of RIBA with Conservation Accreditation, Aidan has built several notable public buildings in the UK and overseas. Aidan grew up in the Black Country where his father was vicar of All Saints Darlaston, making Twentyman a formative influence on his architectural education.

aidanridyard@mac.com
BFF-Architects.com
@AidanRidyard